X-MEN

BLANK GENERATON

MEN: BLANK GENERATION. Contains material originally published in magazine form as X-MEN #30-35. First printing 2013. ISBN# 978-0-7851-6459-3. Published by MARVEL WORLDWIDE, INC., a subsidiary
MARVEL ENTERTAINMENT, LLC. OFFICE OF PUBLICATION: 135 West 50th Street, New York, NY 10020. Copyright © 2012 and 2013 Marvel Characters, Inc. All rights reserved. All characters featured in this issue
d the distinctive names and likenesses thereof, and all related indicia are trademarks of Marvel Characters, Inc. No similarity between any of the names, characters, persons, and/or institutions in this magazine
th those of any living or dead person or institution is intended, and any such similarity which may exist is purely coincidental. **Printed in the U.S.A.** ALAN FINE, EVP - Office of the President, Marvel Worldwide, Inc.
d EVP & CMO Marvel Characters B.V.; DAN BUCKLEY, Publisher & President - Print, Animation & Digital Divisions; JOE QUESADA, Chief Creative Officer; TOM BREVOORT, SVP of Publishing; DAVID BOGART, SVP of
perations & Procurement, Publishing; RUWAN JAYATILLEKE, SVP & Associate Publisher, Publishing; C.B. CEBULSKI, SVP of Creator & Content Development; DAVID GABRIEL, SVP of Publishing Sales & Circulation; JIM
KEEFE, VP of Operations & Logistics; DAN CARR, Executive Director of Publishing Technology; SUSAN CRESPI, Editorial Operations Manager; ALEX MORALES, Publishing Operations Manager; STAN LEE, Chairman
neritus. For information regarding advertising in Marvel Comics or on Marvel.com, please contact Niza Disla, Director of Marvel Partnerships, at ndisla@marvel.com. For Marvel subscription inquiries, please call
0-217-9158. **Manufactured between 12/13/2012 and 1/15/2013 by QUAD/GRAPHICS, DUBUQUE, IA, USA.**

0 9 8 7 6 5 4 3 2 1

X-MEN

BLANK GENERATION

WRITER
BRIAN WOOD

PENCILERS
DAVID LÓPEZ (#30-33 & #35)
& ROLAND BOSCHI (#34-35)

INKERS
ÁLVARO LÓPEZ (#30-33 & #35)
& ROLAND BOSCHI (#34-35)

COLORISTS
RACHELLE ROSENBERG (#30-33)
& DAN BROWN (#34-35)
WITH JIM CHARALAMPIDIS (#35)

LETTERER
VC'S JOE CARAMAGNA

COVER ARTISTS
JORGE MOLINA (#30-34)
& DAVID LÓPEZ (#35)

ASSISTANT EDITORS
JORDAN D. WHITE
& JENNIFER M. SMITH

ASSOCIATE EDITOR
DANIEL KETCHUM

EDITOR
JEANINE SCHAEFER

X-MEN GROUP EDITOR
NICK LOWE

COLLECTION EDITOR: CORY LEVINE
ASSISTANT EDITORS: ALEX STARBUCK & NELSON RIBEIRO
EDITORS, SPECIAL PROJECTS: JENNIFER GRÜNWALD & MARK D. BEAZLEY
SENIOR EDITOR, SPECIAL PROJECTS: JEFF YOUNGQUIST
SENIOR VICE PRESIDENT OF SALES: DAVID GABRIEL

EDITOR IN CHIEF: AXEL ALONSO
CHIEF CREATIVE OFFICER: JOE QUESADA
PUBLISHER: DAN BUCKLEY
EXECUTIVE PRODUCER: ALAN FINE

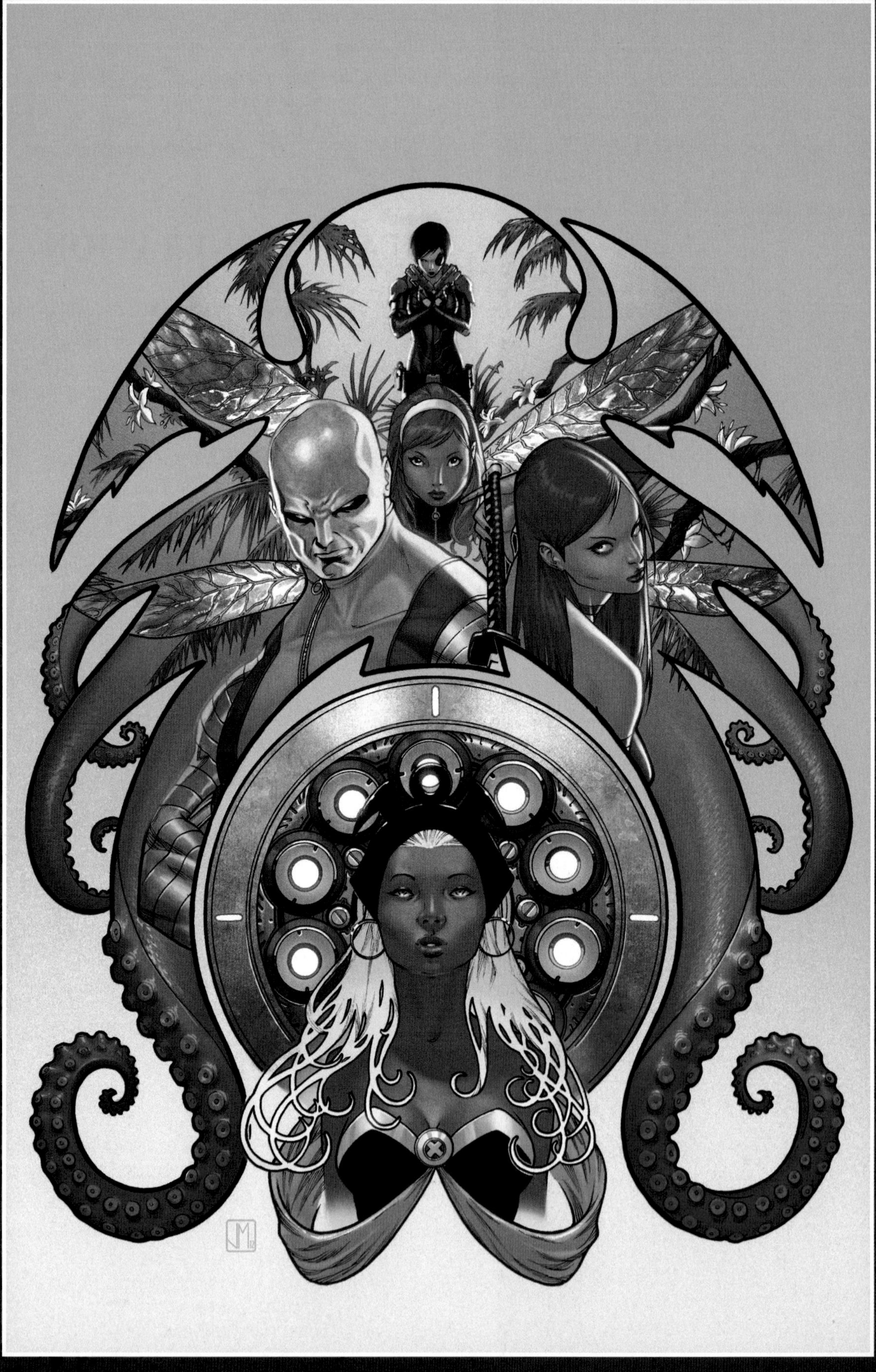

‹THIRTY›

X-MEN

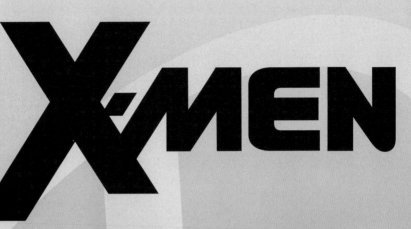

Born with abilities beyond those of normal men, the mutant species has long been hated and feared by the humans around them. The mutant super heroes known as the X-Men are looking to change that, making the world safe for human and mutant alike.

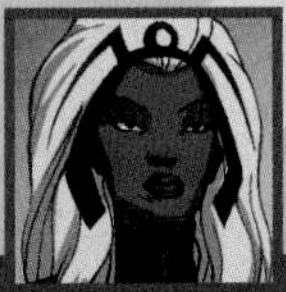

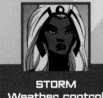

STORM
Weather control

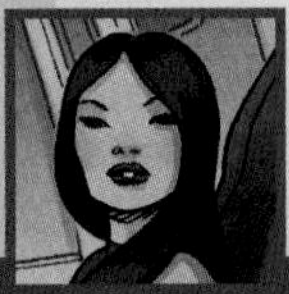

PSYLOCKE
Telepathic ninja

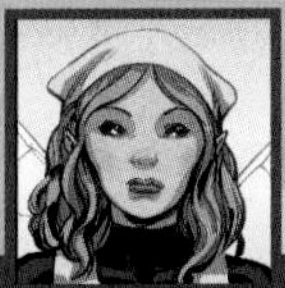

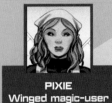

PIXIE
Winged magic-user

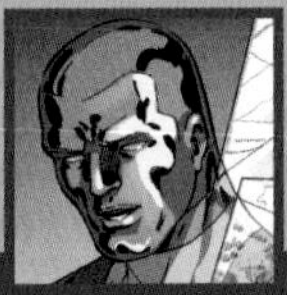

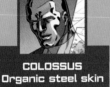

COLOSSUS
Organic steel skin

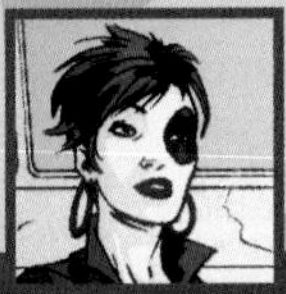

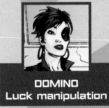

DOMINO
Luck manipulation

PREVIOUSLY

Scott Summers, the mutant know as Cyclops, leads half of mutantkind. He has tasked Storm with putting together a security force to help defend mutantkind, a task Storm has taken seriously. Having dealt with underground sale of Sentinels, hidden cities of vampires, and stranded Skrull soldiers, Storm's elite team has proven they can work together to get the job done. But not content to rest on their laurels, they have decided to up their game, with a little help from Utopia's science team.

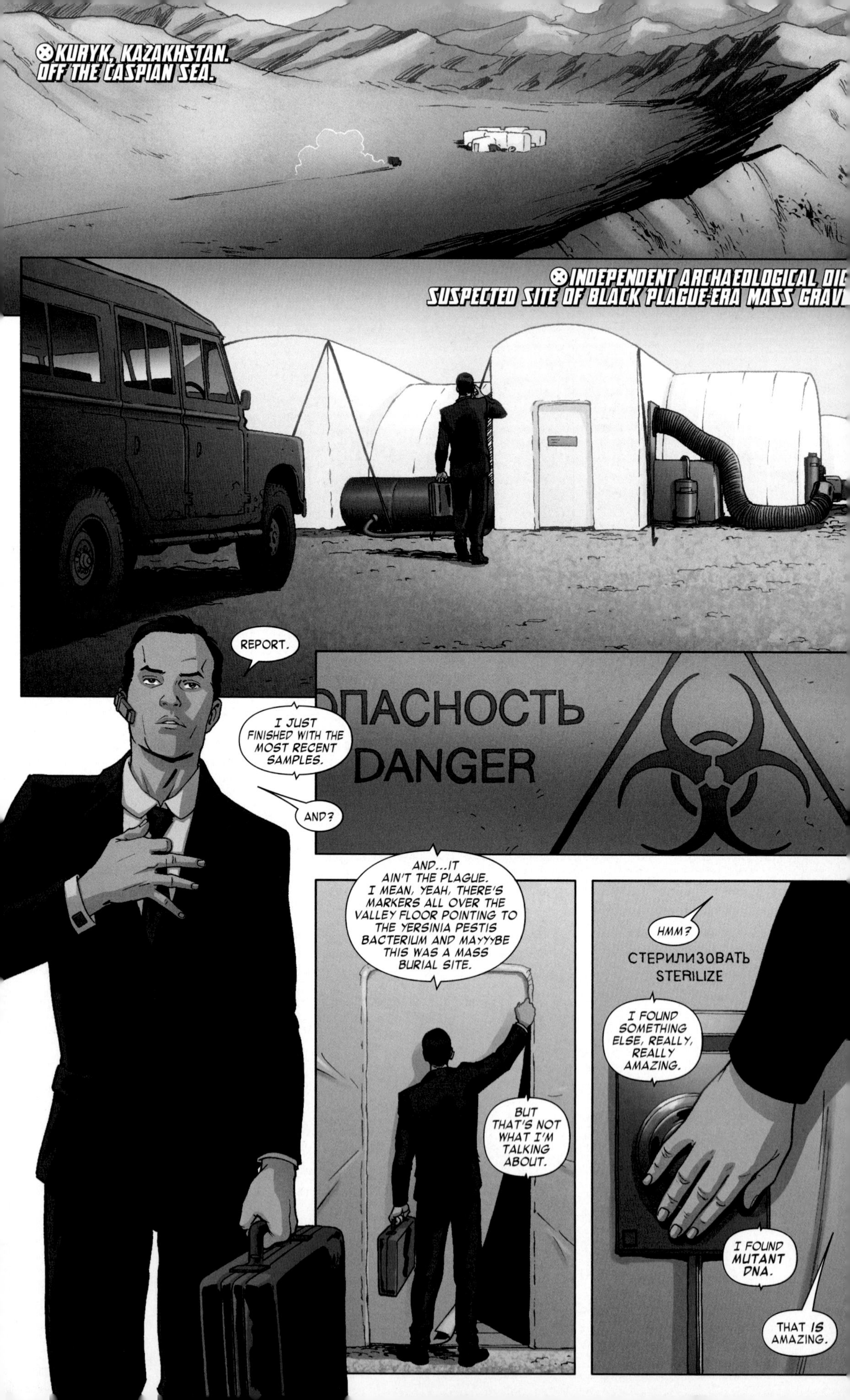
KURYK, KAZAKHSTAN.
OFF THE CASPIAN SEA.
INDEPENDENT ARCHAEOLOGICAL DIG
SUSPECTED SITE OF BLACK PLAGUE-ERA MASS GRAVE
REPORT.
ОПАСНОСТЬ
DANGER
I JUST FINISHED WITH THE MOST RECENT SAMPLES.
AND?
AND...IT AIN'T THE PLAGUE. I MEAN, YEAH, THERE'S MARKERS ALL OVER THE VALLEY FLOOR POINTING TO THE YERSINIA PESTIS BACTERIUM AND MAYYYBE THIS WAS A MASS BURIAL SITE.
BUT THAT'S NOT WHAT I'M TALKING ABOUT.
HMM?
СТЕРИЛИЗОВАТЬ
STERILIZE
I FOUND SOMETHING ELSE, REALLY, REALLY AMAZING.
I FOUND MUTANT DNA.
THAT IS AMAZING.

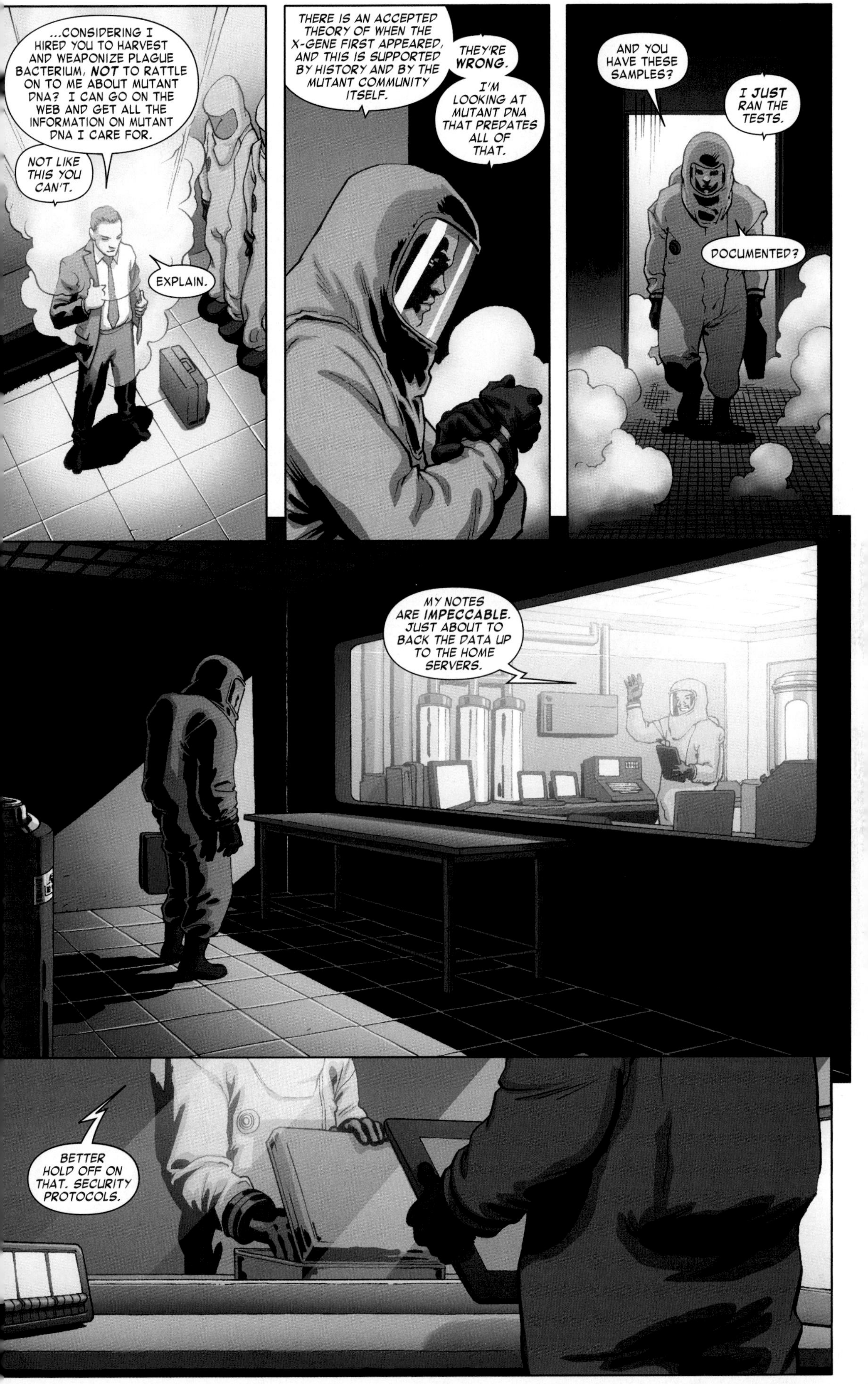
...CONSIDERING I HIRED YOU TO HARVEST AND WEAPONIZE PLAGUE BACTERIUM, NOT TO RATTLE ON TO ME ABOUT MUTANT DNA? I CAN GO ON THE WEB AND GET ALL THE INFORMATION ON MUTANT DNA I CARE FOR.
NOT LIKE THIS YOU CAN'T.
EXPLAIN.
THERE IS AN ACCEPTED THEORY OF WHEN THE X-GENE FIRST APPEARED, AND THIS IS SUPPORTED BY HISTORY AND BY THE MUTANT COMMUNITY ITSELF.
THEY'RE WRONG.
I'M LOOKING AT MUTANT DNA THAT PREDATES ALL OF THAT.
AND YOU HAVE THESE SAMPLES?
I JUST RAN THE TESTS.
DOCUMENTED?
MY NOTES ARE IMPECCABLE. JUST ABOUT TO BACK THE DATA UP TO THE HOME SERVERS.
BETTER HOLD OFF ON THAT. SECURITY PROTOCOLS.

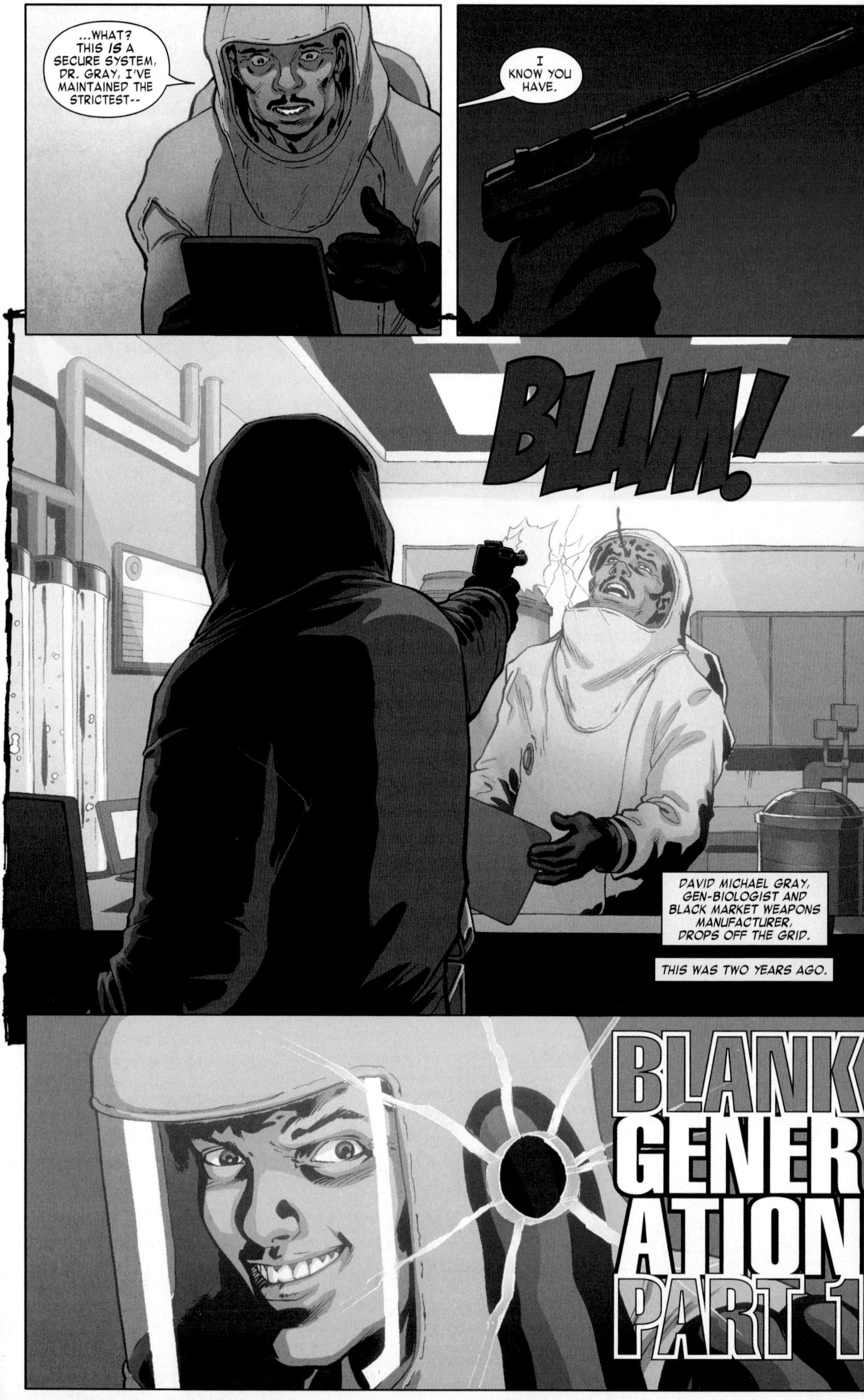
...WHAT? THIS IS A SECURE SYSTEM, DR. GRAY, I'VE MAINTAINED THE STRICTEST--
I KNOW YOU HAVE.
BLAM!
DAVID MICHAEL GRAY, GEN-BIOLOGIST AND BLACK MARKET WEAPONS MANUFACTURER, DROPS OFF THE GRID.
THIS WAS TWO YEARS AGO.
BLANK GENERATION PART 1

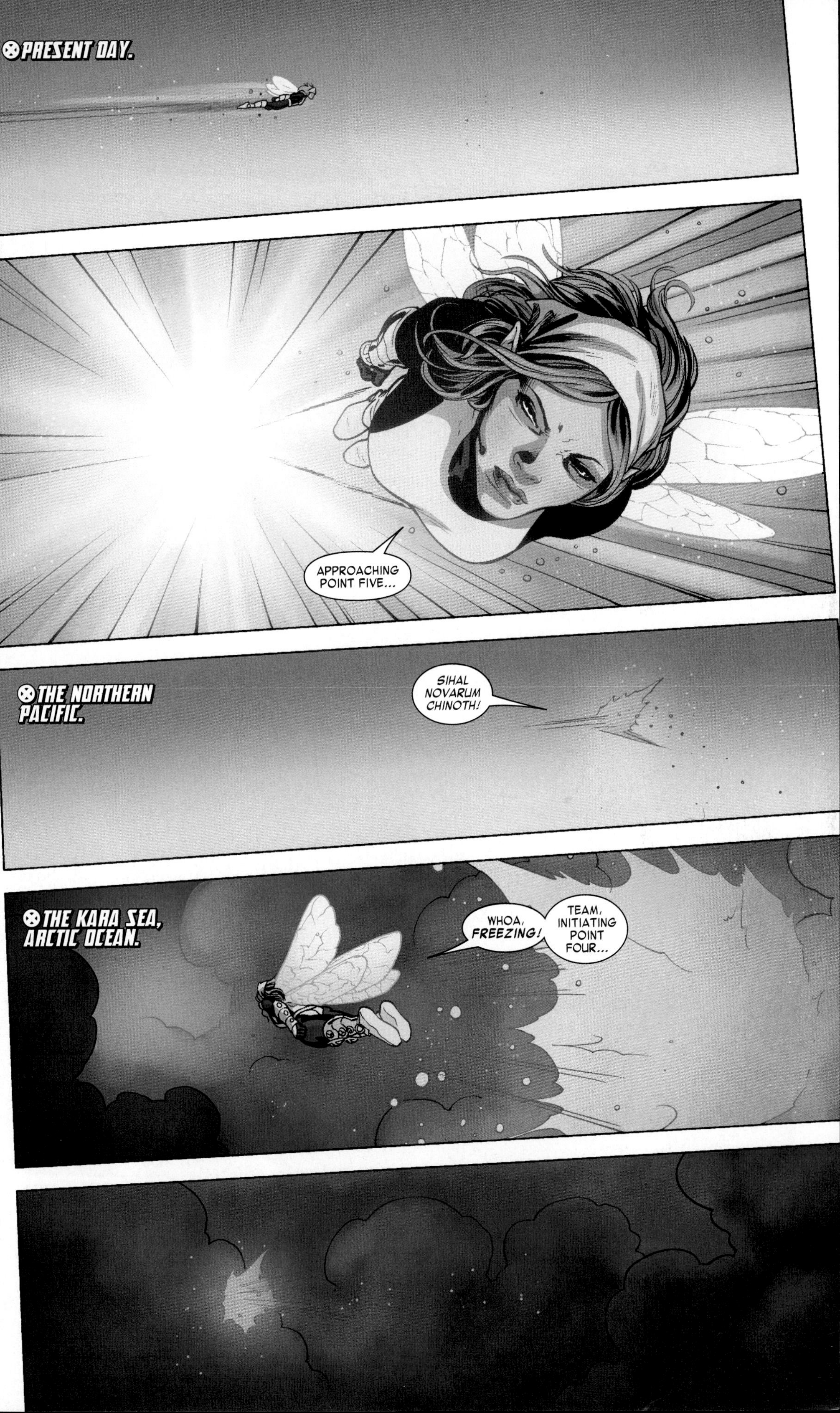
PRESENT DAY.
APPROACHING POINT FIVE...
THE NORTHERN PACIFIC.
SIHAL NOVARUM CHINOTH!
THE KARA SEA, ARCTIC OCEAN.
WHOA, FREEZING!
TEAM, INITIATING POINT FOUR...

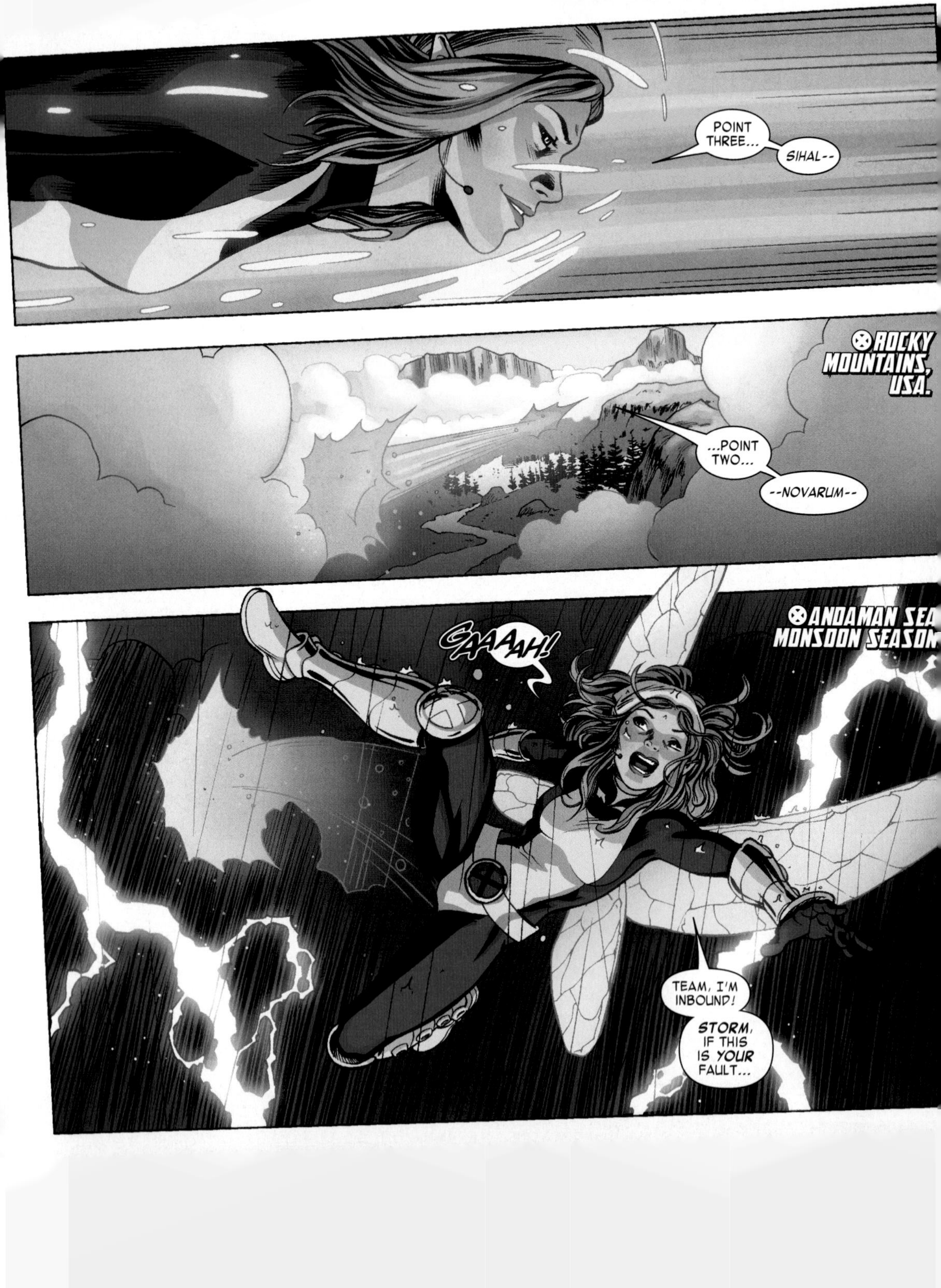
POINT THREE...
SIHAL--
ROCKY MOUNTAINS, USA.
...POINT TWO...
--NOVARUM--
ANDAMAN SEA MONSOON SEASON
GAAAAH!
TEAM, I'M INBOUND!
STORM, IF THIS IS YOUR FAULT...

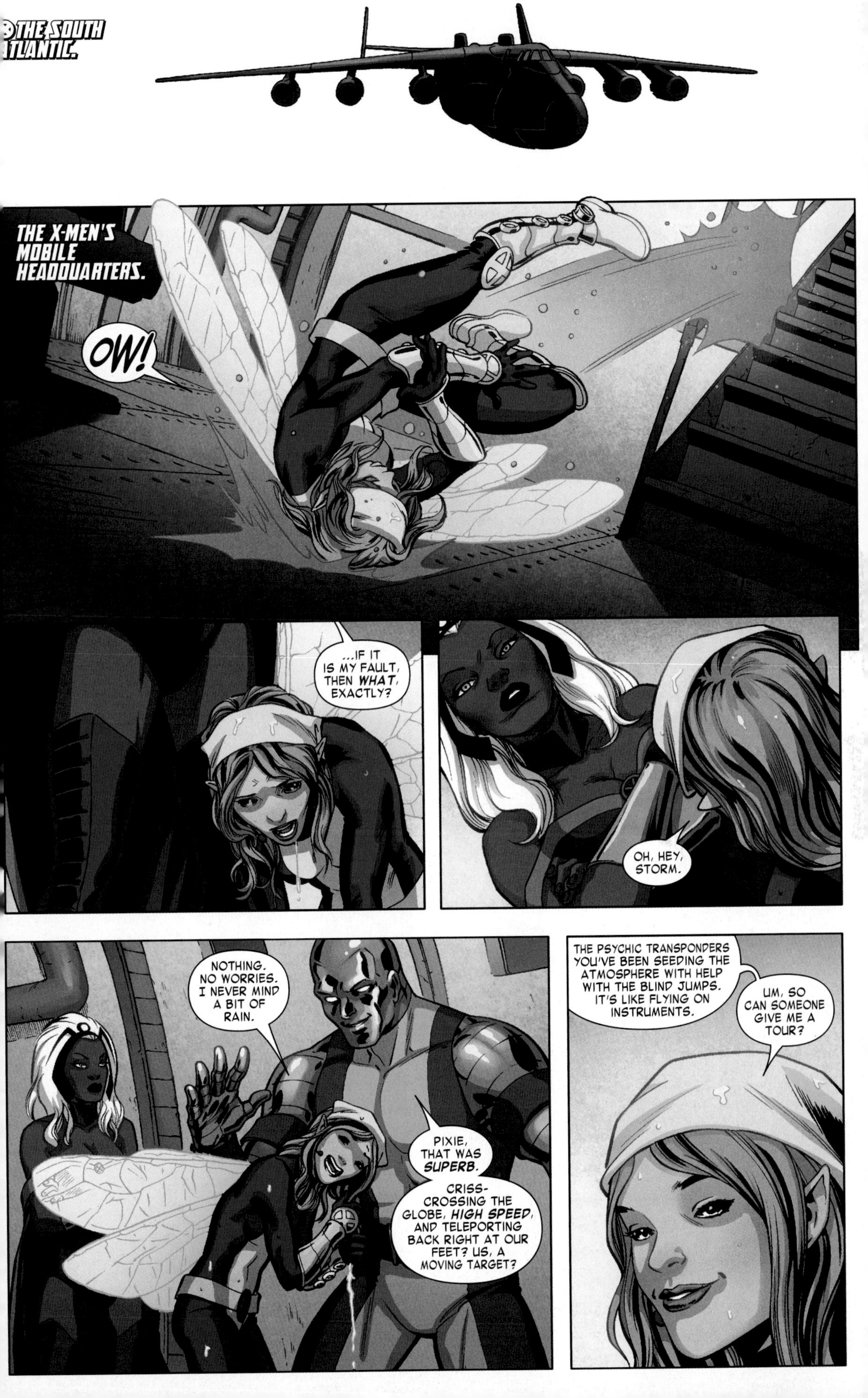
THE SOUTH ATLANTIC.
THE X-MEN'S MOBILE HEADQUARTERS.
OW!
...IF IT IS MY FAULT, THEN WHAT, EXACTLY?
OH, HEY, STORM.
NOTHING. NO WORRIES. I NEVER MIND A BIT OF RAIN.
PIXIE, THAT WAS SUPERB.
CRISS-CROSSING THE GLOBE, HIGH SPEED, AND TELEPORTING BACK RIGHT AT OUR FEET? US, A MOVING TARGET?
THE PSYCHIC TRANSPONDERS YOU'VE BEEN SEEDING THE ATMOSPHERE WITH HELP WITH THE BLIND JUMPS. IT'S LIKE FLYING ON INSTRUMENTS.
UM, SO CAN SOMEONE GIVE ME A TOUR?

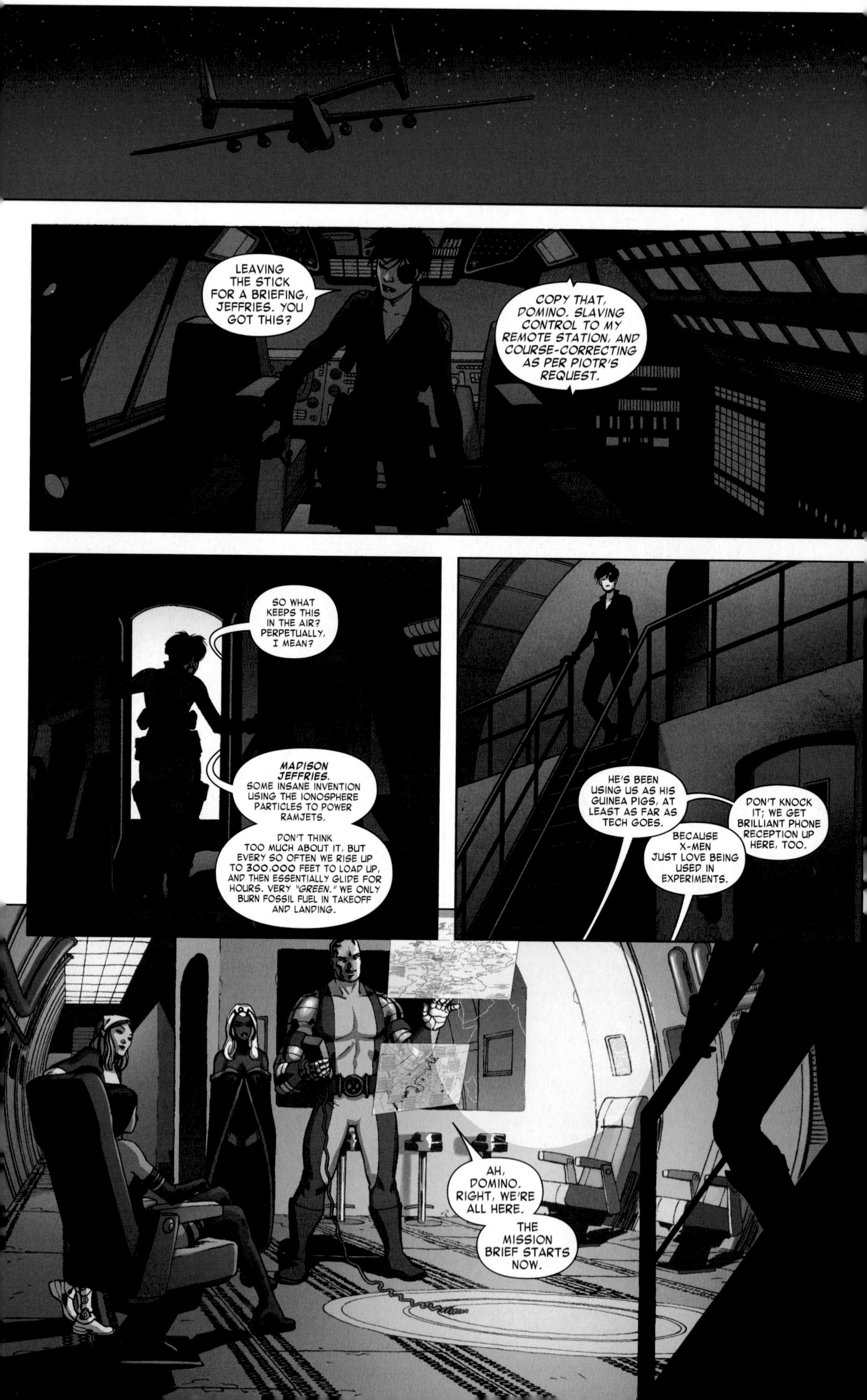
LEAVING THE STICK FOR A BRIEFING, JEFFRIES. YOU GOT THIS?
COPY THAT, DOMINO. SLAVING CONTROL TO MY REMOTE STATION, AND COURSE-CORRECTING AS PER PIOTR'S REQUEST.
SO WHAT KEEPS THIS IN THE AIR? PERPETUALLY, I MEAN?
MADISON JEFFRIES. SOME INSANE INVENTION USING THE IONOSPHERE PARTICLES TO POWER RAMJETS.
DON'T THINK TOO MUCH ABOUT IT, BUT EVERY SO OFTEN WE RISE UP TO 300,000 FEET TO LOAD UP, AND THEN ESSENTIALLY GLIDE FOR HOURS. VERY "GREEN." WE ONLY BURN FOSSIL FUEL IN TAKEOFF AND LANDING.
HE'S BEEN USING US AS HIS GUINEA PIGS, AT LEAST AS FAR AS TECH GOES.
BECAUSE X-MEN JUST LOVE BEING USED IN EXPERIMENTS.
DON'T KNOCK IT; WE GET BRILLIANT PHONE RECEPTION UP HERE, TOO.
AH, DOMINO. RIGHT, WE'RE ALL HERE.
THE MISSION BRIEF STARTS NOW.

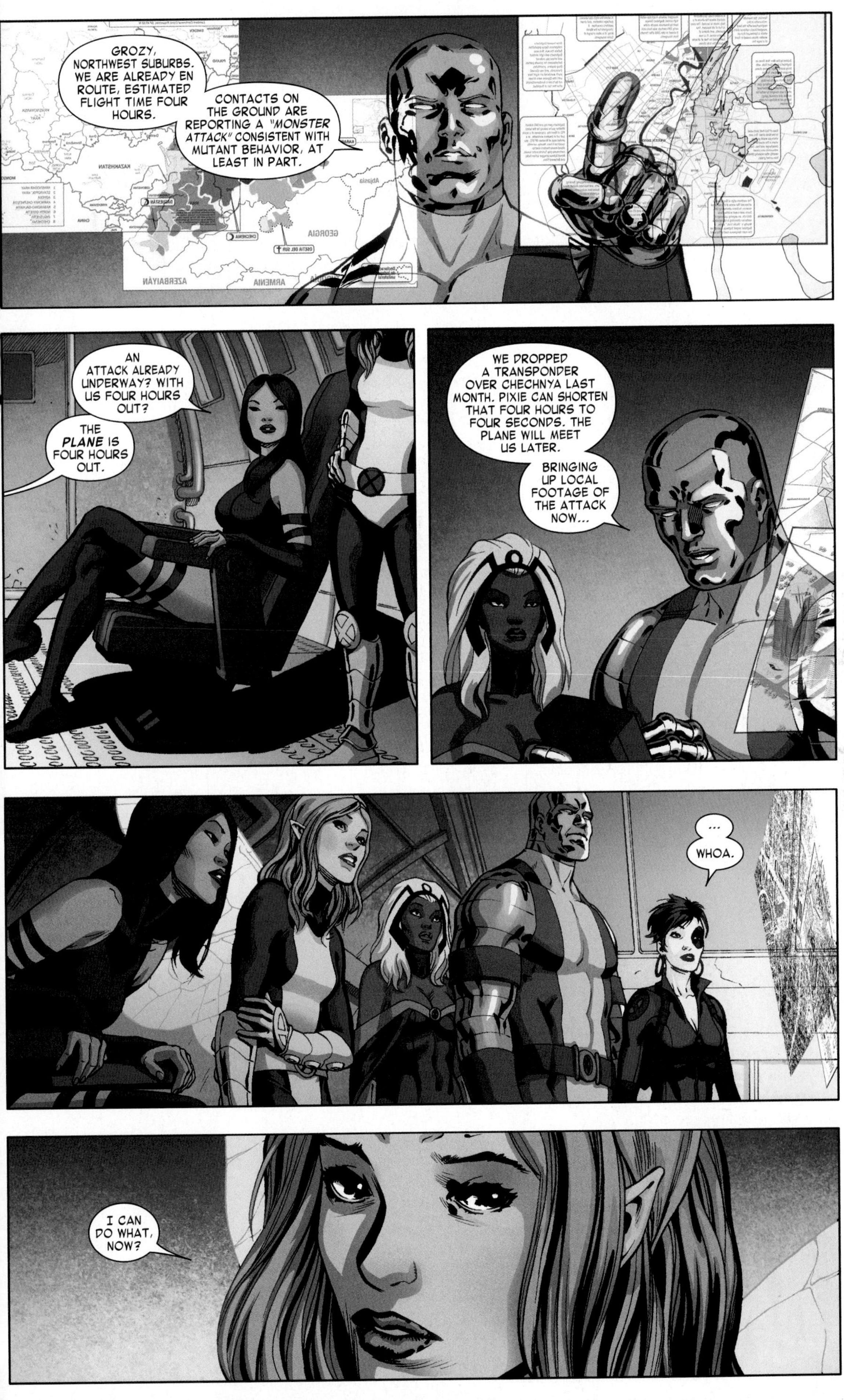
GROZY, NORTHWEST SUBURBS. WE ARE ALREADY EN ROUTE, ESTIMATED FLIGHT TIME FOUR HOURS.
CONTACTS ON THE GROUND ARE REPORTING A "MONSTER ATTACK" CONSISTENT WITH MUTANT BEHAVIOR, AT LEAST IN PART.
KAZAKHSTAN
DAGUESTÁN
CHECHENIA
OSETIA DEL SUR
GEORGIA
Abjasia
AZERBAIYÁN
ARMENIA
AN ATTACK ALREADY UNDERWAY? WITH US FOUR HOURS OUT?
THE *PLANE* IS FOUR HOURS OUT.
WE DROPPED A TRANSPONDER OVER CHECHNYA LAST MONTH. PIXIE CAN SHORTEN THAT FOUR HOURS TO FOUR SECONDS. THE PLANE WILL MEET US LATER.
BRINGING UP LOCAL FOOTAGE OF THE ATTACK NOW...
...
WHOA.
I CAN DO WHAT, NOW?

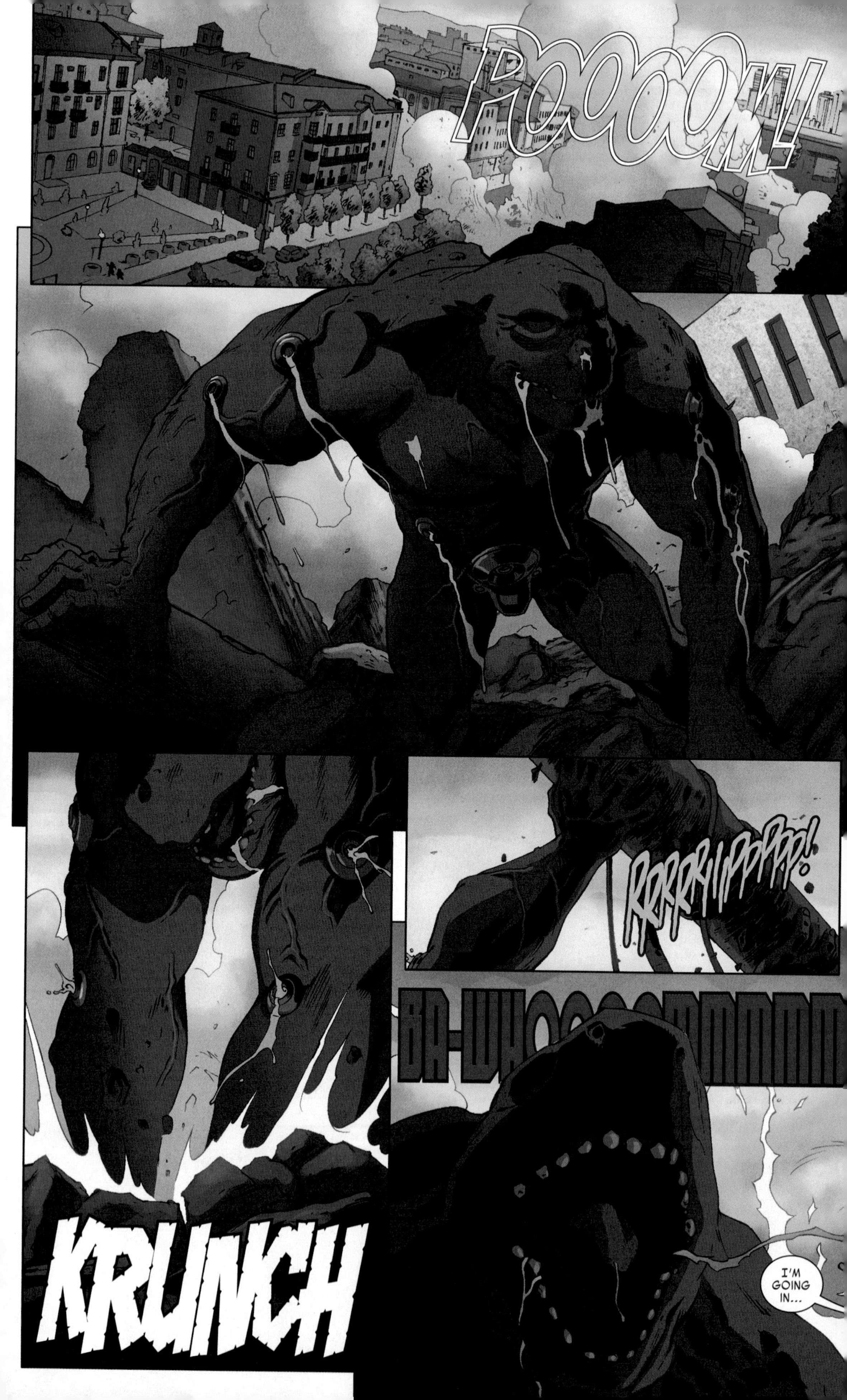
POOOOM!
RRRRRIPPPPP!
BA-WHOOOOMMMMM
KRUNCH
I'M GOING IN...

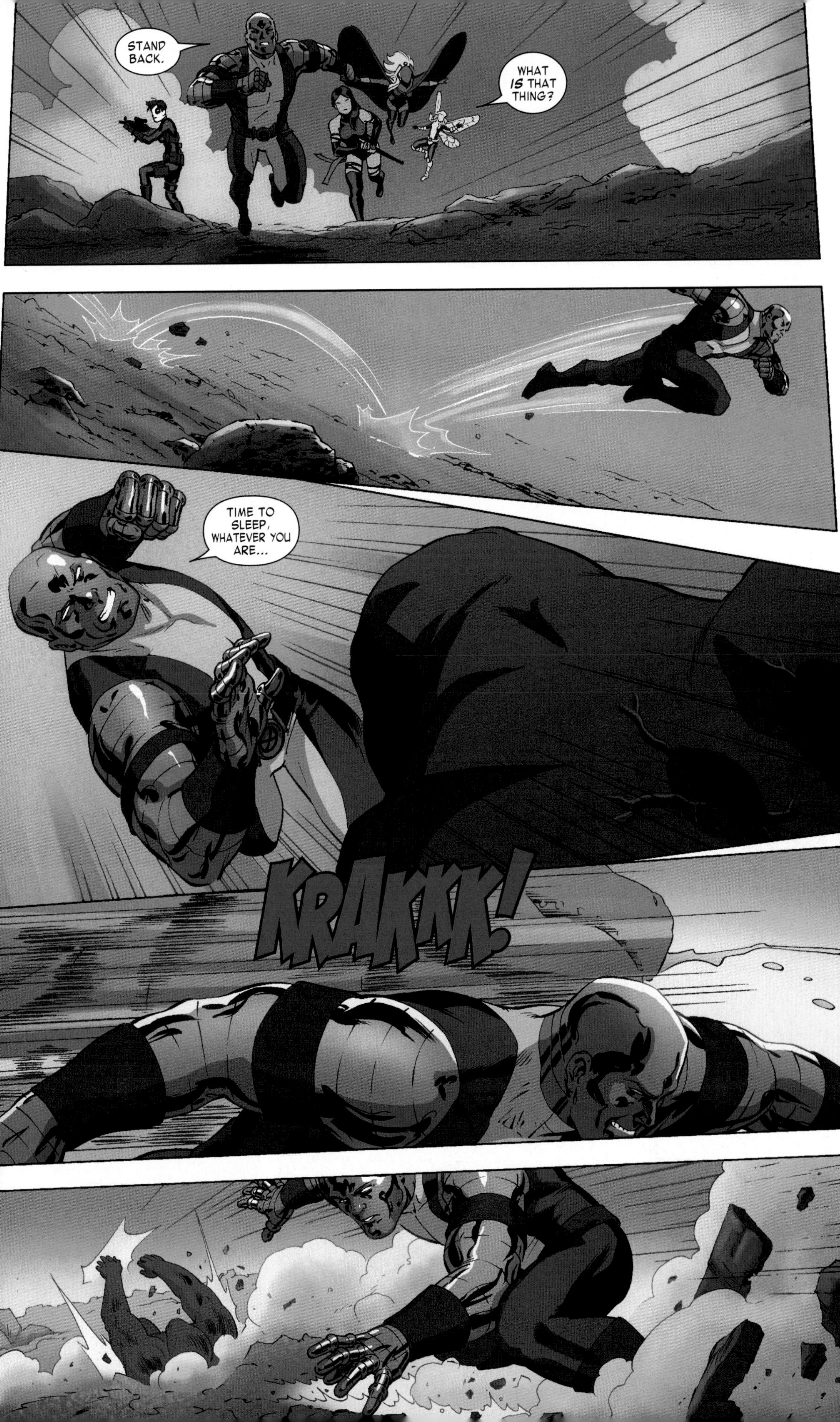
STAND BACK.
WHAT IS THAT THING?
TIME TO SLEEP, WHATEVER YOU ARE...
KRAKKK!

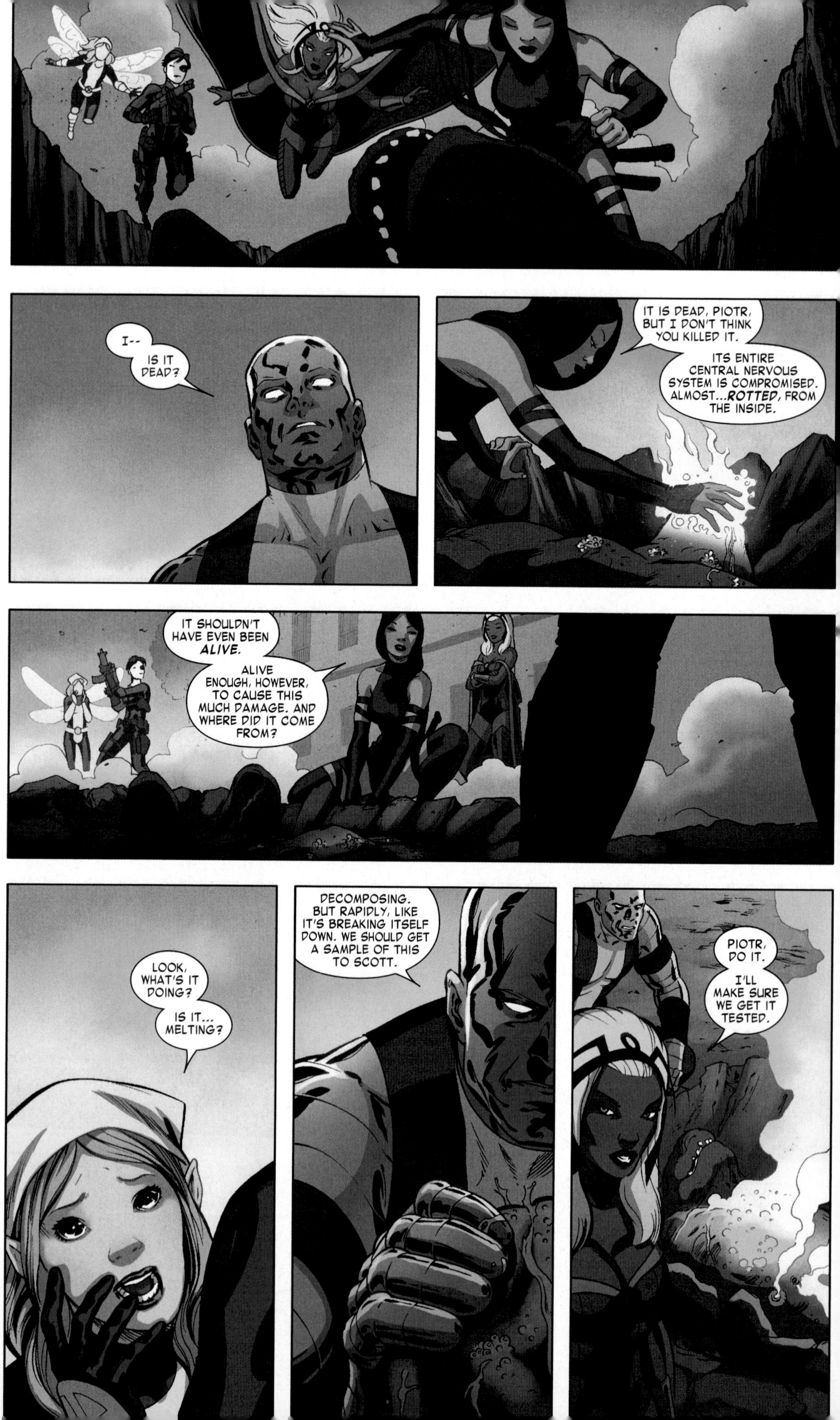
I--
IS IT DEAD?
IT IS DEAD, PIOTR, BUT I DON'T THINK YOU KILLED IT.
ITS ENTIRE CENTRAL NERVOUS SYSTEM IS COMPROMISED. ALMOST...ROTTED, FROM THE INSIDE.
IT SHOULDN'T HAVE EVEN BEEN ALIVE.
ALIVE ENOUGH, HOWEVER, TO CAUSE THIS MUCH DAMAGE. AND WHERE DID IT COME FROM?
LOOK, WHAT'S IT DOING?
IS IT... MELTING?
DECOMPOSING. BUT RAPIDLY, LIKE IT'S BREAKING ITSELF DOWN. WE SHOULD GET A SAMPLE OF THIS TO SCOTT.
PIOTR, DO IT.
I'LL MAKE SURE WE GET IT TESTED.

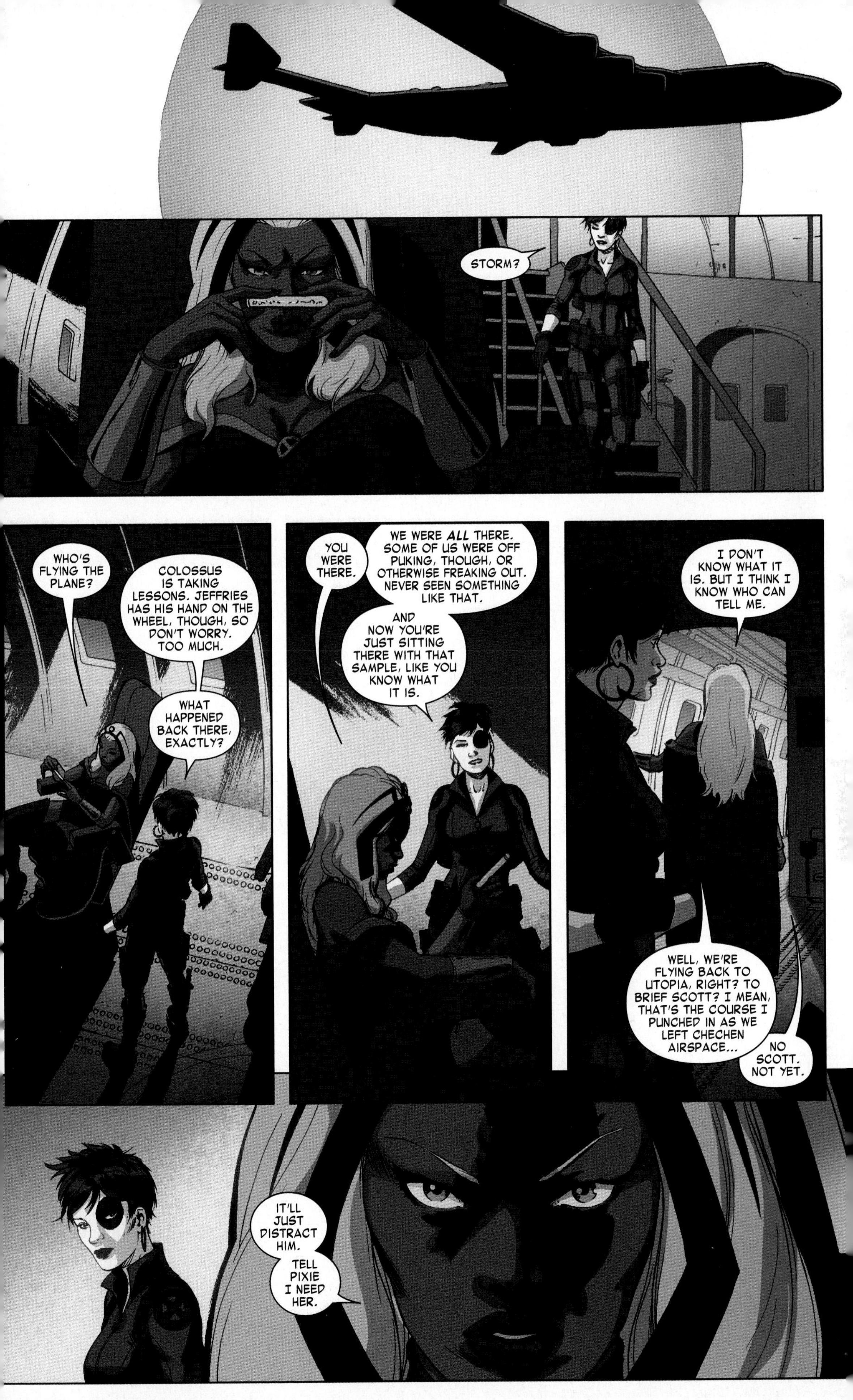
STORM?
WHO'S FLYING THE PLANE?
COLOSSUS IS TAKING LESSONS. JEFFRIES HAS HIS HAND ON THE WHEEL, THOUGH, SO DON'T WORRY. TOO MUCH.
WHAT HAPPENED BACK THERE, EXACTLY?
YOU WERE THERE.
WE WERE *ALL* THERE. SOME OF US WERE OFF PUKING, THOUGH, OR OTHERWISE FREAKING OUT. NEVER SEEN SOMETHING LIKE THAT.
AND NOW YOU'RE JUST SITTING THERE WITH THAT SAMPLE, LIKE YOU KNOW WHAT IT IS.
I DON'T KNOW WHAT IT IS. BUT I THINK I KNOW WHO CAN TELL ME.
WELL, WE'RE FLYING BACK TO UTOPIA, RIGHT? TO BRIEF SCOTT? I MEAN, THAT'S THE COURSE I PUNCHED IN AS WE LEFT CHECHEN AIRSPACE...
NO SCOTT. NOT YET.
IT'LL JUST DISTRACT HIM.
TELL PIXIE I NEED HER.

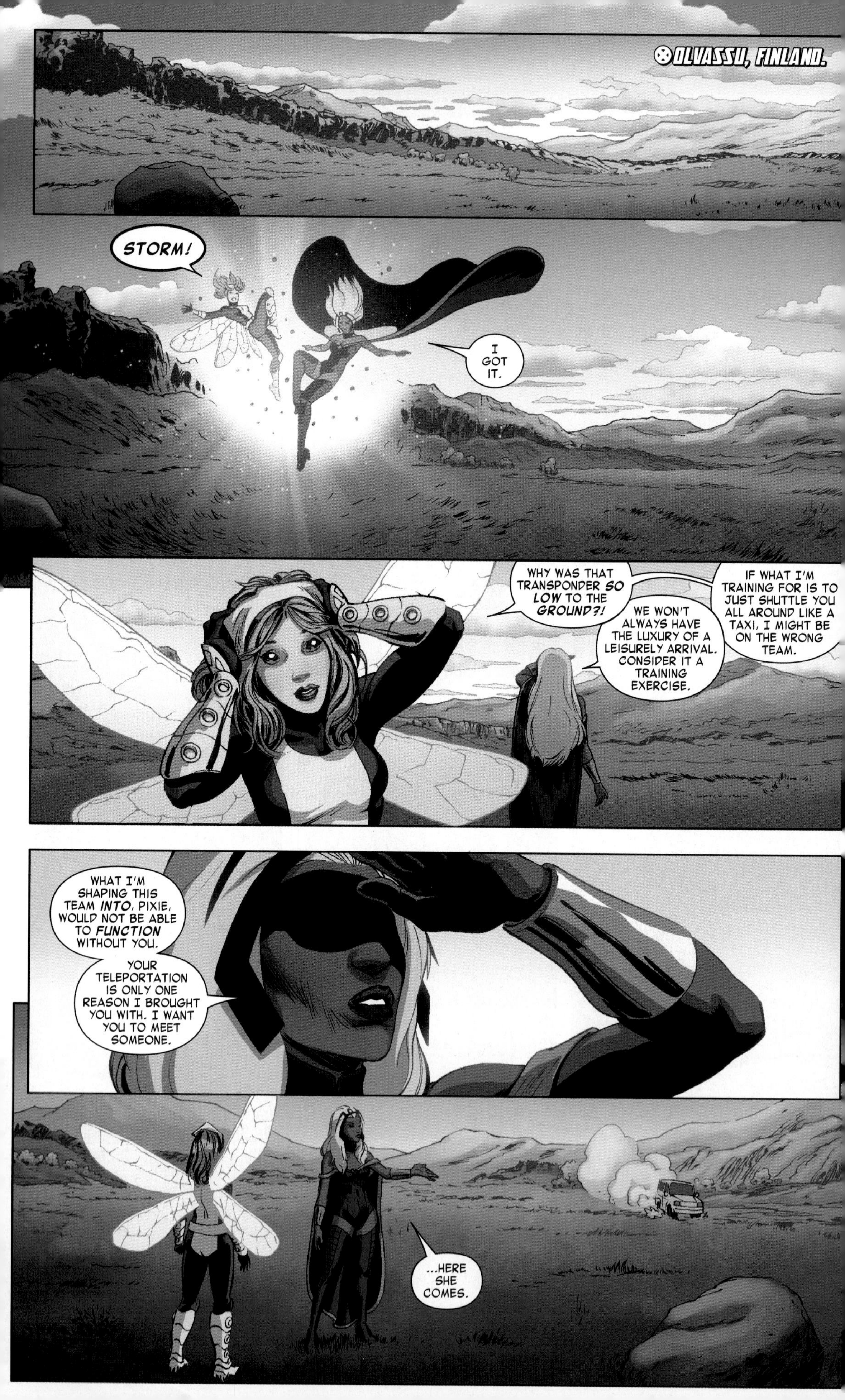
OLVASSU, FINLAND.
STORM!
I GOT IT.
WHY WAS THAT TRANSPONDER **SO LOW** TO THE **GROUND?!**
WE WON'T ALWAYS HAVE THE LUXURY OF A LEISURELY ARRIVAL. CONSIDER IT A TRAINING EXERCISE.
IF WHAT I'M TRAINING FOR IS TO JUST SHUTTLE YOU ALL AROUND LIKE A TAXI, I MIGHT BE ON THE WRONG TEAM.
WHAT I'M SHAPING THIS TEAM **INTO**, PIXIE, WOULD NOT BE ABLE TO **FUNCTION** WITHOUT YOU.
YOUR TELEPORTATION IS ONLY ONE REASON I BROUGHT YOU WITH. I WANT YOU TO MEET SOMEONE.
...HERE SHE COMES.

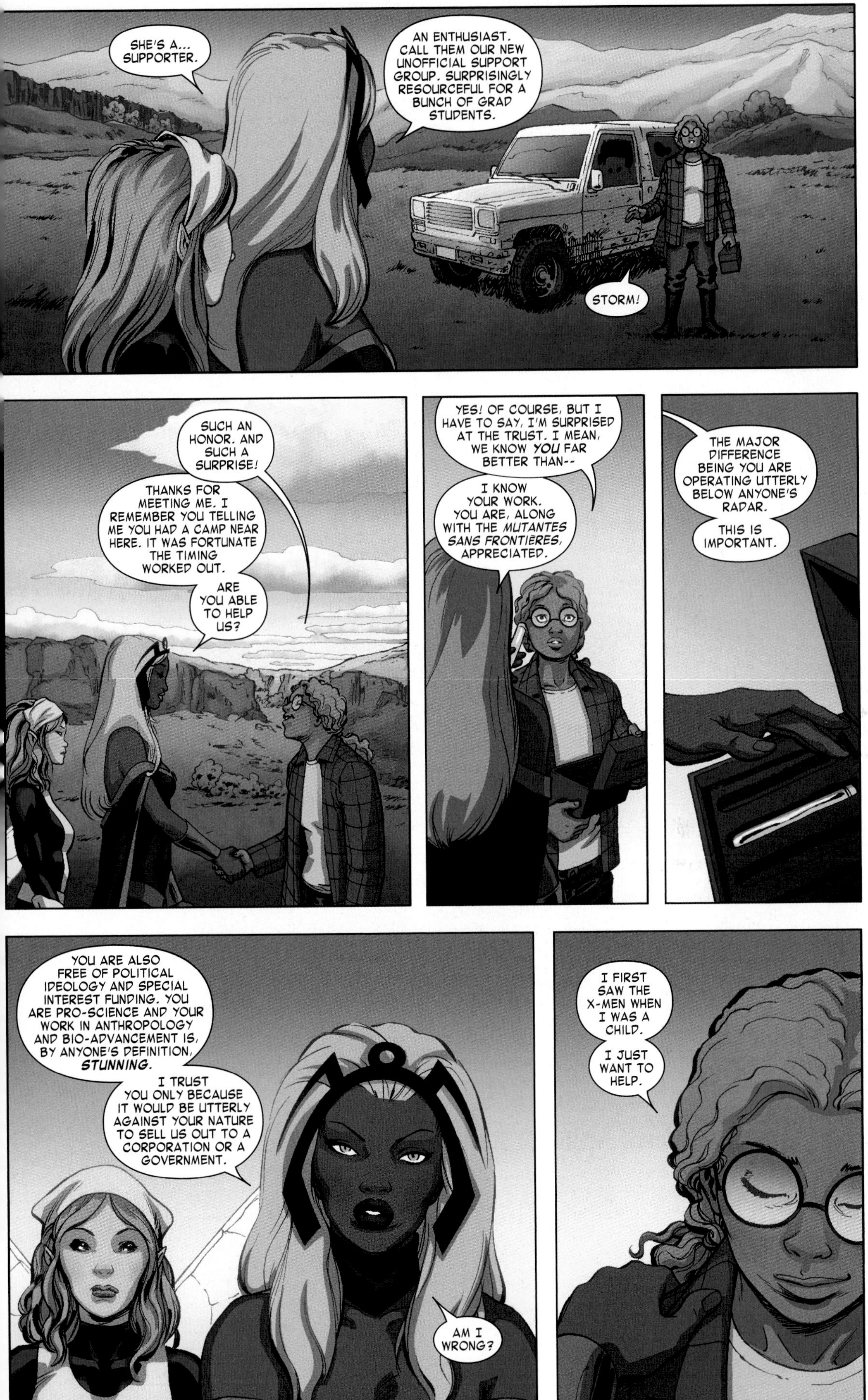
SHE'S A... SUPPORTER.
AN ENTHUSIAST. CALL THEM OUR NEW UNOFFICIAL SUPPORT GROUP. SURPRISINGLY RESOURCEFUL FOR A BUNCH OF GRAD STUDENTS.
STORM!
THANKS FOR MEETING ME. I REMEMBER YOU TELLING ME YOU HAD A CAMP NEAR HERE. IT WAS FORTUNATE THE TIMING WORKED OUT.
SUCH AN HONOR. AND SUCH A SURPRISE!
ARE YOU ABLE TO HELP US?
YES! OF COURSE, BUT I HAVE TO SAY, I'M SURPRISED AT THE TRUST. I MEAN, WE KNOW YOU FAR BETTER THAN--
I KNOW YOUR WORK. YOU ARE, ALONG WITH THE MUTANTES SANS FRONTIÈRES, APPRECIATED.
THE MAJOR DIFFERENCE BEING YOU ARE OPERATING UTTERLY BELOW ANYONE'S RADAR.
THIS IS IMPORTANT.
YOU ARE ALSO FREE OF POLITICAL IDEOLOGY AND SPECIAL INTEREST FUNDING. YOU ARE PRO-SCIENCE AND YOUR WORK IN ANTHROPOLOGY AND BIO-ADVANCEMENT IS, BY ANYONE'S DEFINITION, STUNNING.
I TRUST YOU ONLY BECAUSE IT WOULD BE UTTERLY AGAINST YOUR NATURE TO SELL US OUT TO A CORPORATION OR A GOVERNMENT.
AM I WRONG?
I FIRST SAW THE X-MEN WHEN I WAS A CHILD.
I JUST WANT TO HELP.

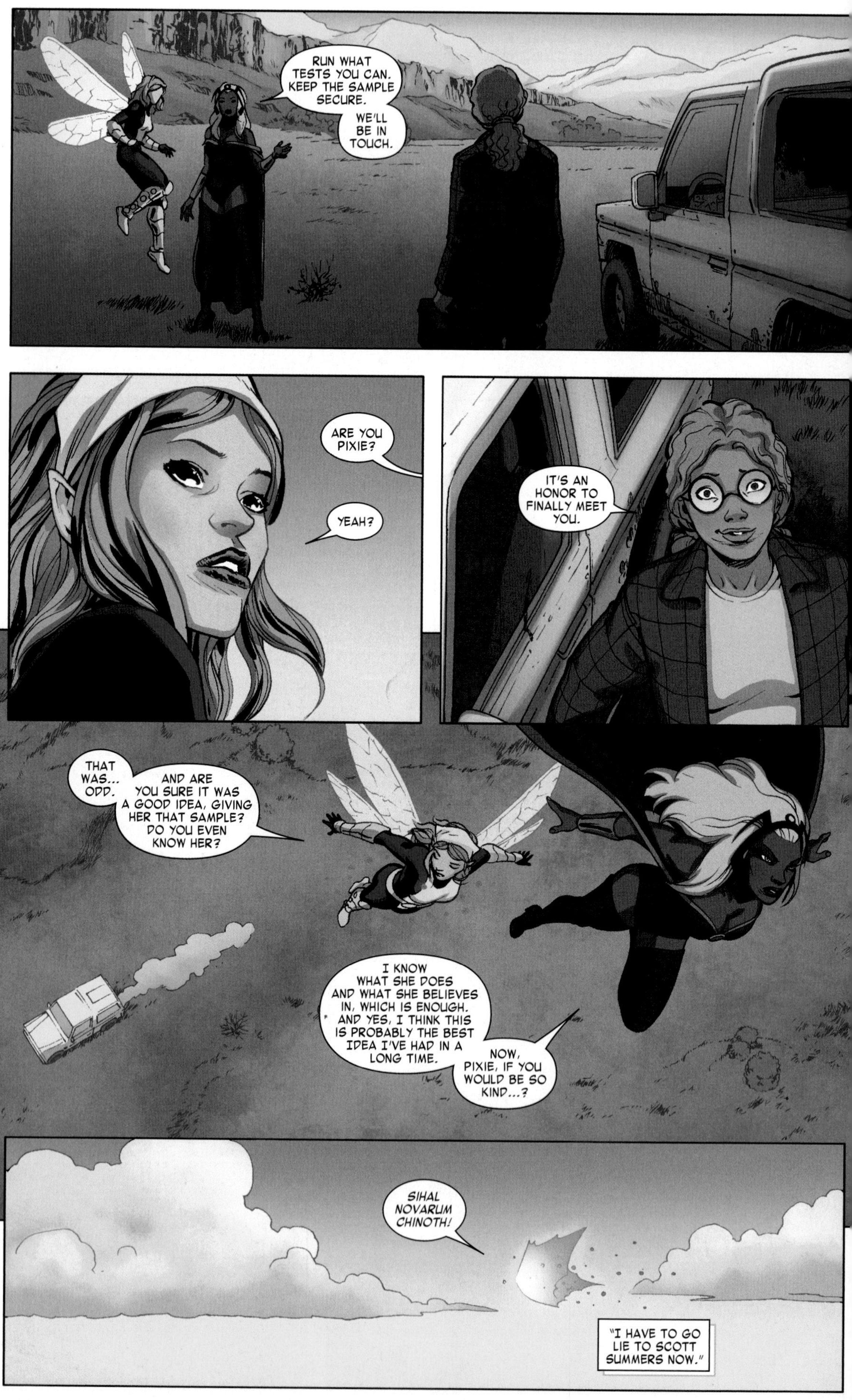
RUN WHAT TESTS YOU CAN. KEEP THE SAMPLE SECURE.
WE'LL BE IN TOUCH.
ARE YOU PIXIE?
YEAH?
IT'S AN HONOR TO FINALLY MEET YOU.
THAT WAS... ODD.
AND ARE YOU SURE IT WAS A GOOD IDEA, GIVING HER THAT SAMPLE? DO YOU EVEN KNOW HER?
I KNOW WHAT SHE DOES AND WHAT SHE BELIEVES IN, WHICH IS ENOUGH. AND YES, I THINK THIS IS PROBABLY THE BEST IDEA I'VE HAD IN A LONG TIME.
NOW, PIXIE, IF YOU WOULD BE SO KIND...?
SIHAL NOVARUM CHINOTH!
"I HAVE TO GO LIE TO SCOTT SUMMERS NOW."

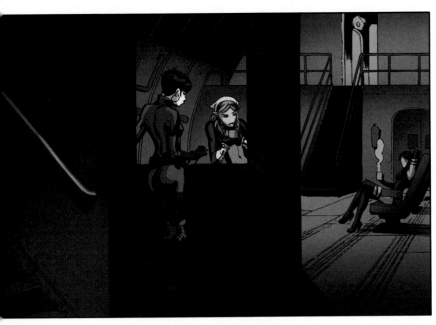

I TOLD YOU...

IF I'M TO TAKE THE "SECURITY TEAM" CONCEPT TO ITS FULLEST POTENTIAL, I NEED SOME LEEWAY...

...A LOT OF LEEWAY. I CAN'T HAVE YOU MICRO-MANAGING THIS. TRUST US.

I JUST WANT UPDATES, ORORO. I WANT FACE-TO-FACE VISITS. I NEED TO BE IN THE LOOP.

HOW MANY TIMES HAVE YOU BLOWN ME OFF THIS PAST MONTH?

OUR MANDATE INSISTS WE STOP AND RESPOND WHEN NEEDED.

SCOTT, I WRITE YOU TERRIFIC BRIEFS AND YOU KNOW IT.

FINE. SO, GROZNY. I READ YOUR REPORT.

SOCIAL MEDIA GOT THE NEWS OUT FIRST, I'M SORRY TO SAY, BUT THE REGIME IN POWER SHUT ACCESS DOWN FAST AND I BELIEVE THE STORY IS LARGELY CONTAINED.

AND THE... SUBJECT?

NON-HUMAN ENTITY, SEMI-SENTIENT, DESTROYING CITY BLOCKS. COLOSSUS TOOK IT OUT WITH ONE PUNCH.

...SERIOUSLY?

NO DISREPECT TO PIOTR, BUT THE CREATURE APPEARED TO BE ON ITS LAST LEGS ANYWAY.

THEN IT DISSOLVED.

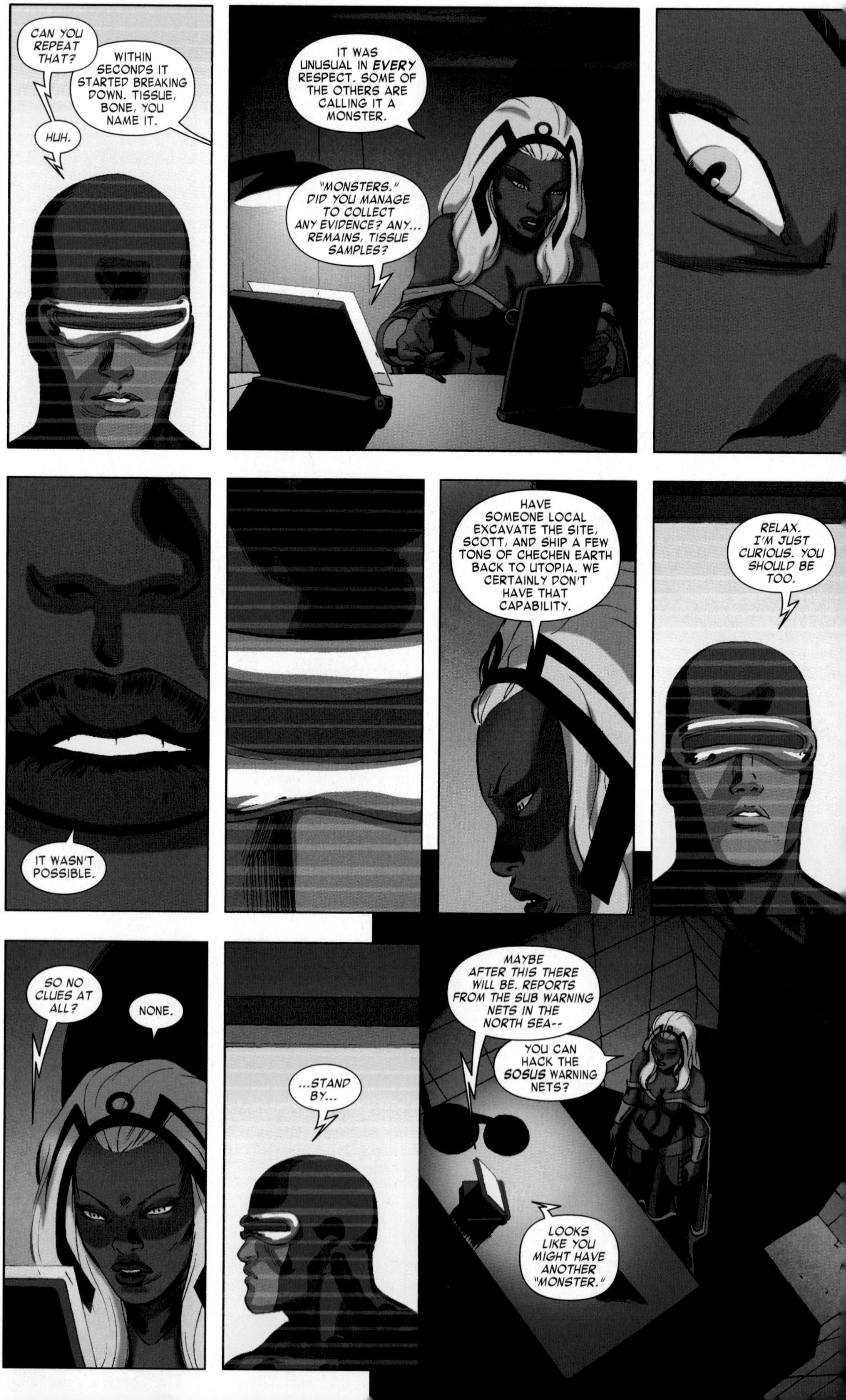
CAN YOU REPEAT THAT?
WITHIN SECONDS IT STARTED BREAKING DOWN. TISSUE, BONE, YOU NAME IT.
HUH.
IT WAS UNUSUAL IN EVERY RESPECT. SOME OF THE OTHERS ARE CALLING IT A MONSTER.
"MONSTERS." DID YOU MANAGE TO COLLECT ANY EVIDENCE? ANY... REMAINS, TISSUE SAMPLES?
IT WASN'T POSSIBLE.
HAVE SOMEONE LOCAL EXCAVATE THE SITE, SCOTT, AND SHIP A FEW TONS OF CHECHEN EARTH BACK TO UTOPIA. WE CERTAINLY DON'T HAVE THAT CAPABILITY.
RELAX. I'M JUST CURIOUS. YOU SHOULD BE TOO.
SO NO CLUES AT ALL?
NONE.
...STAND BY...
MAYBE AFTER THIS THERE WILL BE. REPORTS FROM THE SUB WARNING NETS IN THE NORTH SEA--
YOU CAN HACK THE SOSUS WARNING NETS?
LOOKS LIKE YOU MIGHT HAVE ANOTHER "MONSTER."

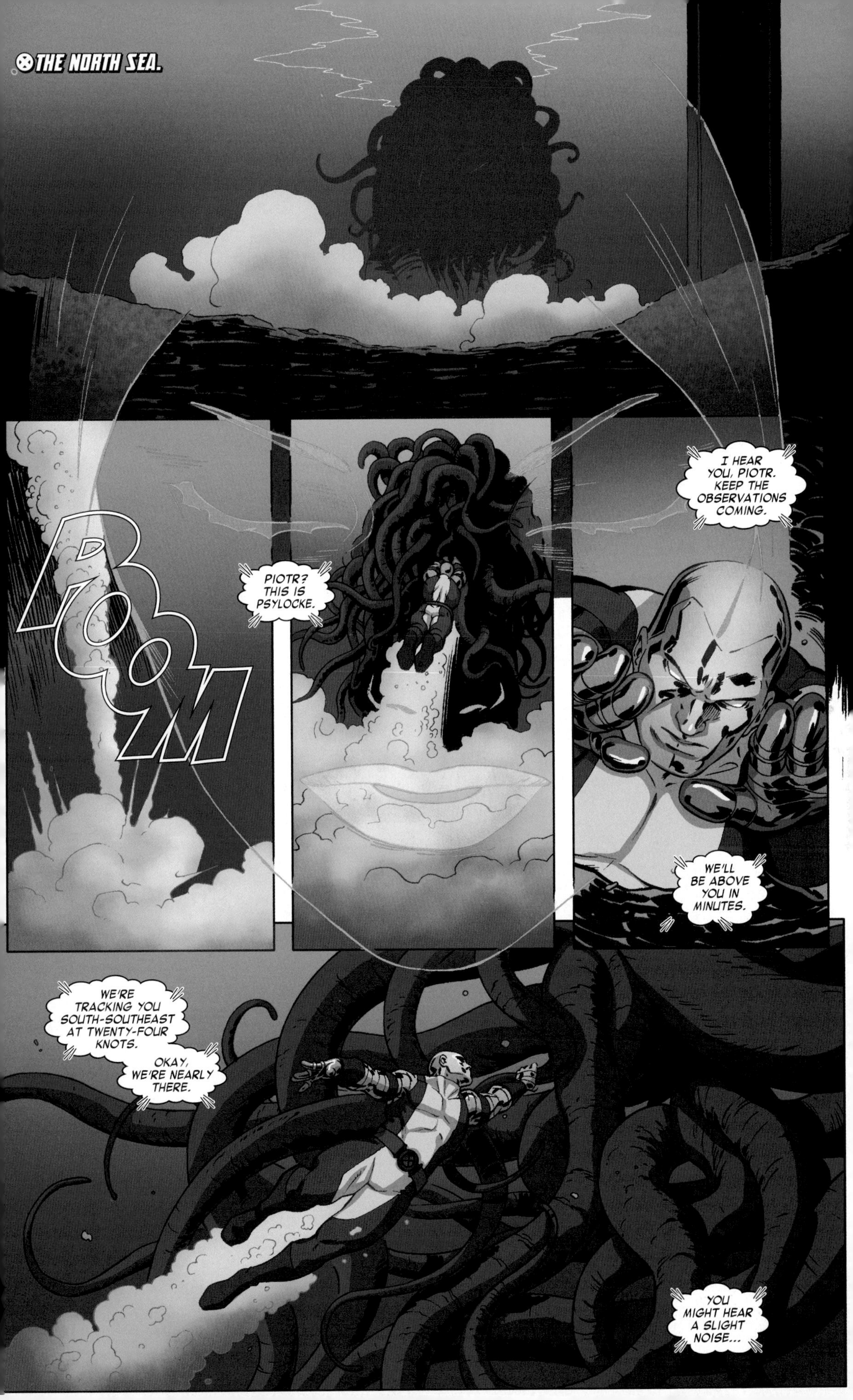
THE NORTH SEA.
BOOM
PIOTR? THIS IS PSYLOCKE.
I HEAR YOU, PIOTR. KEEP THE OBSERVATIONS COMING.
WE'LL BE ABOVE YOU IN MINUTES.
WE'RE TRACKING YOU SOUTH-SOUTHEAST AT TWENTY-FOUR KNOTS.
OKAY, WE'RE NEARLY THERE.
YOU MIGHT HEAR A SLIGHT NOISE...

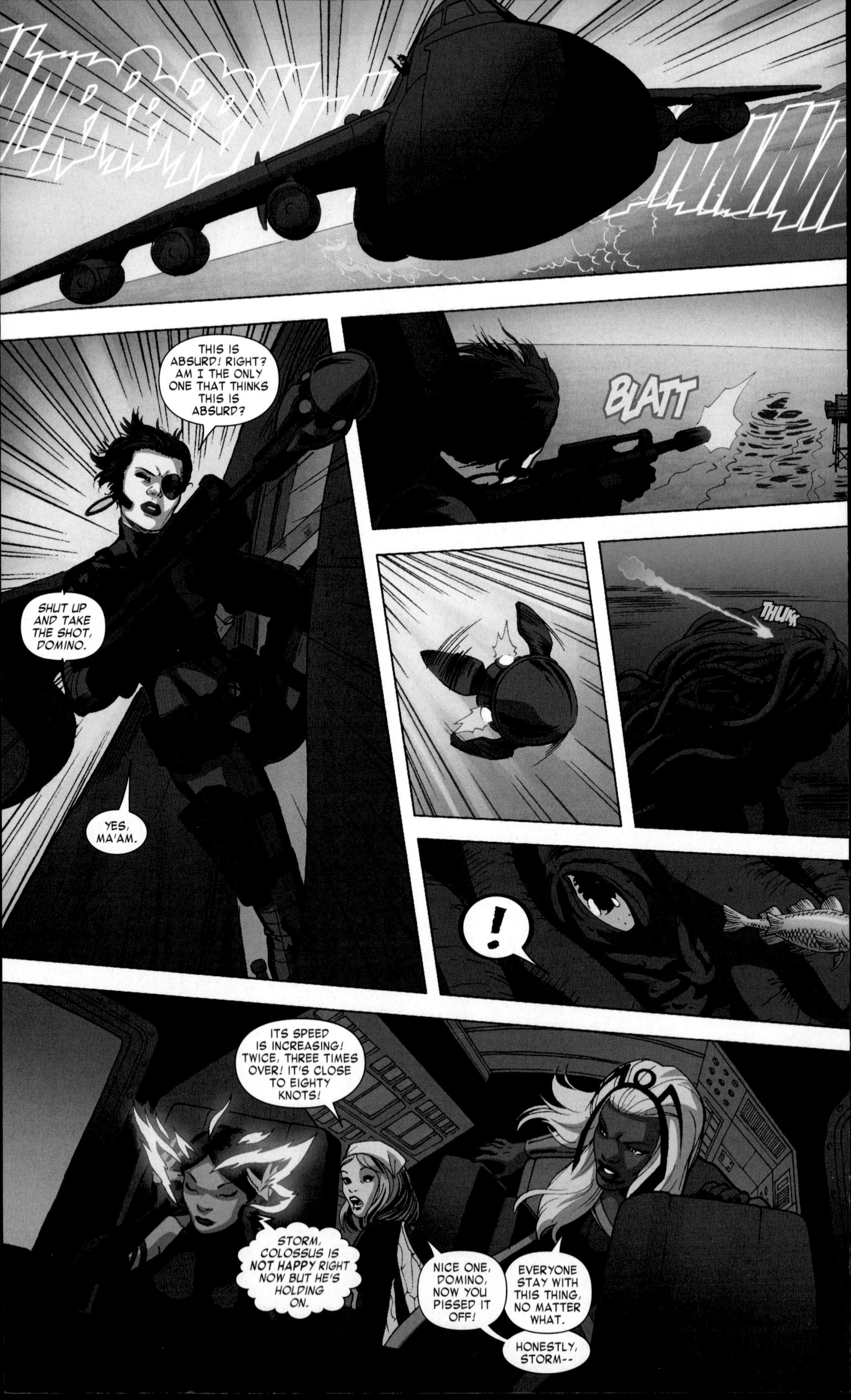

THIS IS ABSURD! RIGHT? AM I THE ONLY ONE THAT THINKS THIS IS ABSURD?
SHUT UP AND TAKE THE SHOT, DOMINO.
YES, MA'AM.
BLATT
THUKK
!
ITS SPEED IS INCREASING! TWICE, THREE TIMES OVER! IT'S CLOSE TO EIGHTY KNOTS!
STORM, COLOSSUS IS **NOT HAPPY** RIGHT NOW BUT HE'S HOLDING ON.
NICE ONE, DOMINO, NOW YOU PISSED IT OFF!
EVERYONE STAY WITH THIS THING, NO MATTER WHAT.
HONESTLY, STORM--

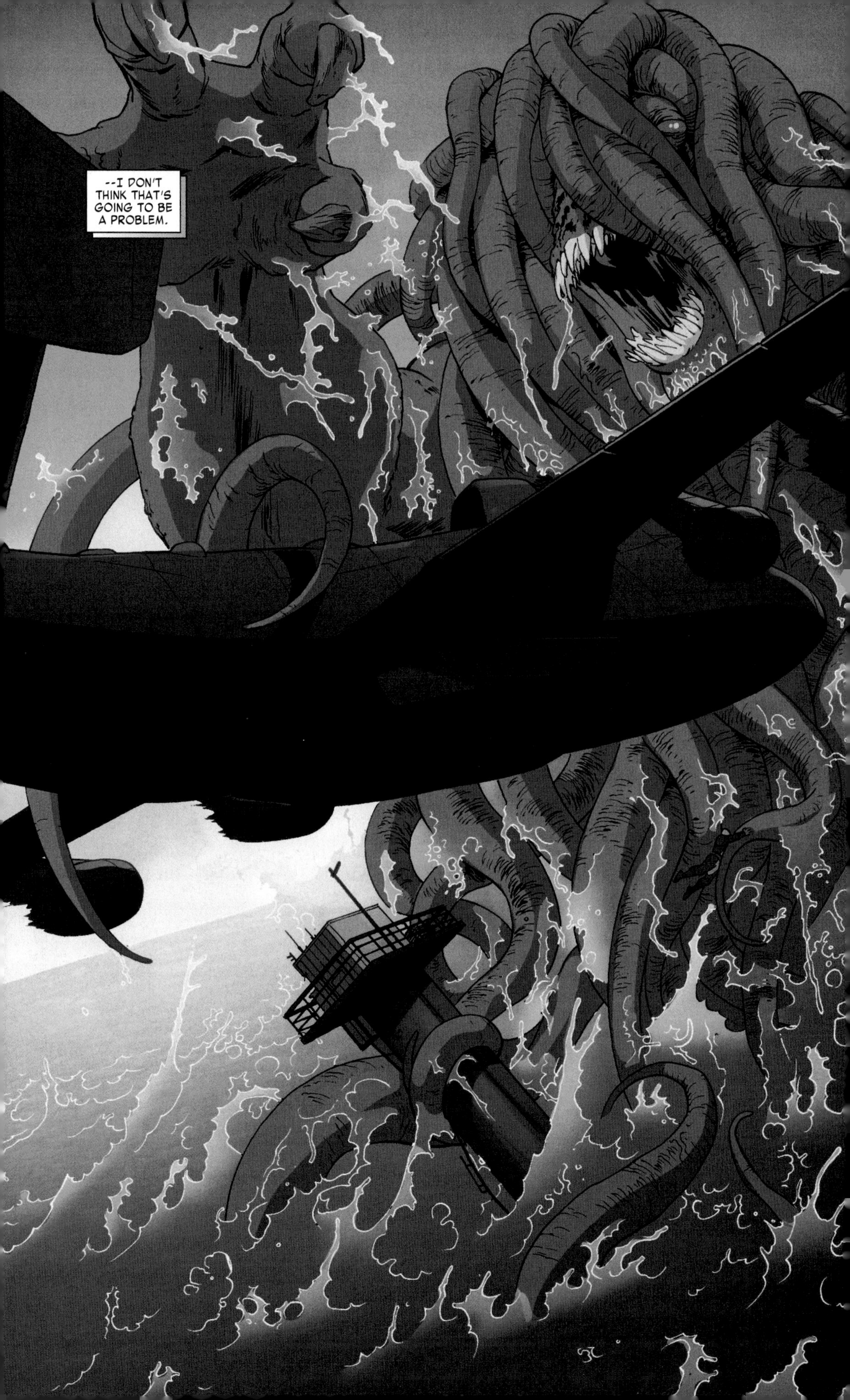
--I DON'T THINK THAT'S GOING TO BE A PROBLEM.

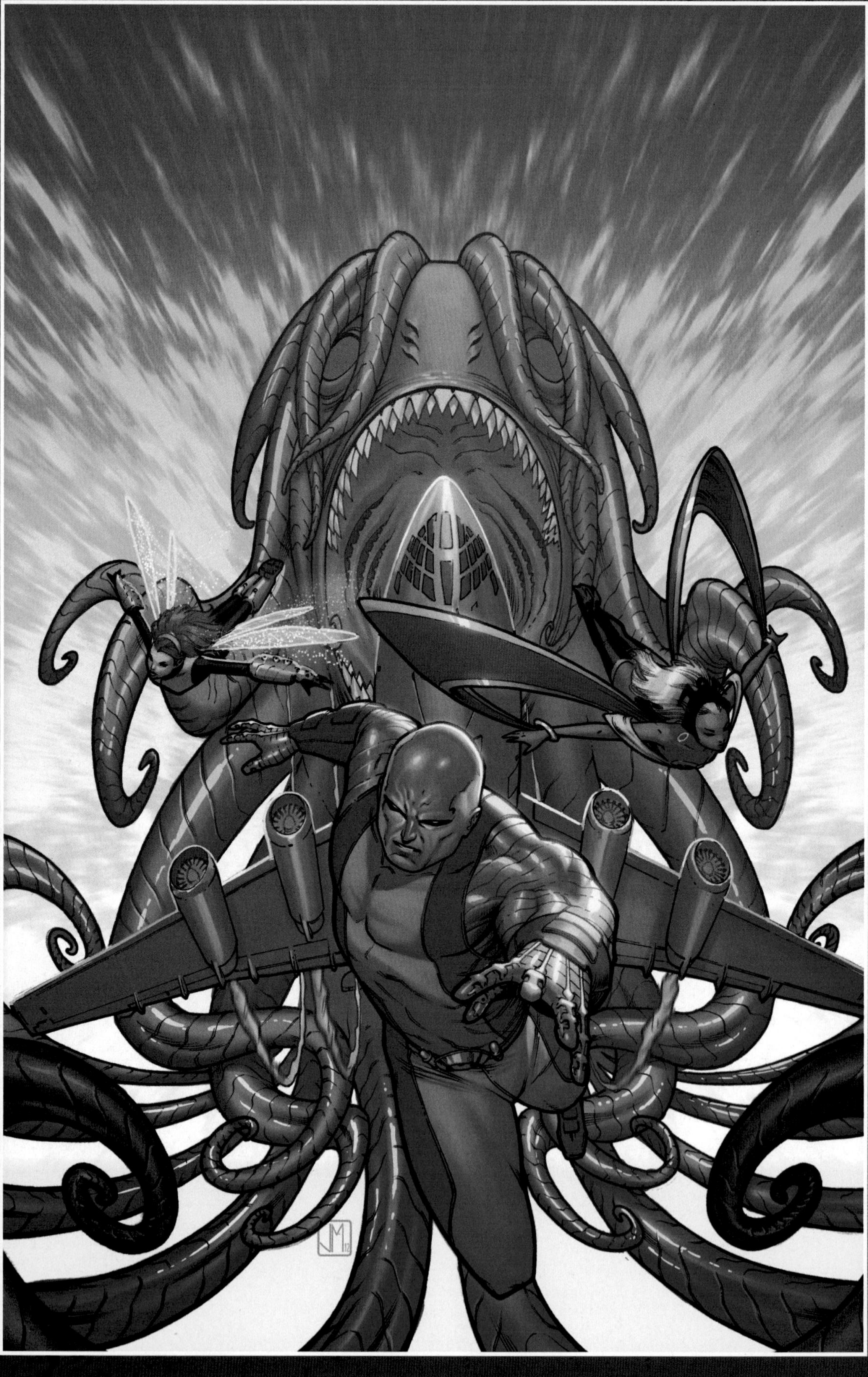

THIRTY-ONE

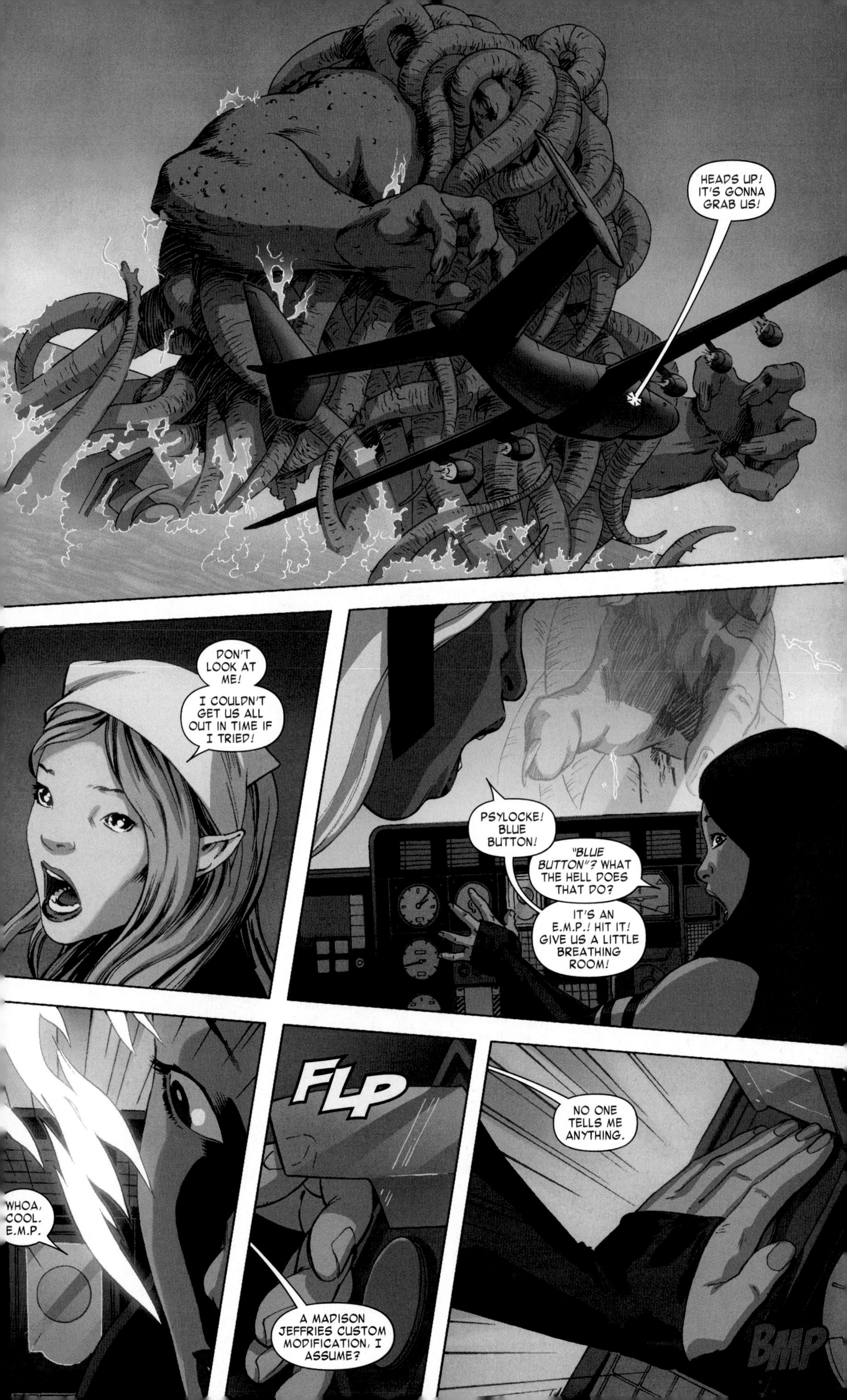
HEADS UP! IT'S GONNA GRAB US!
DON'T LOOK AT ME!
I COULDN'T GET US ALL OUT IN TIME IF I TRIED!
PSYLOCKE! BLUE BUTTON!
"BLUE BUTTON"? WHAT THE HELL DOES THAT DO?
IT'S AN E.M.P.! HIT IT! GIVE US A LITTLE BREATHING ROOM!
WHOA, COOL. E.M.P.
FLP
A MADISON JEFFRIES CUSTOM MODIFICATION, I ASSUME?
NO ONE TELLS ME ANYTHING.
BMP

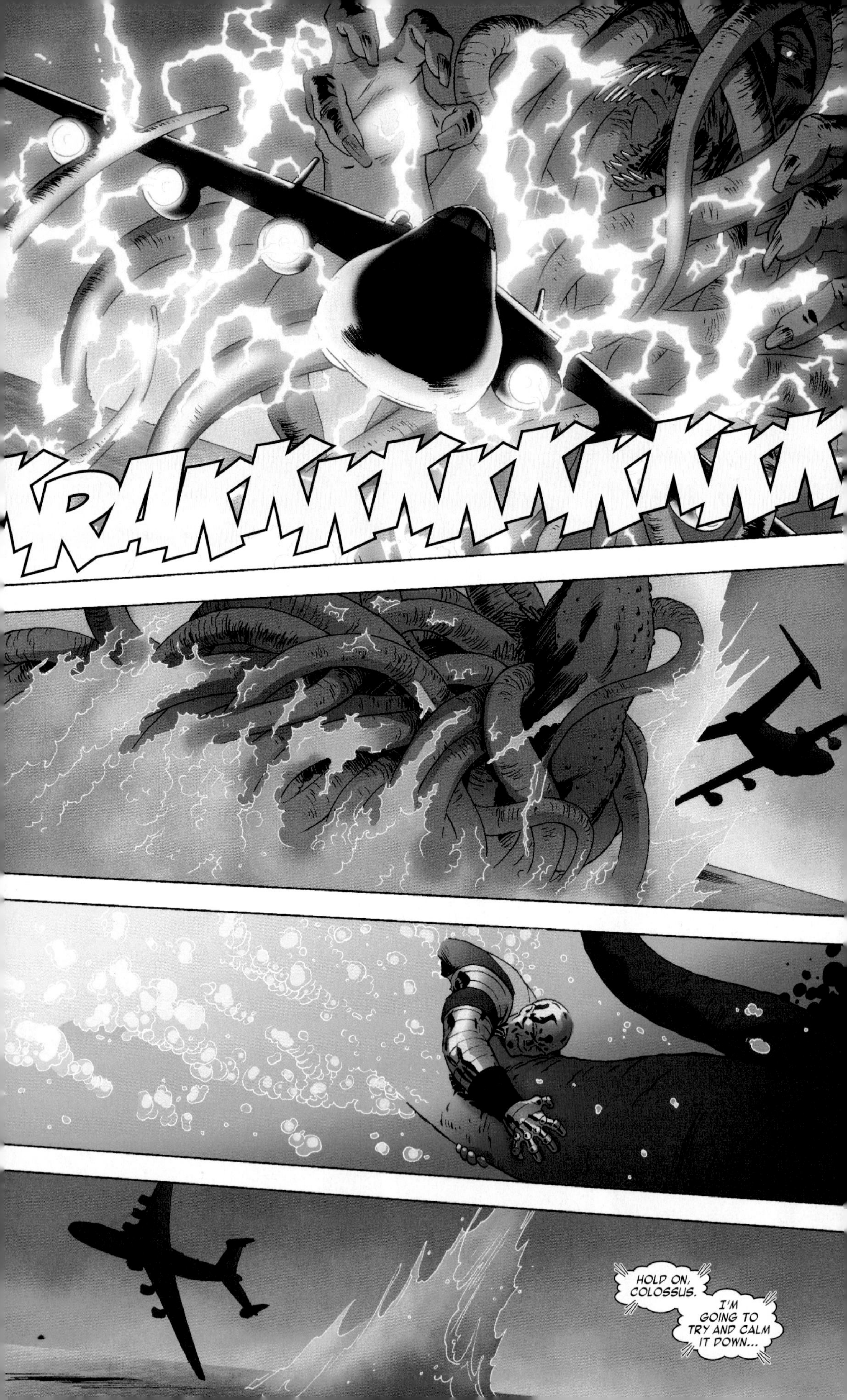
KRAKKKKKKKKKKK
HOLD ON, COLOSSUS.
I'M GOING TO TRY AND CALM IT DOWN...

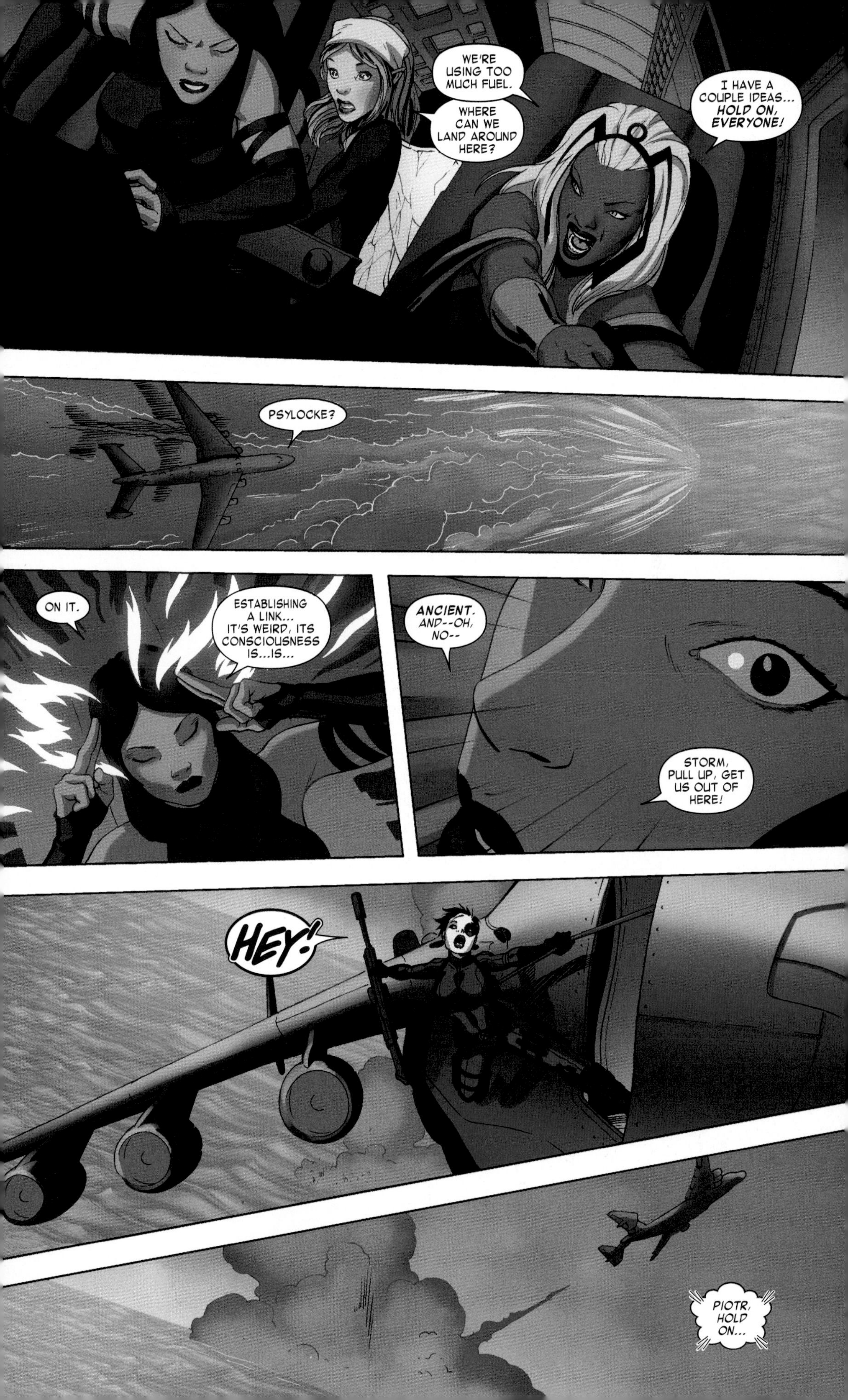
WE'RE USING TOO MUCH FUEL.
WHERE CAN WE LAND AROUND HERE?
I HAVE A COUPLE IDEAS... HOLD ON, EVERYONE!
PSYLOCKE?
ON IT.
ESTABLISHING A LINK... IT'S WEIRD, ITS CONSCIOUSNESS IS...IS...
ANCIENT. AND--OH, NO--
STORM, PULL UP, GET US OUT OF HERE!
HEY!
PIOTR, HOLD ON...

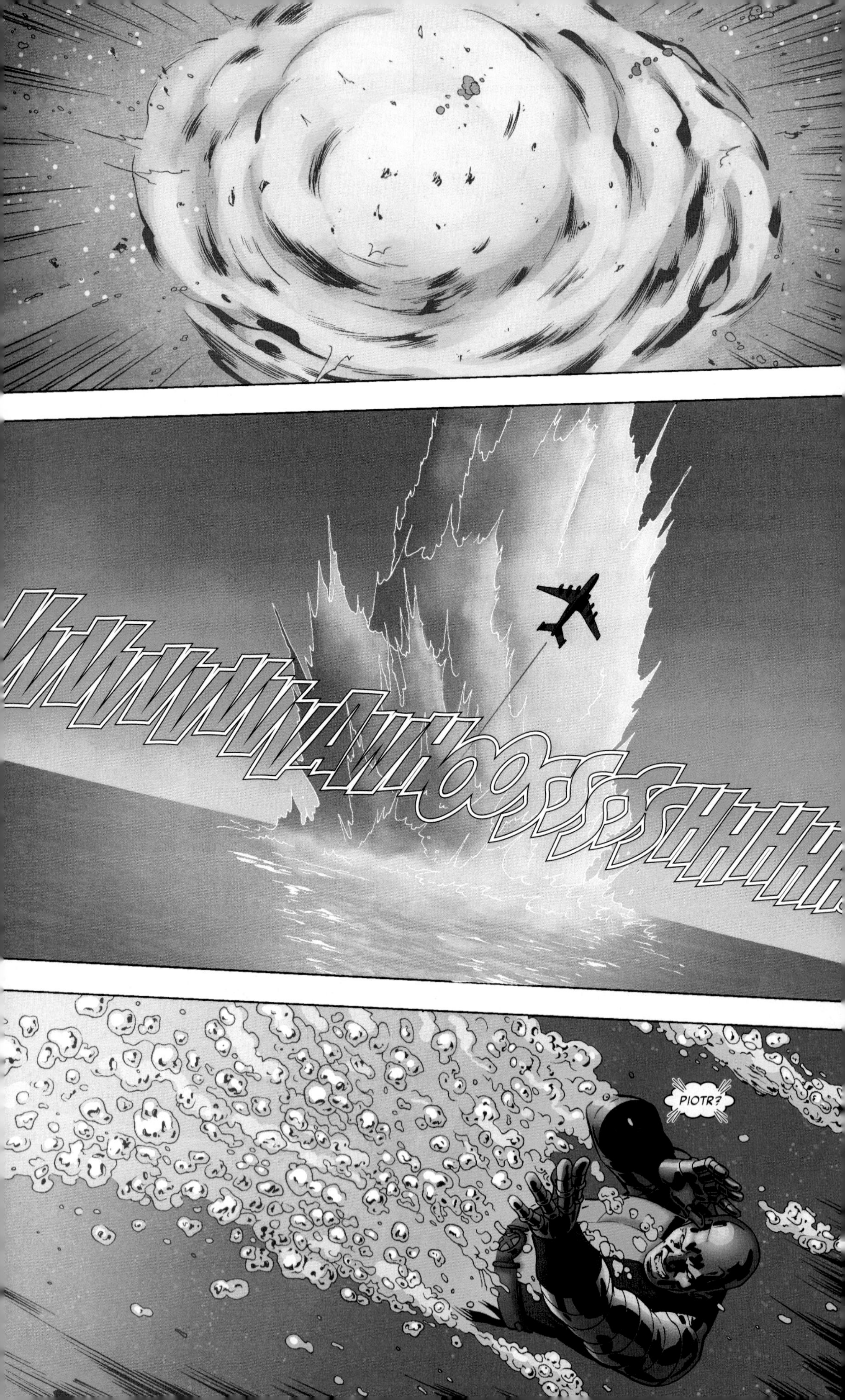
PIOTR?

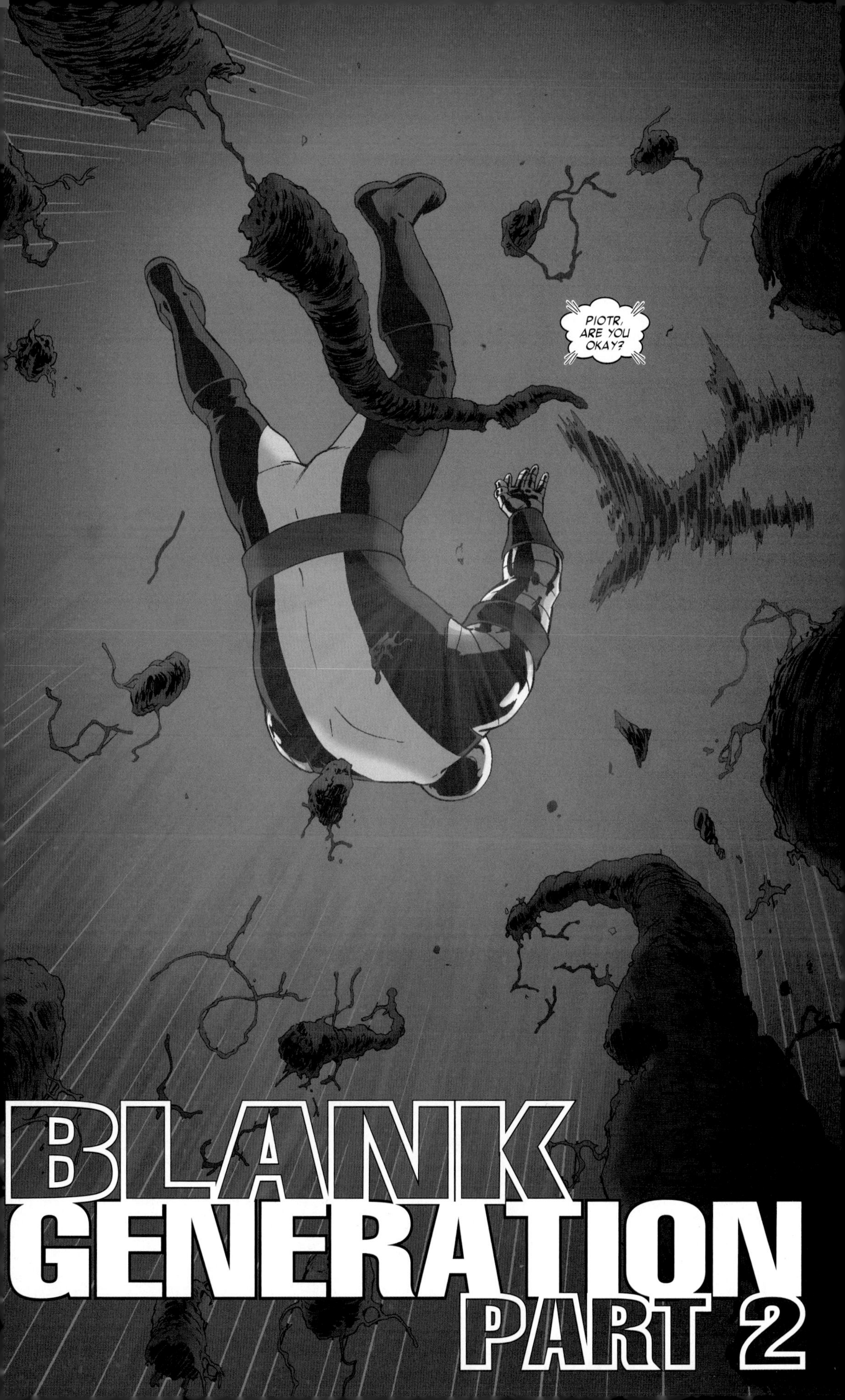
PIOTR, ARE YOU OKAY?
BLANK GENERATION PART 2

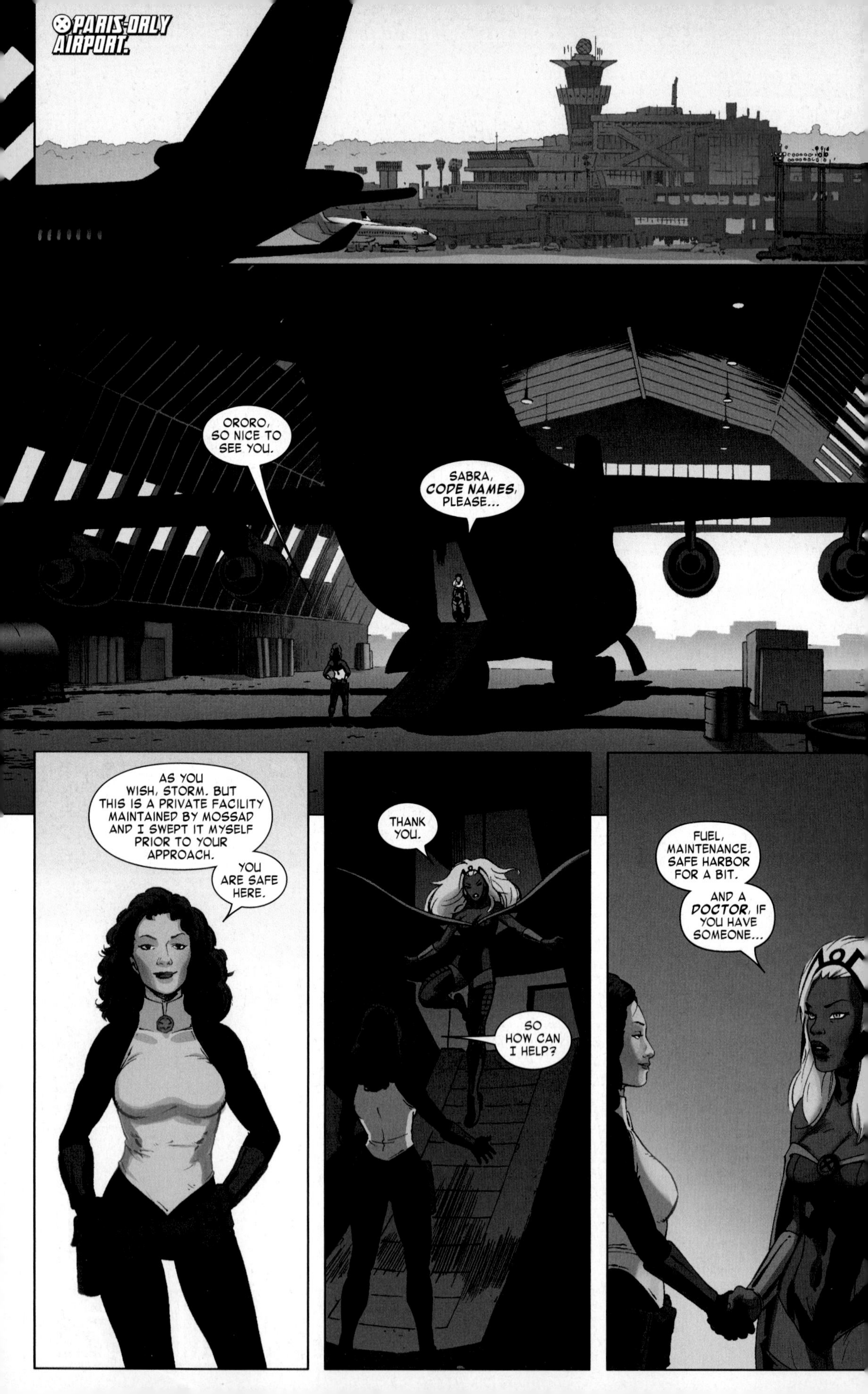
PARIS-ORLY AIRPORT.
ORORO, SO NICE TO SEE YOU.
SABRA, CODE NAMES, PLEASE...
AS YOU WISH, STORM. BUT THIS IS A PRIVATE FACILITY MAINTAINED BY MOSSAD AND I SWEPT IT MYSELF PRIOR TO YOUR APPROACH.
YOU ARE SAFE HERE.
THANK YOU.
SO HOW CAN I HELP?
FUEL, MAINTENANCE. SAFE HARBOR FOR A BIT.
AND A DOCTOR, IF YOU HAVE SOMEONE...

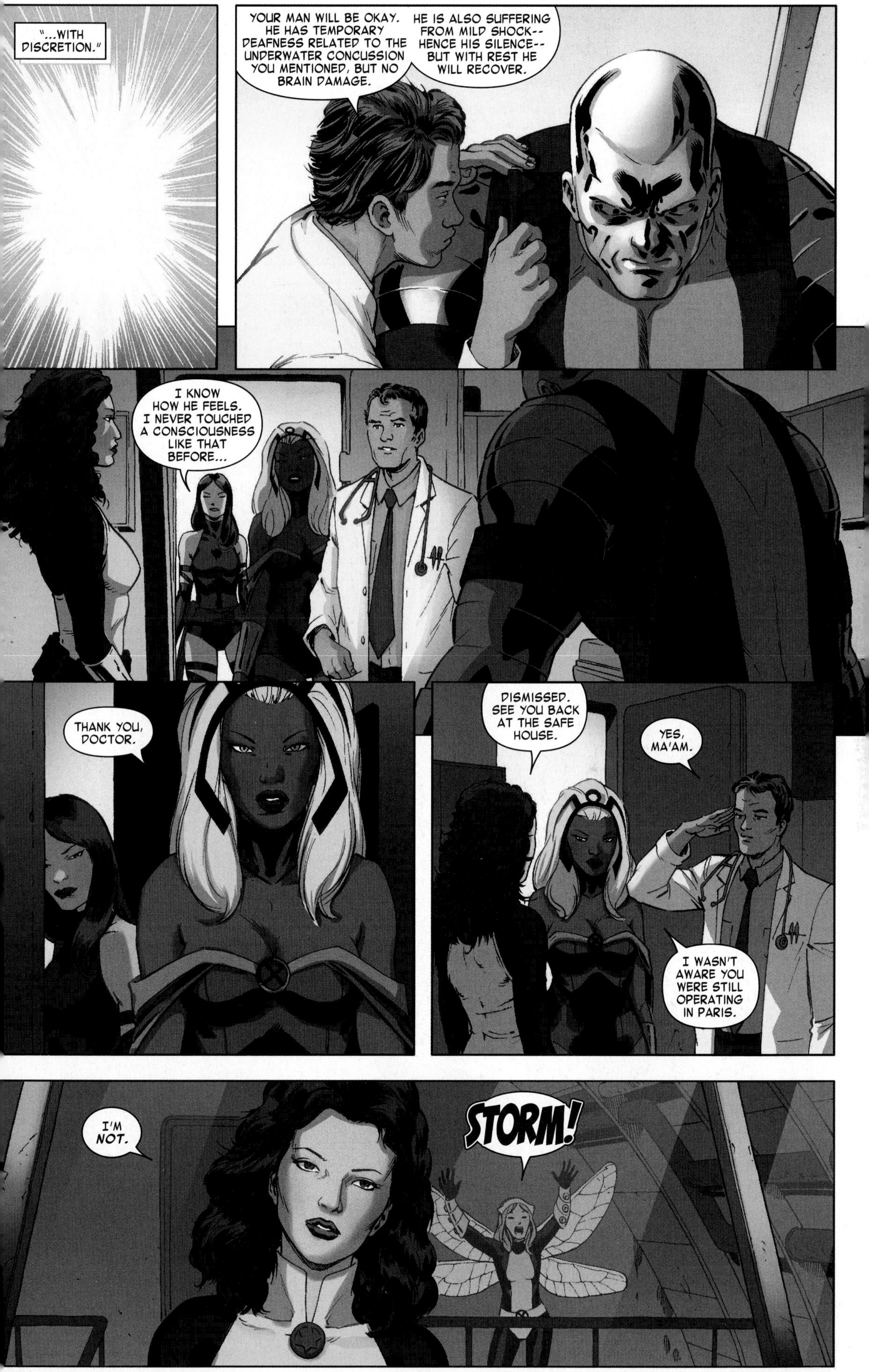
"...WITH DISCRETION."
YOUR MAN WILL BE OKAY. HE HAS TEMPORARY DEAFNESS RELATED TO THE UNDERWATER CONCUSSION YOU MENTIONED, BUT NO BRAIN DAMAGE.
HE IS ALSO SUFFERING FROM MILD SHOCK-- HENCE HIS SILENCE-- BUT WITH REST HE WILL RECOVER.
I KNOW HOW HE FEELS. I NEVER TOUCHED A CONSCIOUSNESS LIKE THAT BEFORE...
THANK YOU, DOCTOR.
DISMISSED. SEE YOU BACK AT THE SAFE HOUSE.
YES, MA'AM.
I WASN'T AWARE YOU WERE STILL OPERATING IN PARIS.
I'M NOT.
STORM!

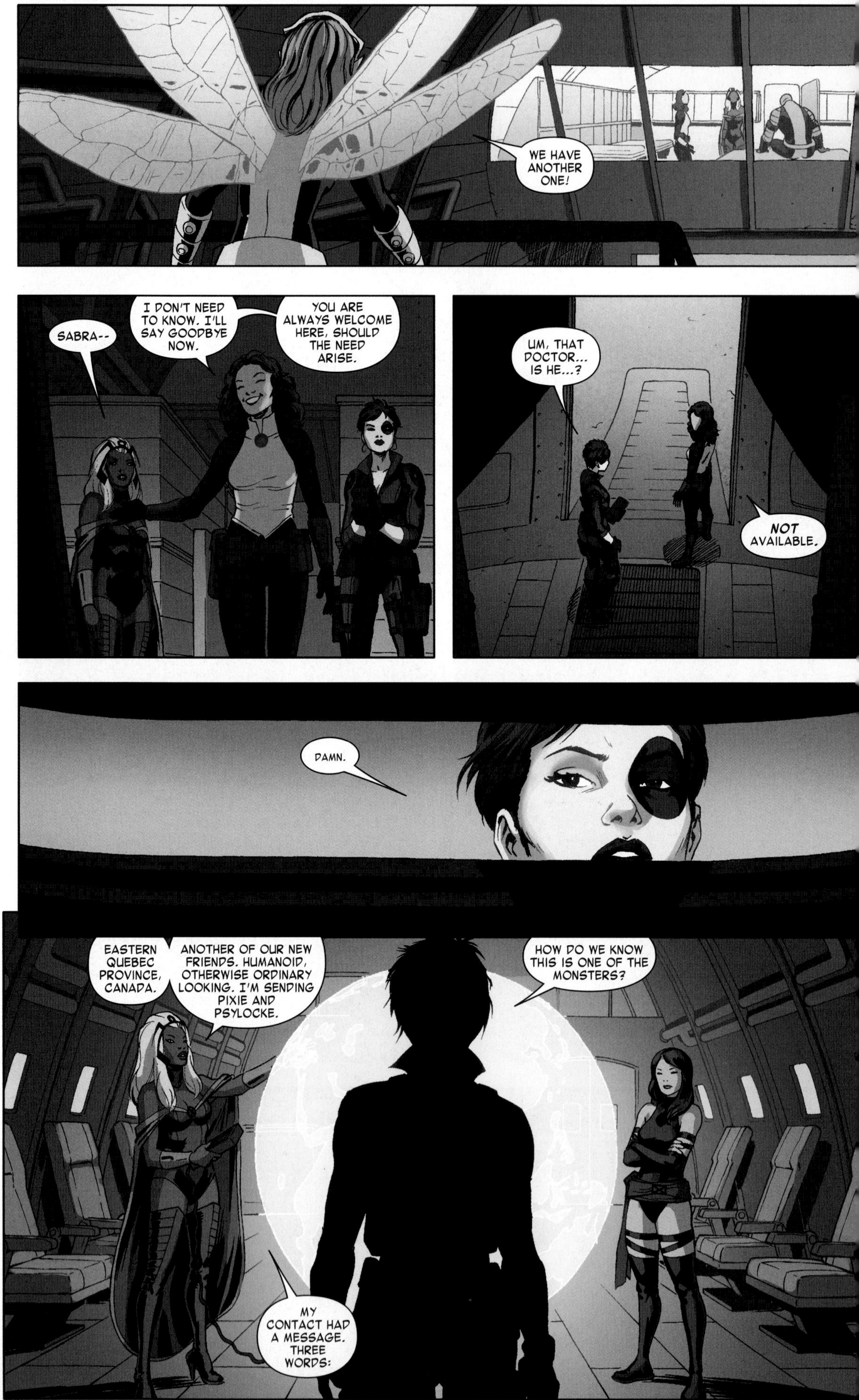
WE HAVE ANOTHER ONE!
SABRA--
I DON'T NEED TO KNOW. I'LL SAY GOODBYE NOW.
YOU ARE ALWAYS WELCOME HERE, SHOULD THE NEED ARISE.
UM, THAT DOCTOR... IS HE...?
NOT AVAILABLE.
DAMN.
EASTERN QUEBEC PROVINCE, CANADA.
ANOTHER OF OUR NEW FRIENDS. HUMANOID, OTHERWISE ORDINARY LOOKING. I'M SENDING PIXIE AND PSYLOCKE.
HOW DO WE KNOW THIS IS ONE OF THE MONSTERS?
MY CONTACT HAD A MESSAGE. THREE WORDS:

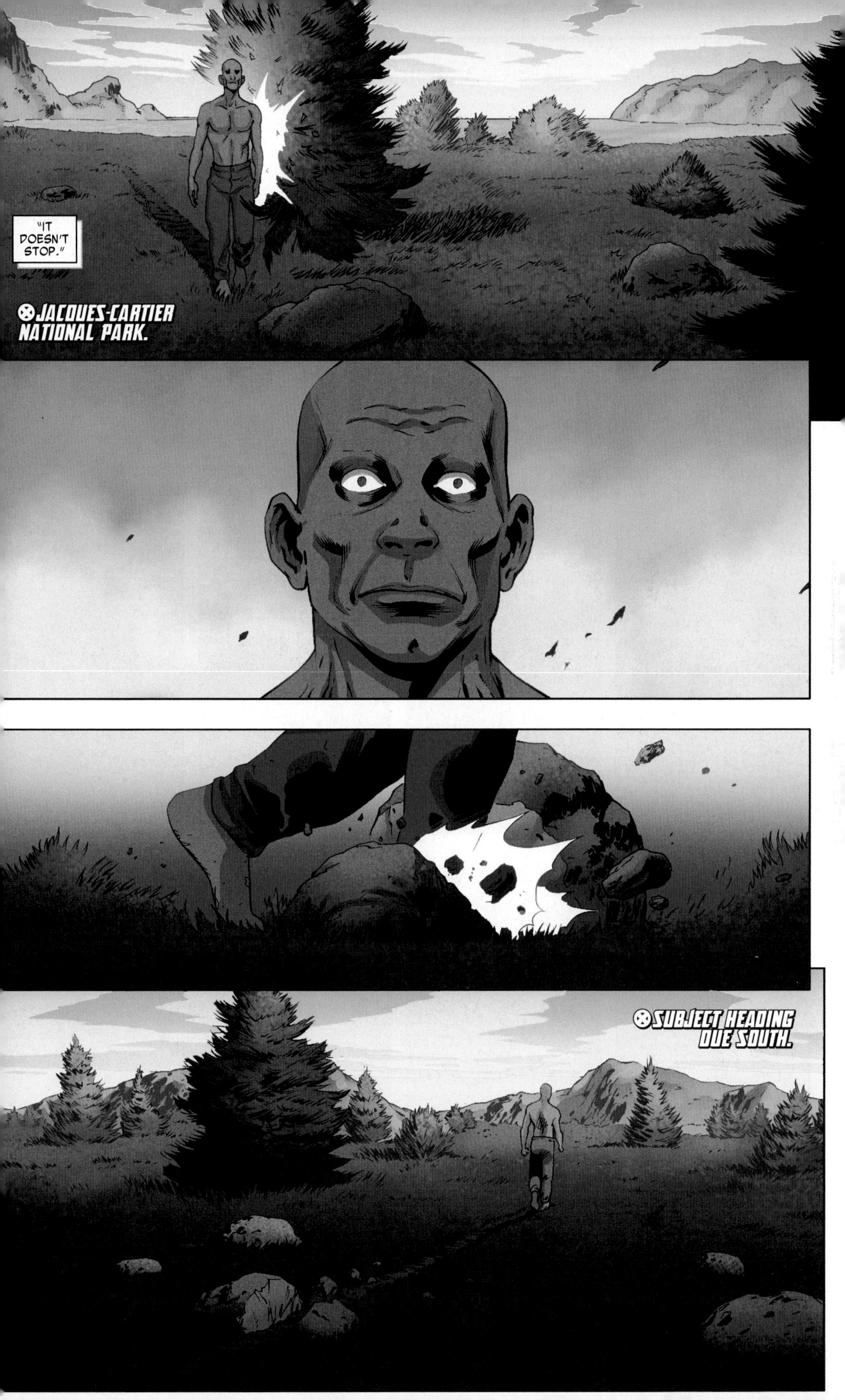
"IT DOESN'T STOP."
JACQUES-CARTIER NATIONAL PARK.
SUBJECT HEADING DUE SOUTH.

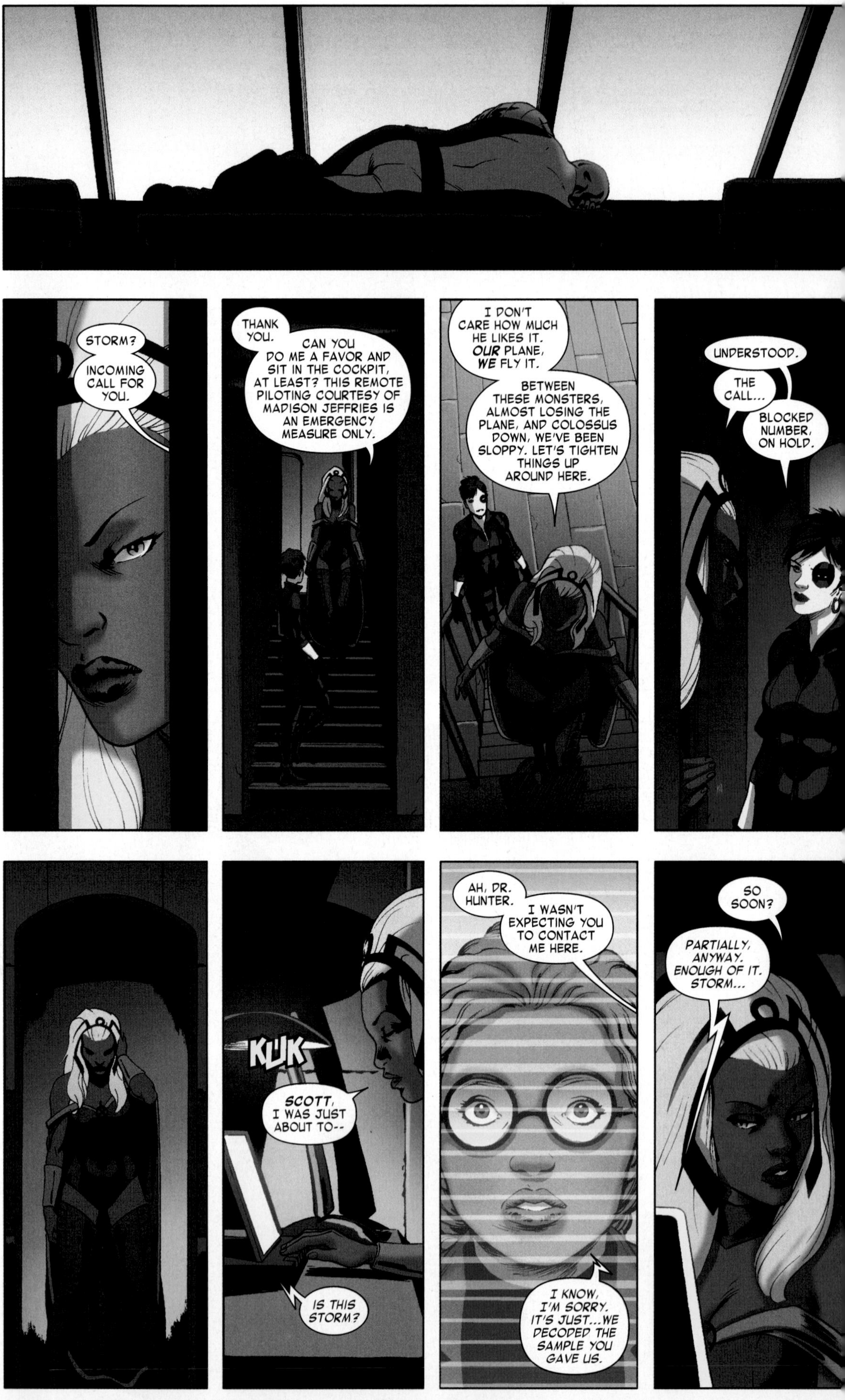
STORM?
INCOMING CALL FOR YOU.
THANK YOU.
CAN YOU DO ME A FAVOR AND SIT IN THE COCKPIT, AT LEAST? THIS REMOTE PILOTING COURTESY OF MADISON JEFFRIES IS AN EMERGENCY MEASURE ONLY.
I DON'T CARE HOW MUCH HE LIKES IT. OUR PLANE, WE FLY IT.
BETWEEN THESE MONSTERS, ALMOST LOSING THE PLANE, AND COLOSSUS DOWN, WE'VE BEEN SLOPPY. LET'S TIGHTEN THINGS UP AROUND HERE.
UNDERSTOOD.
THE CALL...
BLOCKED NUMBER, ON HOLD.
KLIK
SCOTT, I WAS JUST ABOUT TO--
IS THIS STORM?
AH, DR. HUNTER.
I WASN'T EXPECTING YOU TO CONTACT ME HERE.
I KNOW, I'M SORRY. IT'S JUST...WE DECODED THE SAMPLE YOU GAVE US.
SO SOON?
PARTIALLY, ANYWAY. ENOUGH OF IT. STORM...

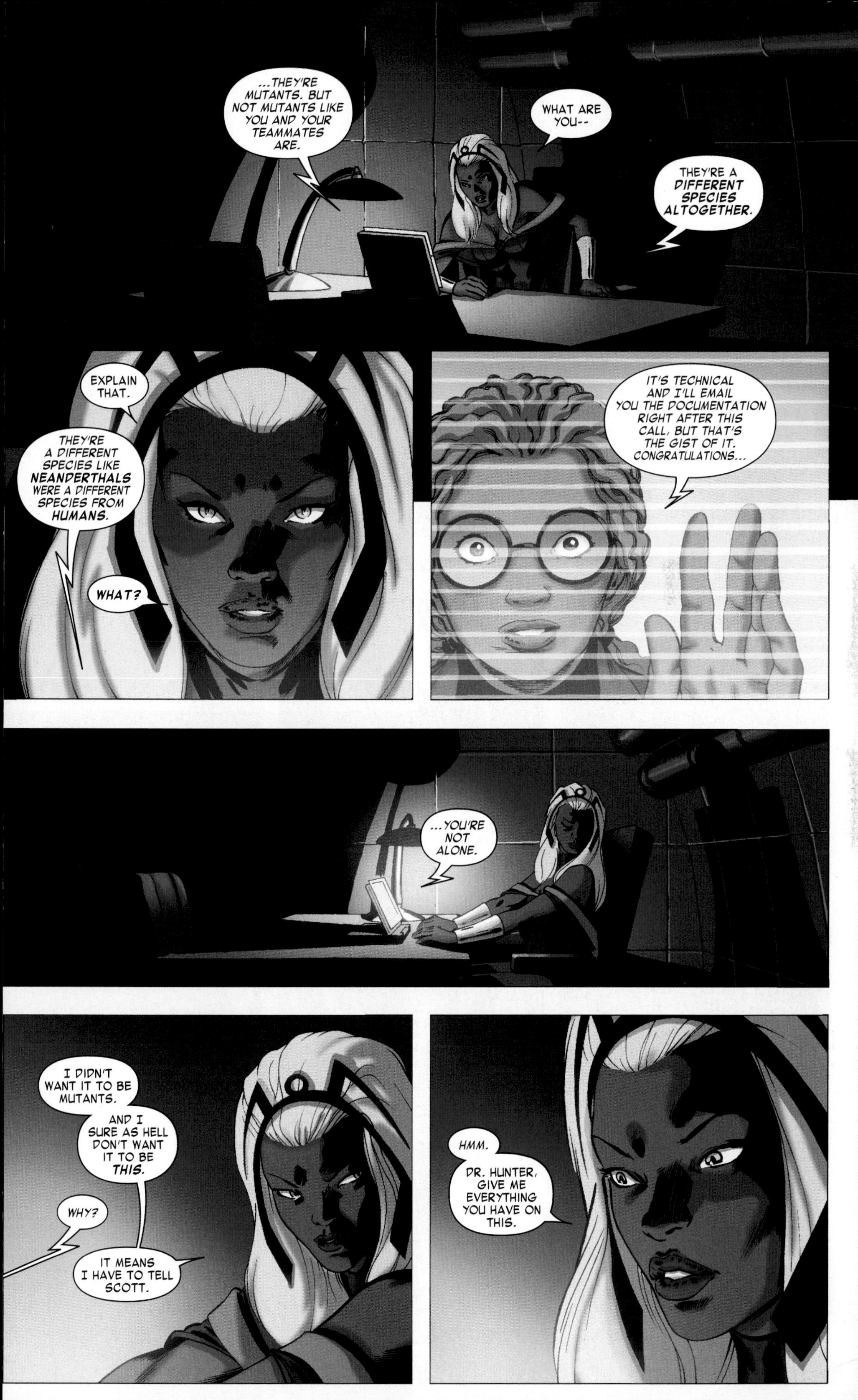
...THEY'RE MUTANTS. BUT NOT MUTANTS LIKE YOU AND YOUR TEAMMATES ARE.
WHAT ARE YOU--
THEY'RE A DIFFERENT SPECIES ALTOGETHER.
EXPLAIN THAT.
THEY'RE A DIFFERENT SPECIES LIKE NEANDERTHALS WERE A DIFFERENT SPECIES FROM HUMANS.
WHAT?
IT'S TECHNICAL AND I'LL EMAIL YOU THE DOCUMENTATION RIGHT AFTER THIS CALL, BUT THAT'S THE GIST OF IT. CONGRATULATIONS...
...YOU'RE NOT ALONE.
I DIDN'T WANT IT TO BE MUTANTS.
AND I SURE AS HELL DON'T WANT IT TO BE THIS.
WHY?
IT MEANS I HAVE TO TELL SCOTT.
HMM.
DR. HUNTER, GIVE ME EVERYTHING YOU HAVE ON THIS.

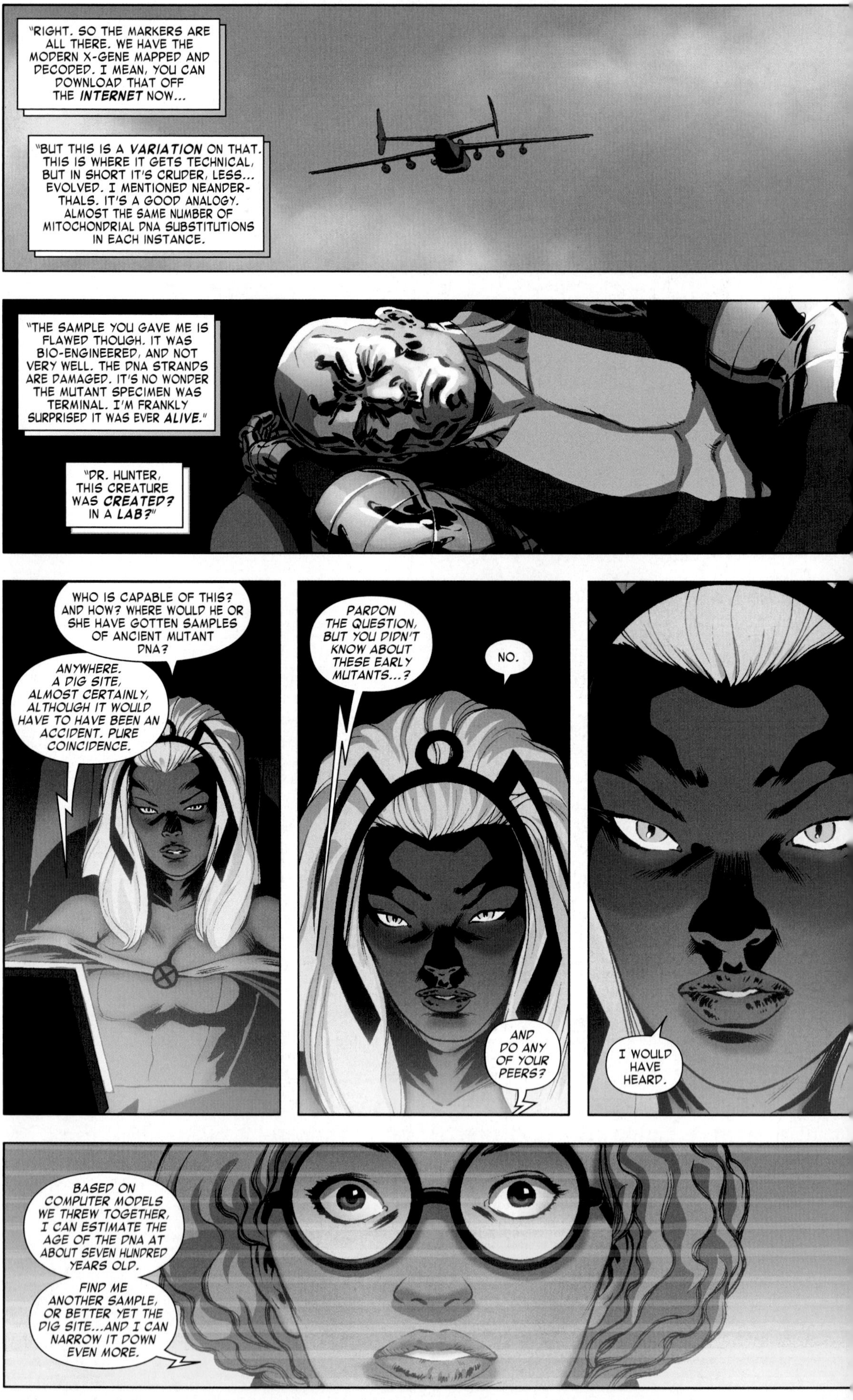
"RIGHT. SO THE MARKERS ARE ALL THERE. WE HAVE THE MODERN X-GENE MAPPED AND DECODED. I MEAN, YOU CAN DOWNLOAD THAT OFF THE INTERNET NOW...
"BUT THIS IS A VARIATION ON THAT. THIS IS WHERE IT GETS TECHNICAL, BUT IN SHORT IT'S CRUDER, LESS... EVOLVED. I MENTIONED NEANDERTHALS. IT'S A GOOD ANALOGY. ALMOST THE SAME NUMBER OF MITOCHONDRIAL DNA SUBSTITUTIONS IN EACH INSTANCE.
"THE SAMPLE YOU GAVE ME IS FLAWED THOUGH. IT WAS BIO-ENGINEERED, AND NOT VERY WELL. THE DNA STRANDS ARE DAMAGED. IT'S NO WONDER THE MUTANT SPECIMEN WAS TERMINAL. I'M FRANKLY SURPRISED IT WAS EVER ALIVE."
"DR. HUNTER, THIS CREATURE WAS CREATED? IN A LAB?"
WHO IS CAPABLE OF THIS? AND HOW? WHERE WOULD HE OR SHE HAVE GOTTEN SAMPLES OF ANCIENT MUTANT DNA?
ANYWHERE. A DIG SITE, ALMOST CERTAINLY, ALTHOUGH IT WOULD HAVE TO HAVE BEEN AN ACCIDENT. PURE COINCIDENCE.
PARDON THE QUESTION, BUT YOU DIDN'T KNOW ABOUT THESE EARLY MUTANTS...?
NO.
AND DO ANY OF YOUR PEERS?
I WOULD HAVE HEARD.
BASED ON COMPUTER MODELS WE THREW TOGETHER, I CAN ESTIMATE THE AGE OF THE DNA AT ABOUT SEVEN HUNDRED YEARS OLD.
FIND ME ANOTHER SAMPLE, OR BETTER YET THE DIG SITE...AND I CAN NARROW IT DOWN EVEN MORE.

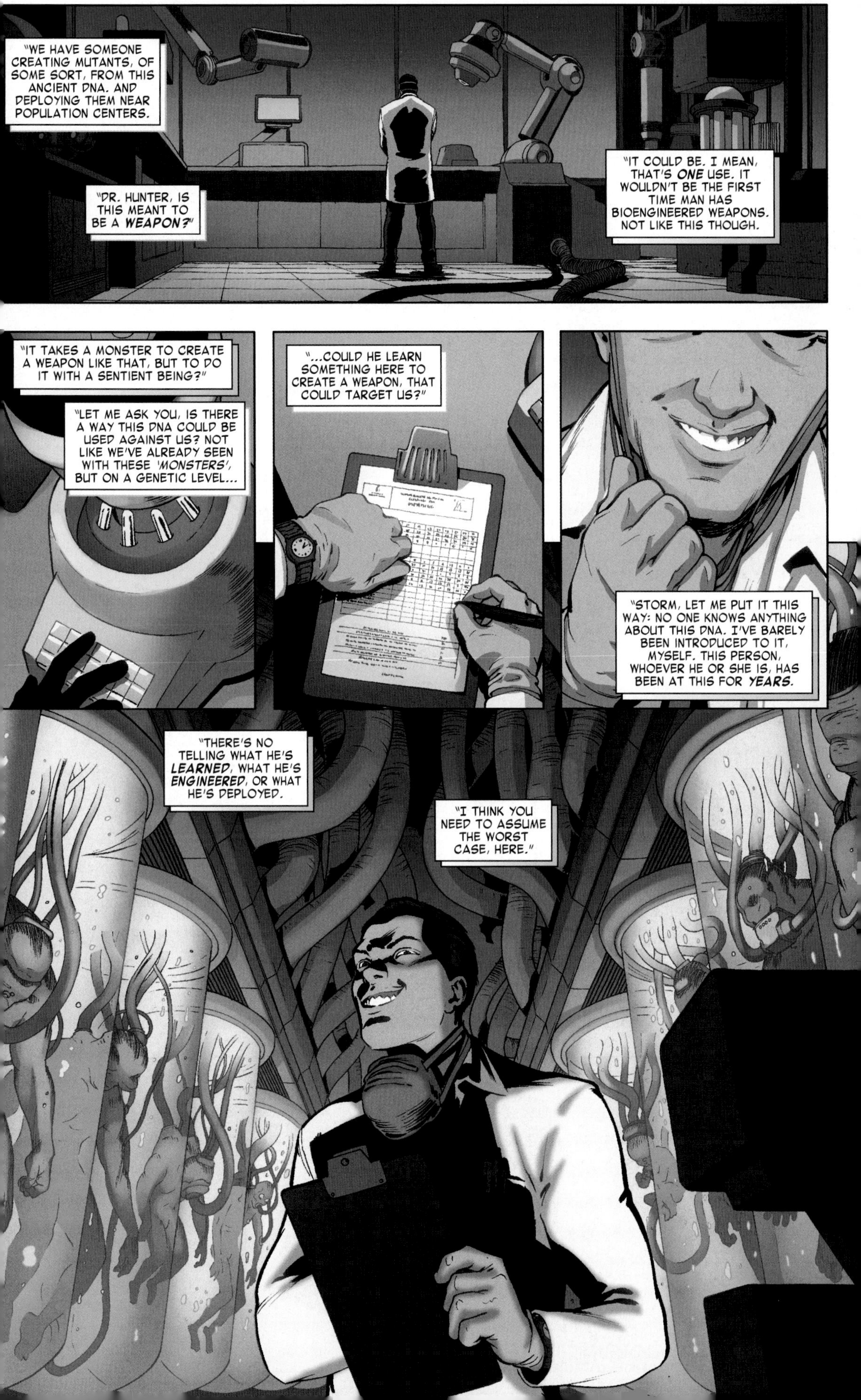
"WE HAVE SOMEONE CREATING MUTANTS, OF SOME SORT, FROM THIS ANCIENT DNA. AND DEPLOYING THEM NEAR POPULATION CENTERS.
"DR. HUNTER, IS THIS MEANT TO BE A *WEAPON?*"
"IT COULD BE. I MEAN, THAT'S *ONE* USE. IT WOULDN'T BE THE FIRST TIME MAN HAS BIOENGINEERED WEAPONS. NOT LIKE THIS THOUGH.
"IT TAKES A MONSTER TO CREATE A WEAPON LIKE THAT, BUT TO DO IT WITH A SENTIENT BEING?"
"LET ME ASK YOU, IS THERE A WAY THIS DNA COULD BE USED AGAINST US? NOT LIKE WE'VE ALREADY SEEN WITH THESE *'MONSTERS'*, BUT ON A GENETIC LEVEL...
"...COULD HE LEARN SOMETHING HERE TO CREATE A WEAPON, THAT COULD TARGET US?"
"STORM, LET ME PUT IT THIS WAY: NO ONE KNOWS ANYTHING ABOUT THIS DNA. I'VE BARELY BEEN INTRODUCED TO IT, MYSELF. THIS PERSON, WHOEVER HE OR SHE IS, HAS BEEN AT THIS FOR *YEARS*.
"THERE'S NO TELLING WHAT HE'S *LEARNED*, WHAT HE'S *ENGINEERED*, OR WHAT HE'S DEPLOYED.
"I THINK YOU NEED TO ASSUME THE WORST CASE, HERE."

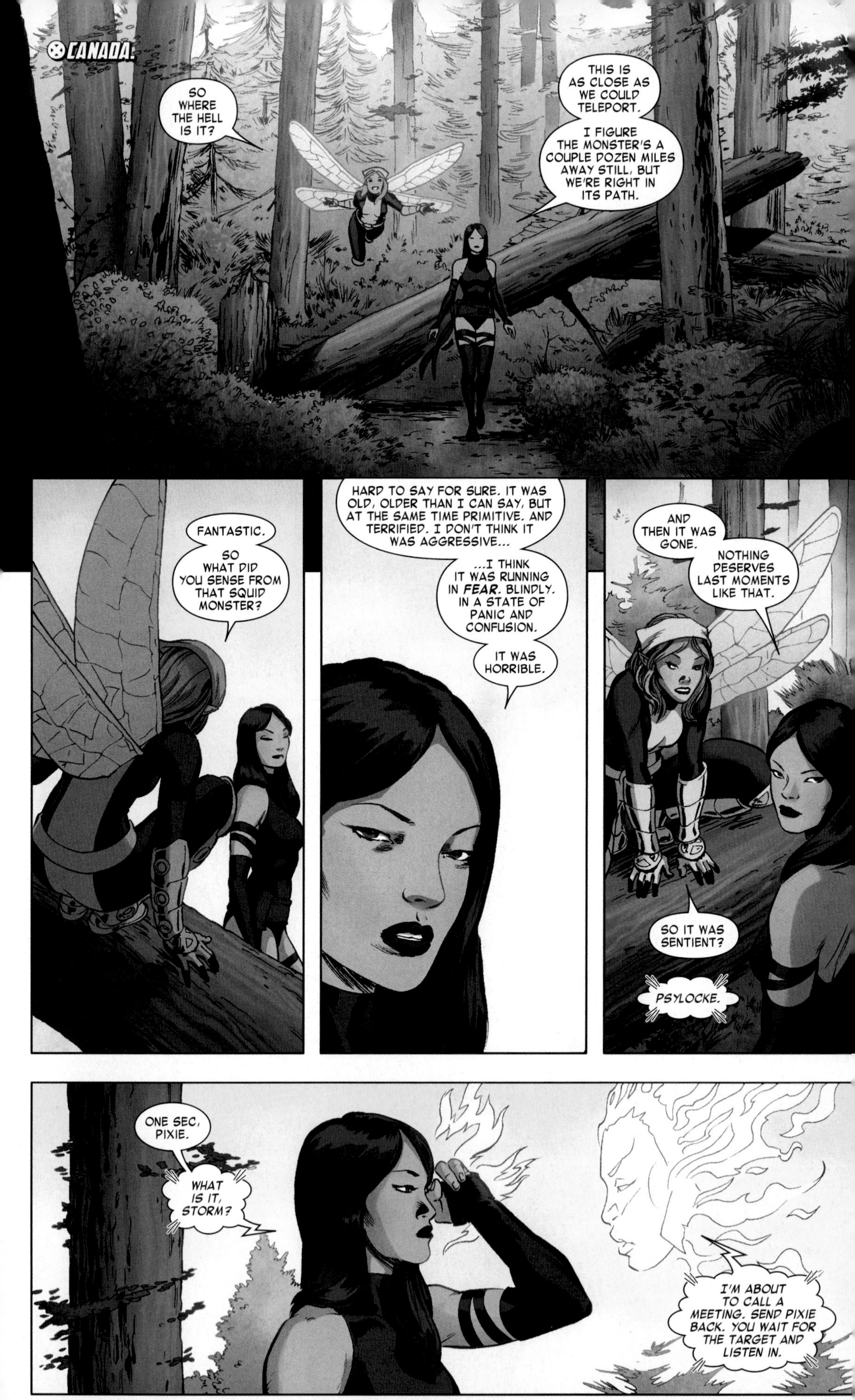
CANADA.
SO WHERE THE HELL IS IT?
THIS IS AS CLOSE AS WE COULD TELEPORT.
I FIGURE THE MONSTER'S A COUPLE DOZEN MILES AWAY STILL, BUT WE'RE RIGHT IN ITS PATH.
FANTASTIC.
SO WHAT DID YOU SENSE FROM THAT SQUID MONSTER?
HARD TO SAY FOR SURE. IT WAS OLD, OLDER THAN I CAN SAY, BUT AT THE SAME TIME PRIMITIVE. AND TERRIFIED. I DON'T THINK IT WAS AGGRESSIVE...
...I THINK IT WAS RUNNING IN FEAR. BLINDLY. IN A STATE OF PANIC AND CONFUSION.
IT WAS HORRIBLE.
AND THEN IT WAS GONE.
NOTHING DESERVES LAST MOMENTS LIKE THAT.
SO IT WAS SENTIENT?
PSYLOCKE.
ONE SEC, PIXIE.
WHAT IS IT, STORM?
I'M ABOUT TO CALL A MEETING. SEND PIXIE BACK. YOU WAIT FOR THE TARGET AND LISTEN IN.

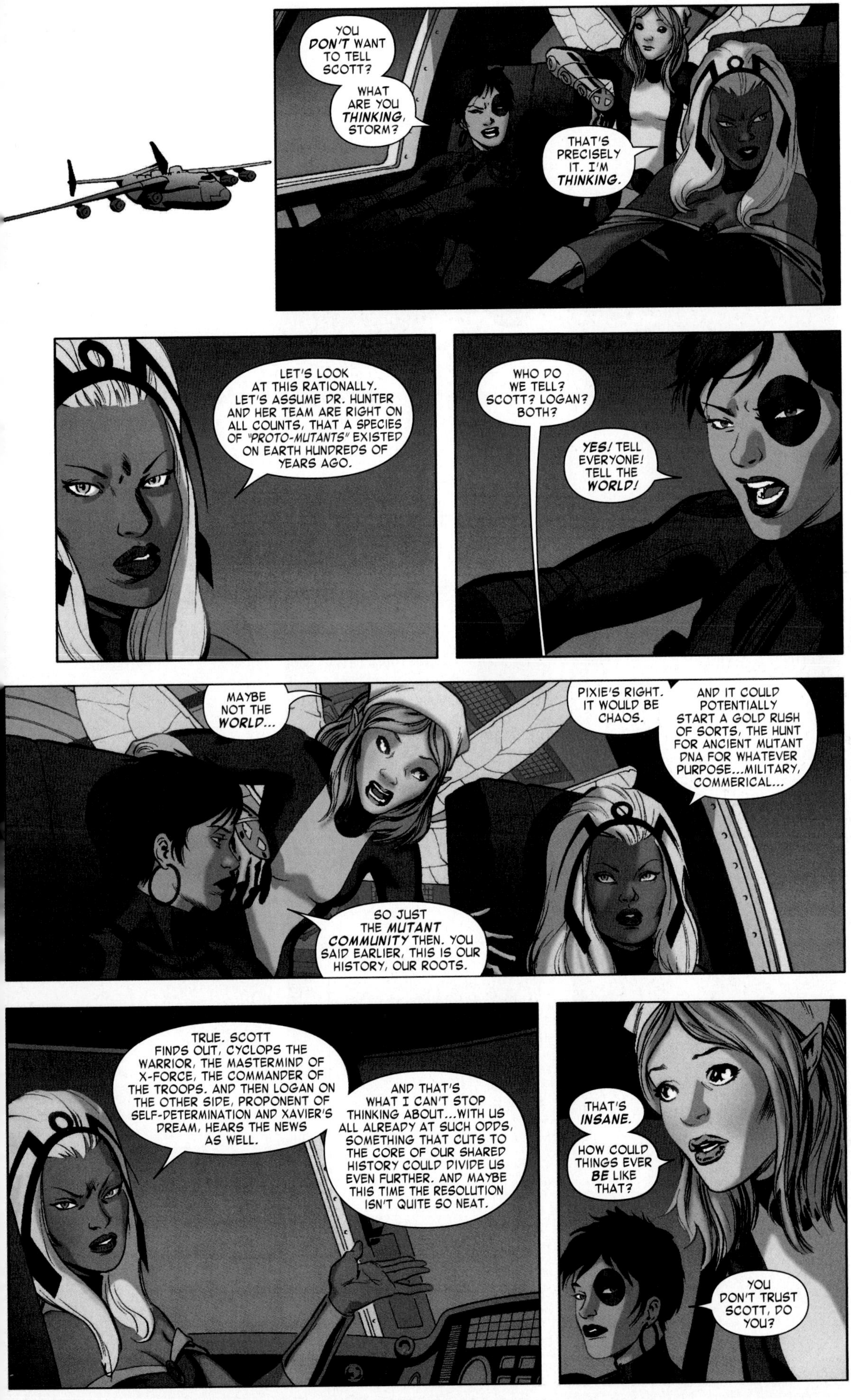
YOU DON'T WANT TO TELL SCOTT?
WHAT ARE YOU THINKING, STORM?
THAT'S PRECISELY IT. I'M THINKING.
LET'S LOOK AT THIS RATIONALLY. LET'S ASSUME DR. HUNTER AND HER TEAM ARE RIGHT ON ALL COUNTS, THAT A SPECIES OF "PROTO-MUTANTS" EXISTED ON EARTH HUNDREDS OF YEARS AGO.
WHO DO WE TELL? SCOTT? LOGAN? BOTH?
YES! TELL EVERYONE! TELL THE WORLD!
MAYBE NOT THE WORLD...
PIXIE'S RIGHT. IT WOULD BE CHAOS.
AND IT COULD POTENTIALLY START A GOLD RUSH OF SORTS, THE HUNT FOR ANCIENT MUTANT DNA FOR WHATEVER PURPOSE...MILITARY, COMMERICAL...
SO JUST THE MUTANT COMMUNITY THEN. YOU SAID EARLIER, THIS IS OUR HISTORY, OUR ROOTS.
TRUE. SCOTT FINDS OUT, CYCLOPS THE WARRIOR, THE MASTERMIND OF X-FORCE, THE COMMANDER OF THE TROOPS. AND THEN LOGAN ON THE OTHER SIDE, PROPONENT OF SELF-DETERMINATION AND XAVIER'S DREAM, HEARS THE NEWS AS WELL.
AND THAT'S WHAT I CAN'T STOP THINKING ABOUT...WITH US ALL ALREADY AT SUCH ODDS, SOMETHING THAT CUTS TO THE CORE OF OUR SHARED HISTORY COULD DIVIDE US EVEN FURTHER. AND MAYBE THIS TIME THE RESOLUTION ISN'T QUITE SO NEAT.
THAT'S INSANE.
HOW COULD THINGS EVER BE LIKE THAT?
YOU DON'T TRUST SCOTT, DO YOU?

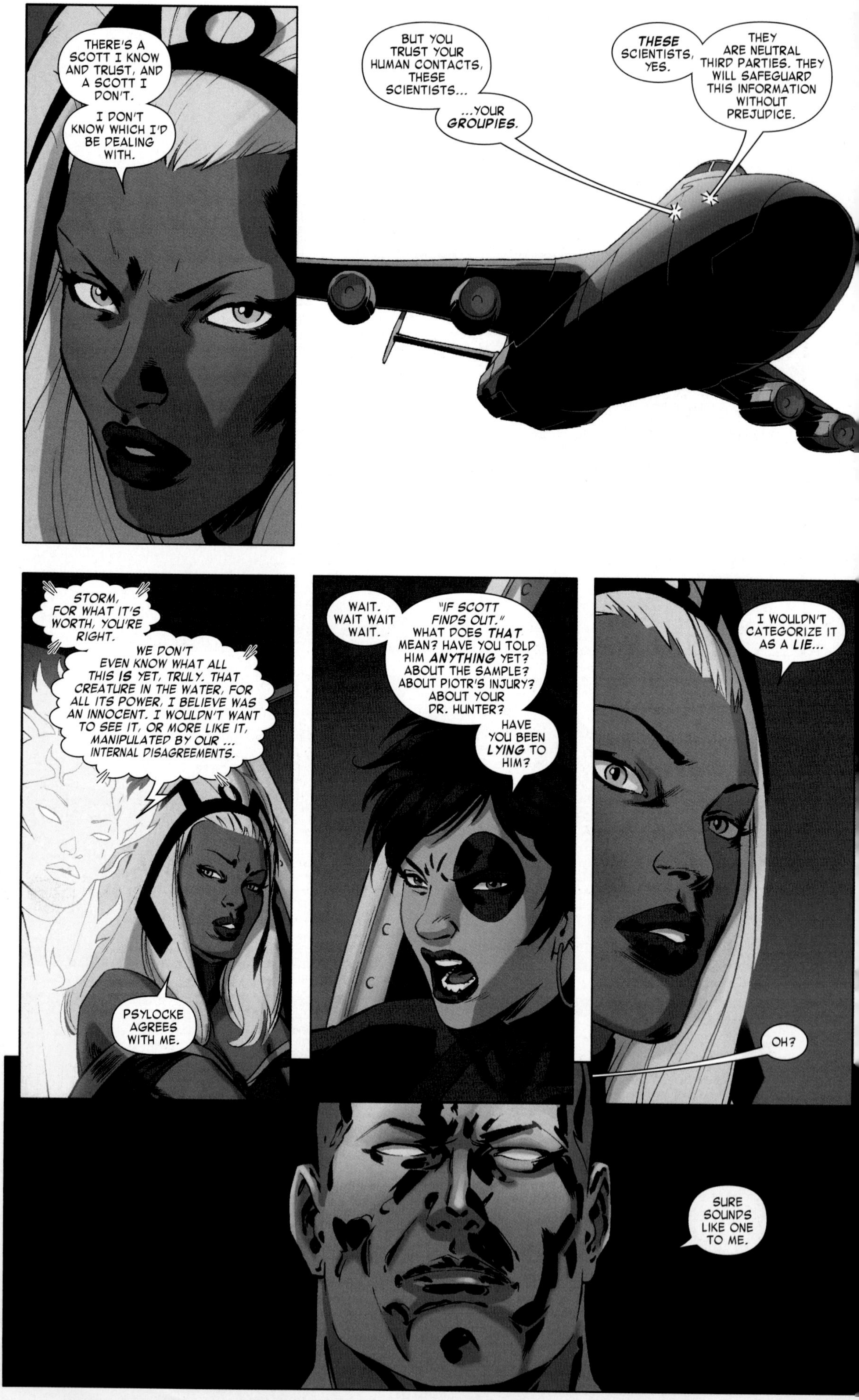
THERE'S A SCOTT I KNOW AND TRUST, AND A SCOTT I DON'T.
I DON'T KNOW WHICH I'D BE DEALING WITH.
BUT YOU TRUST YOUR HUMAN CONTACTS, THESE SCIENTISTS...
...YOUR GROUPIES.
THESE SCIENTISTS, YES.
THEY ARE NEUTRAL THIRD PARTIES. THEY WILL SAFEGUARD THIS INFORMATION WITHOUT PREJUDICE.
STORM, FOR WHAT IT'S WORTH, YOU'RE RIGHT.
WE DON'T EVEN KNOW WHAT ALL THIS IS YET, TRULY. THAT CREATURE IN THE WATER, FOR ALL ITS POWER, I BELIEVE WAS AN INNOCENT. I WOULDN'T WANT TO SEE IT, OR MORE LIKE IT, MANIPULATED BY OUR ... INTERNAL DISAGREEMENTS.
PSYLOCKE AGREES WITH ME.
WAIT. WAIT WAIT WAIT.
"IF SCOTT FINDS OUT." WHAT DOES THAT MEAN? HAVE YOU TOLD HIM ANYTHING YET? ABOUT THE SAMPLE? ABOUT PIOTR'S INJURY? ABOUT YOUR DR. HUNTER?
HAVE YOU BEEN LYING TO HIM?
I WOULDN'T CATEGORIZE IT AS A LIE...
OH?
SURE SOUNDS LIKE ONE TO ME.

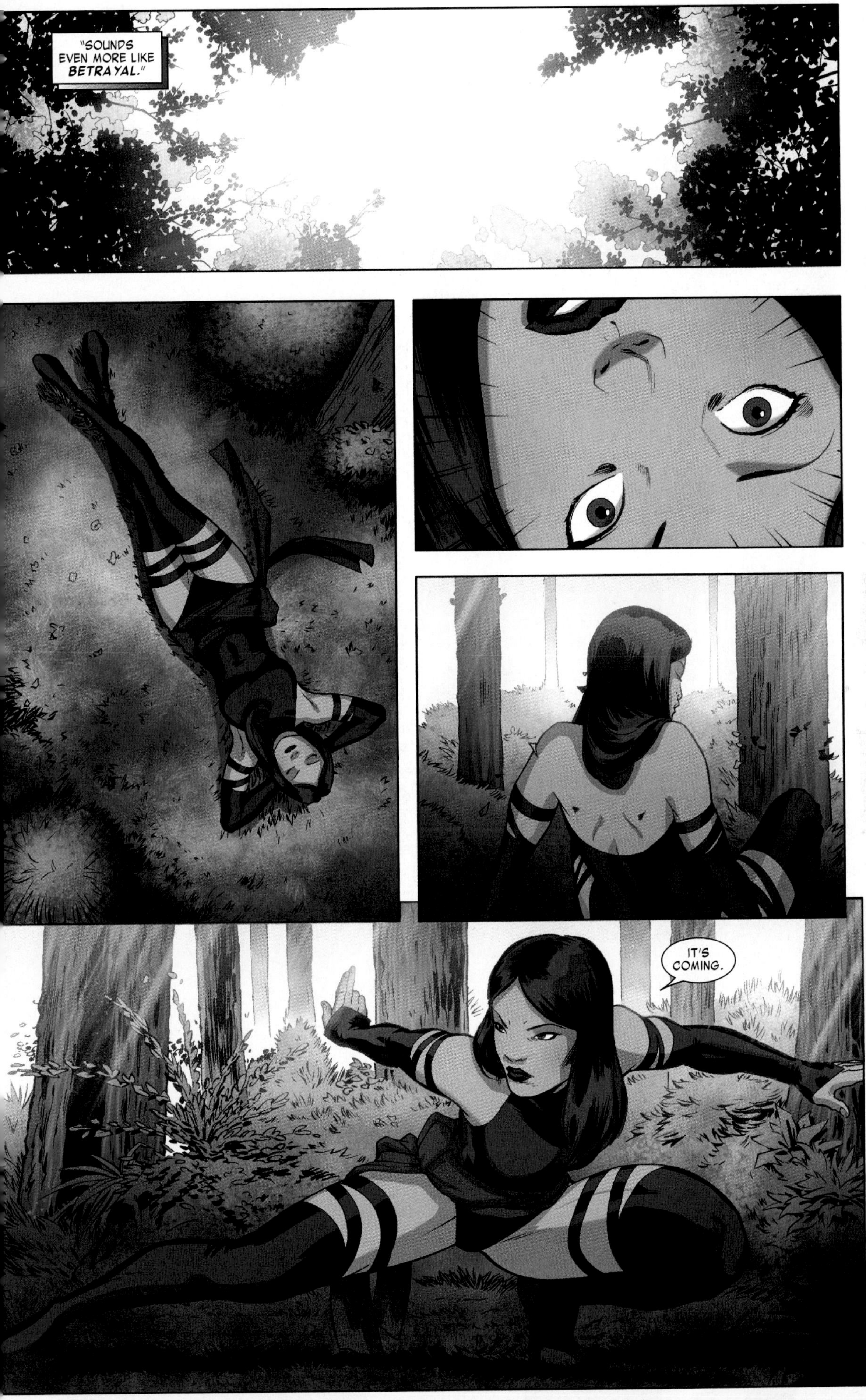
"SOUNDS EVEN MORE LIKE BETRAYAL."
IT'S COMING.

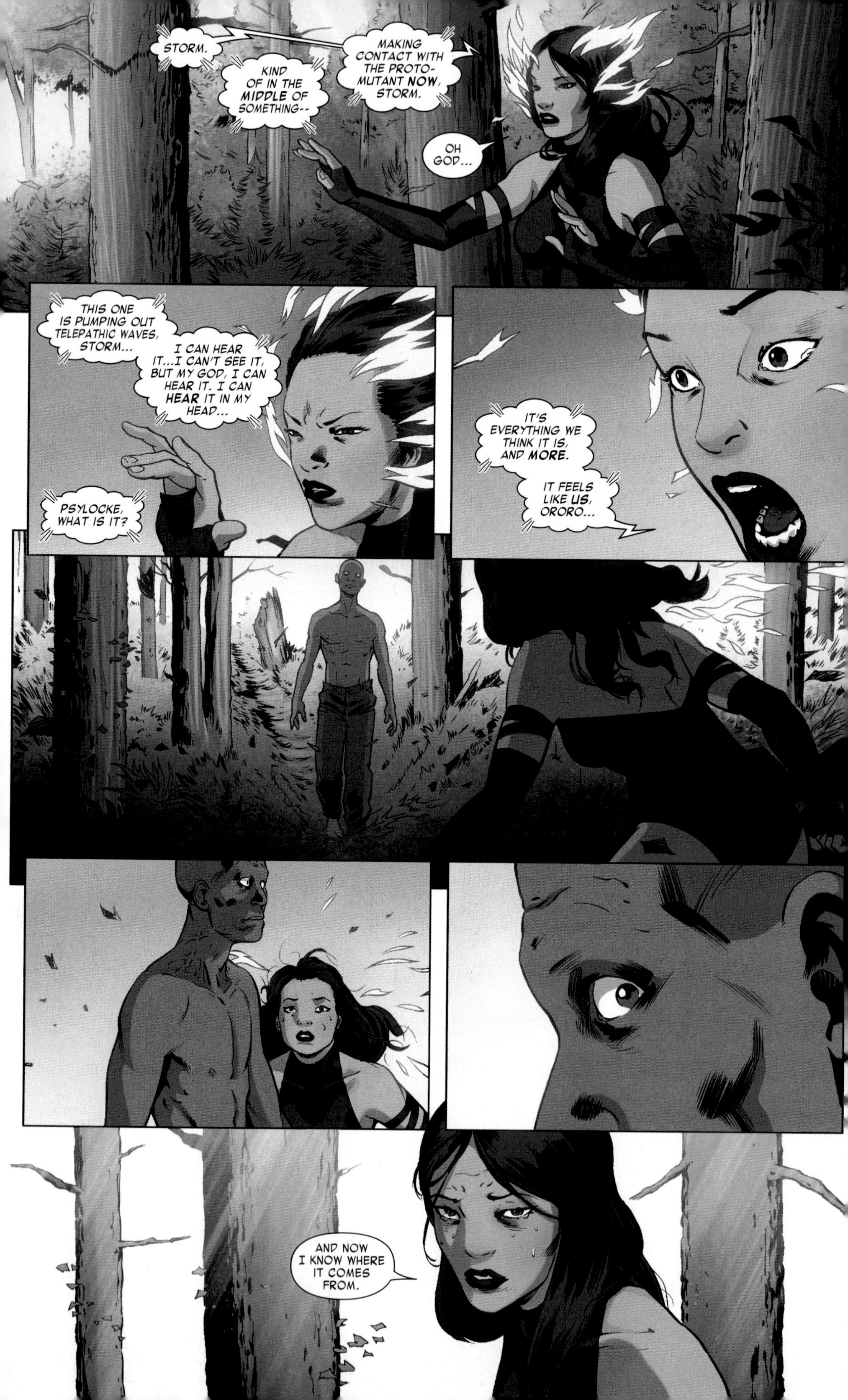
STORM.
KIND OF IN THE MIDDLE OF SOMETHING--
MAKING CONTACT WITH THE PROTO-MUTANT NOW, STORM.
OH GOD...
THIS ONE IS PUMPING OUT TELEPATHIC WAVES, STORM...
I CAN HEAR IT...I CAN'T SEE IT, BUT MY GOD, I CAN HEAR IT. I CAN HEAR IT IN MY HEAD...
PSYLOCKE, WHAT IS IT?
IT'S EVERYTHING WE THINK IT IS, AND MORE.
IT FEELS LIKE US, ORORO...
AND NOW I KNOW WHERE IT COMES FROM.

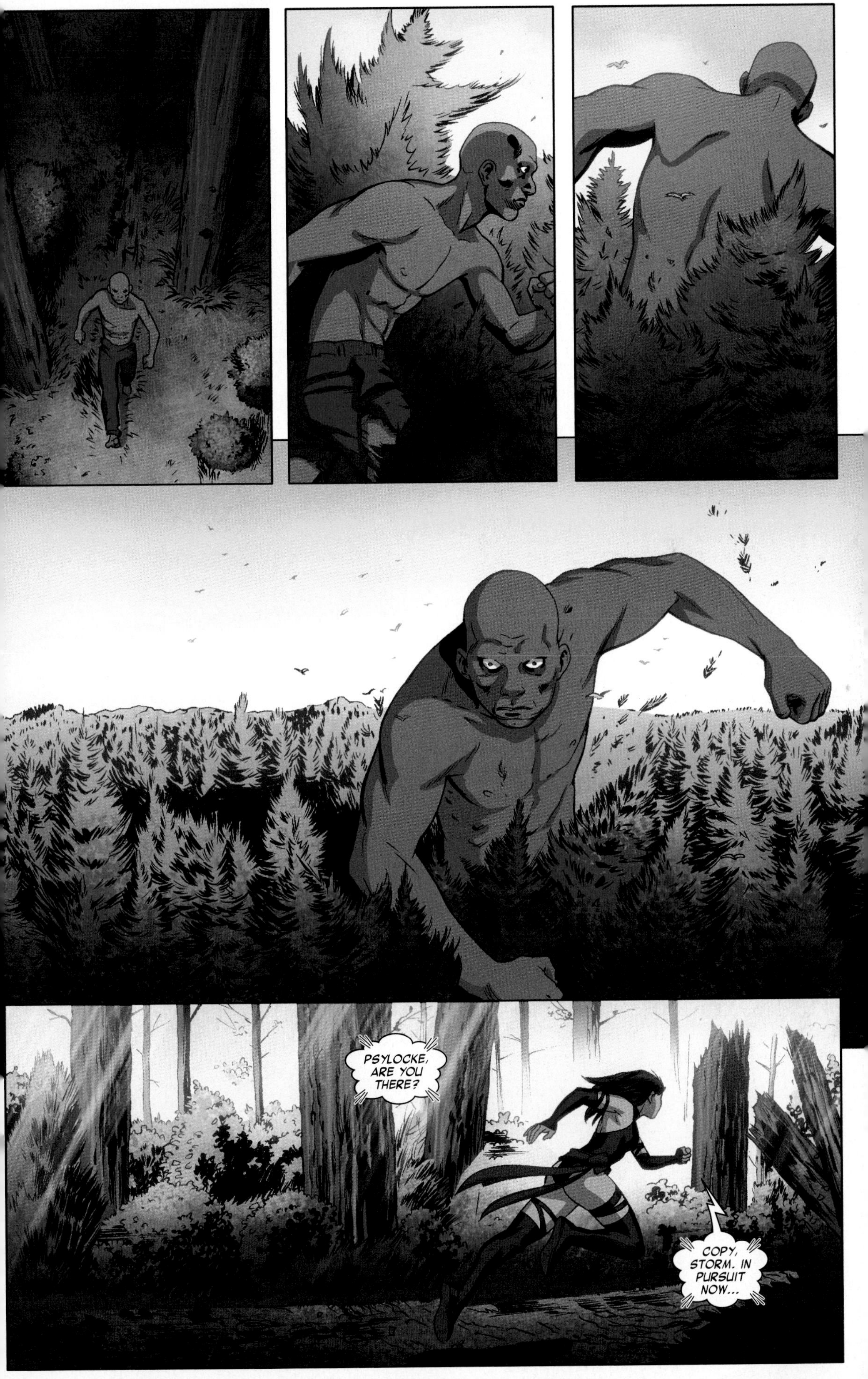
PSYLOCKE, ARE YOU THERE?
COPY, STORM. IN PURSUIT NOW...

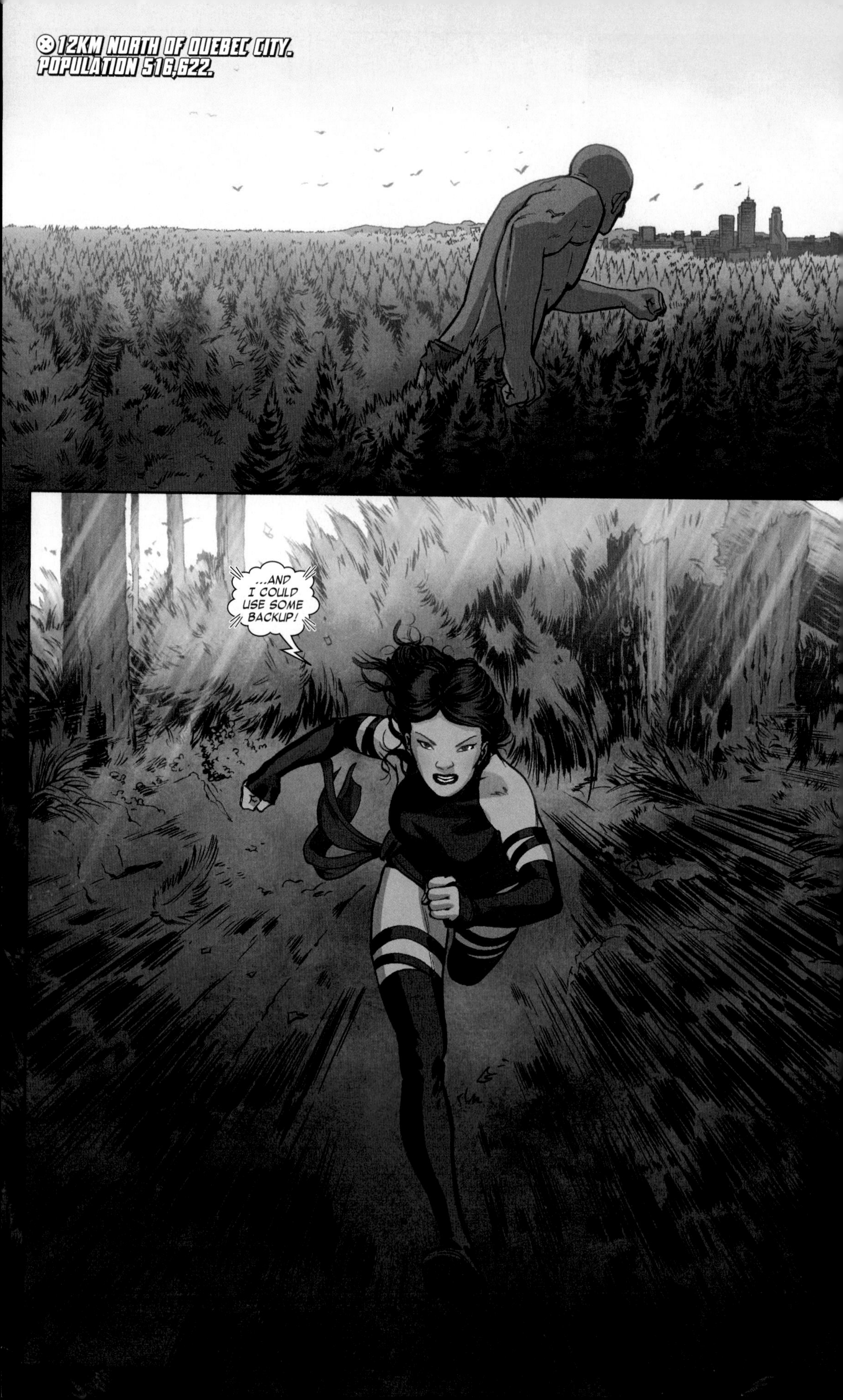
12KM NORTH OF QUEBEC CITY. POPULATION 516,622.
...AND I COULD USE SOME BACKUP!

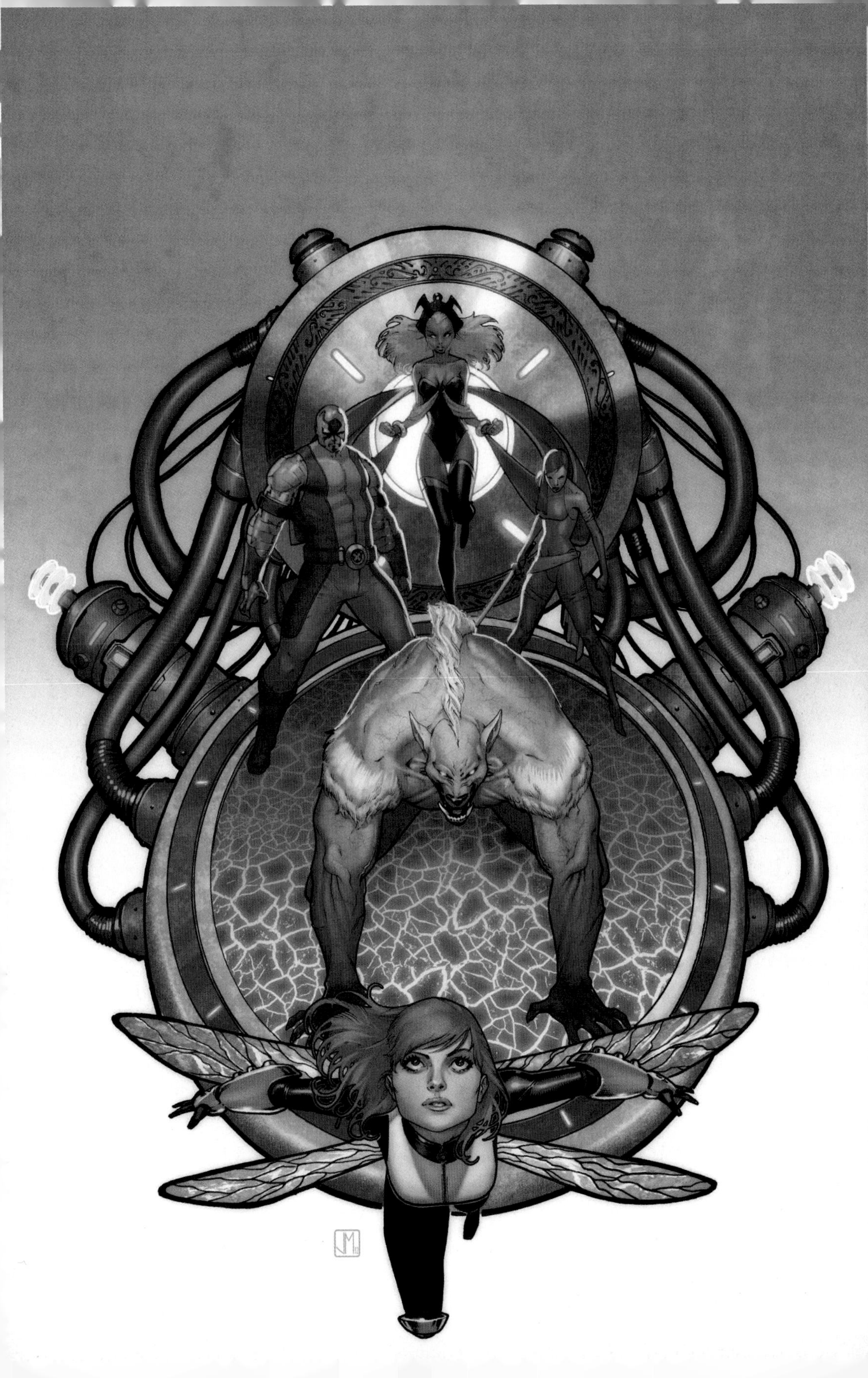

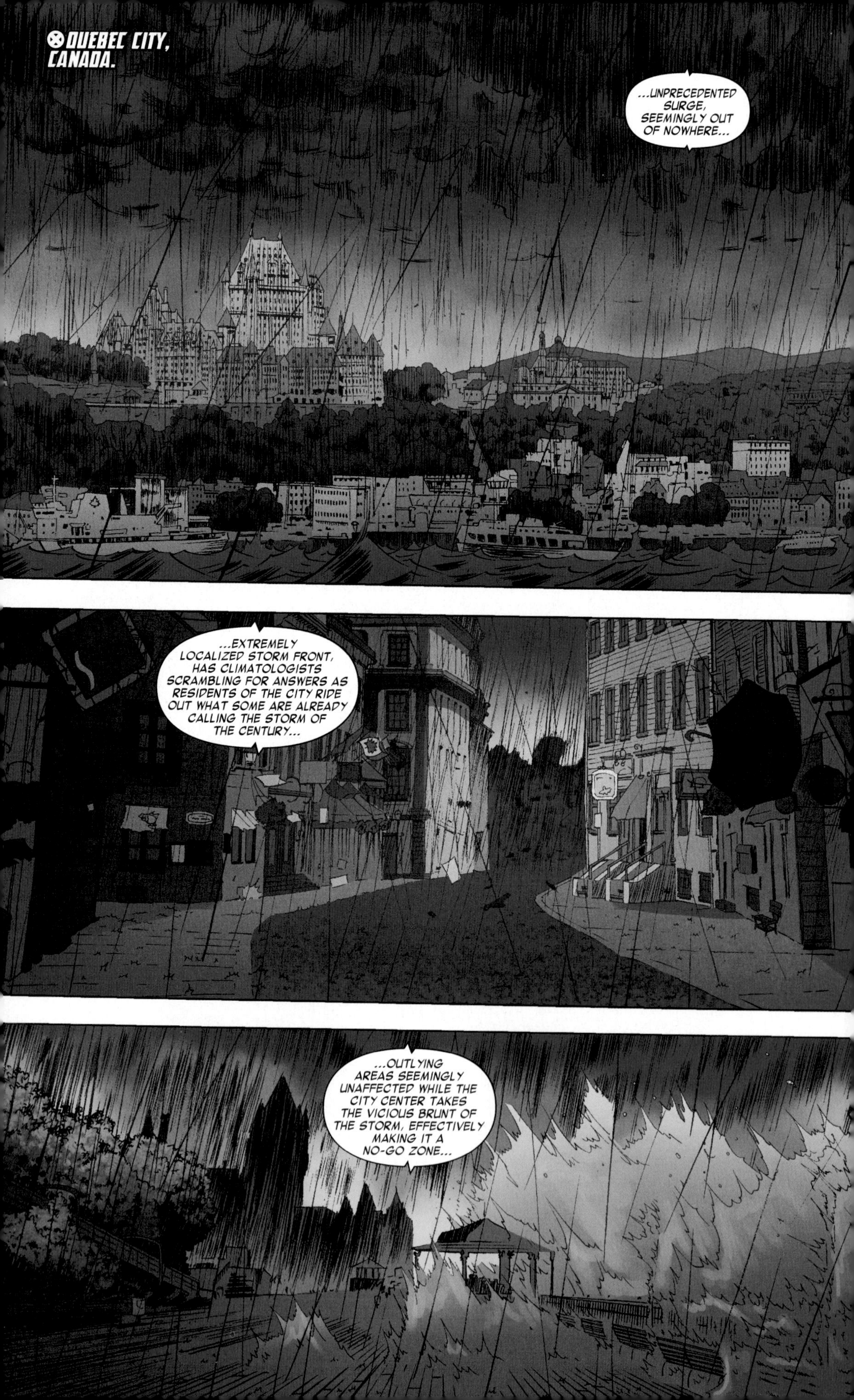
QUEBEC CITY, CANADA.
...UNPRECEDENTED SURGE, SEEMINGLY OUT OF NOWHERE...
...EXTREMELY LOCALIZED STORM FRONT, HAS CLIMATOLOGISTS SCRAMBLING FOR ANSWERS AS RESIDENTS OF THE CITY RIDE OUT WHAT SOME ARE ALREADY CALLING THE STORM OF THE CENTURY...
...OUTLYING AREAS SEEMINGLY UNAFFECTED WHILE THE CITY CENTER TAKES THE VICIOUS BRUNT OF THE STORM, EFFECTIVELY MAKING IT A NO-GO ZONE...

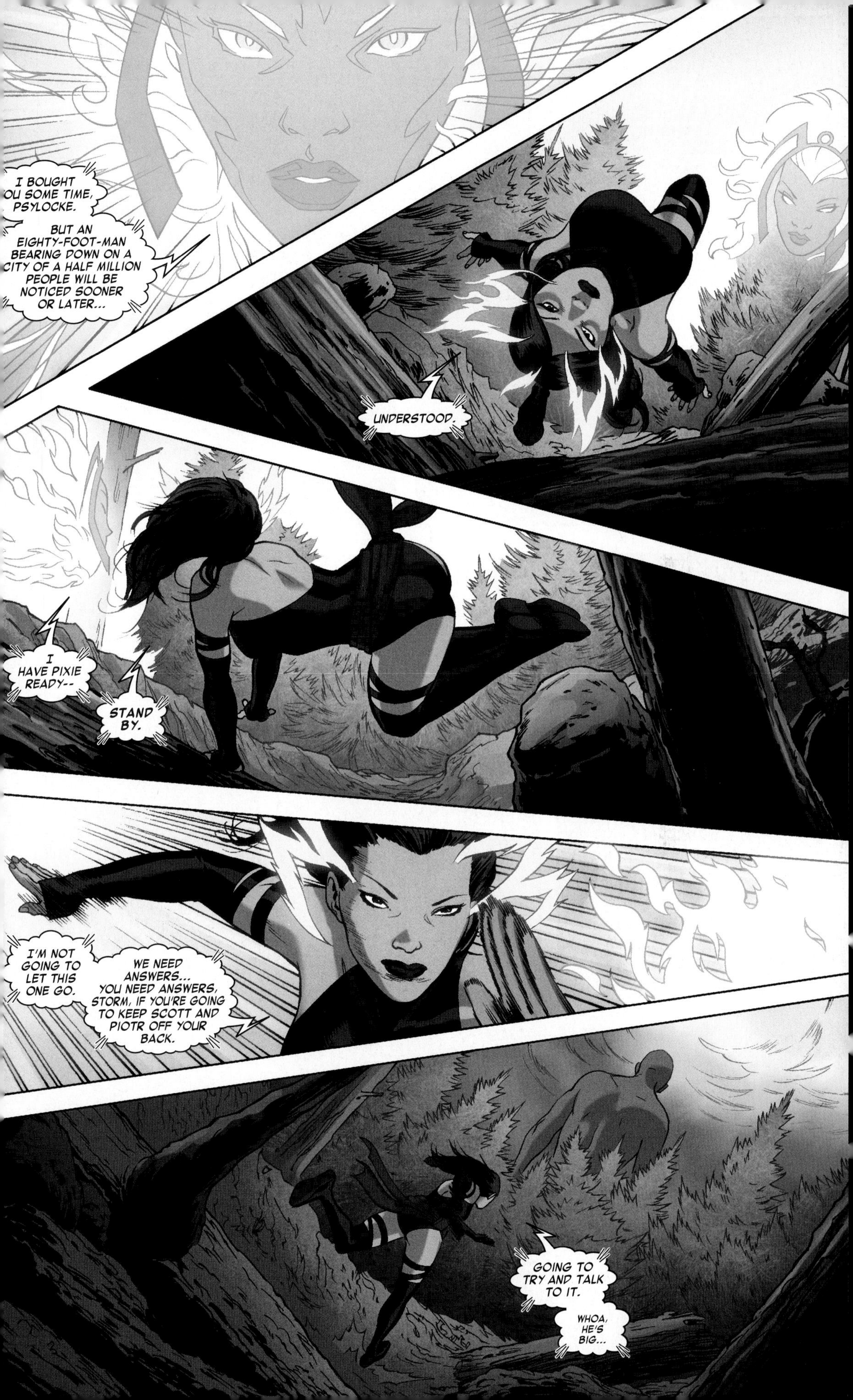
I BOUGHT OU SOME TIME, PSYLOCKE.
BUT AN EIGHTY-FOOT-MAN BEARING DOWN ON A CITY OF A HALF MILLION PEOPLE WILL BE NOTICED SOONER OR LATER...
UNDERSTOOD.
I HAVE PIXIE READY--
STAND BY.
I'M NOT GOING TO LET THIS ONE GO.
WE NEED ANSWERS... YOU NEED ANSWERS, STORM, IF YOU'RE GOING TO KEEP SCOTT AND PIOTR OFF YOUR BACK.
GOING TO TRY AND TALK TO IT.
WHOA, HE'S BIG...

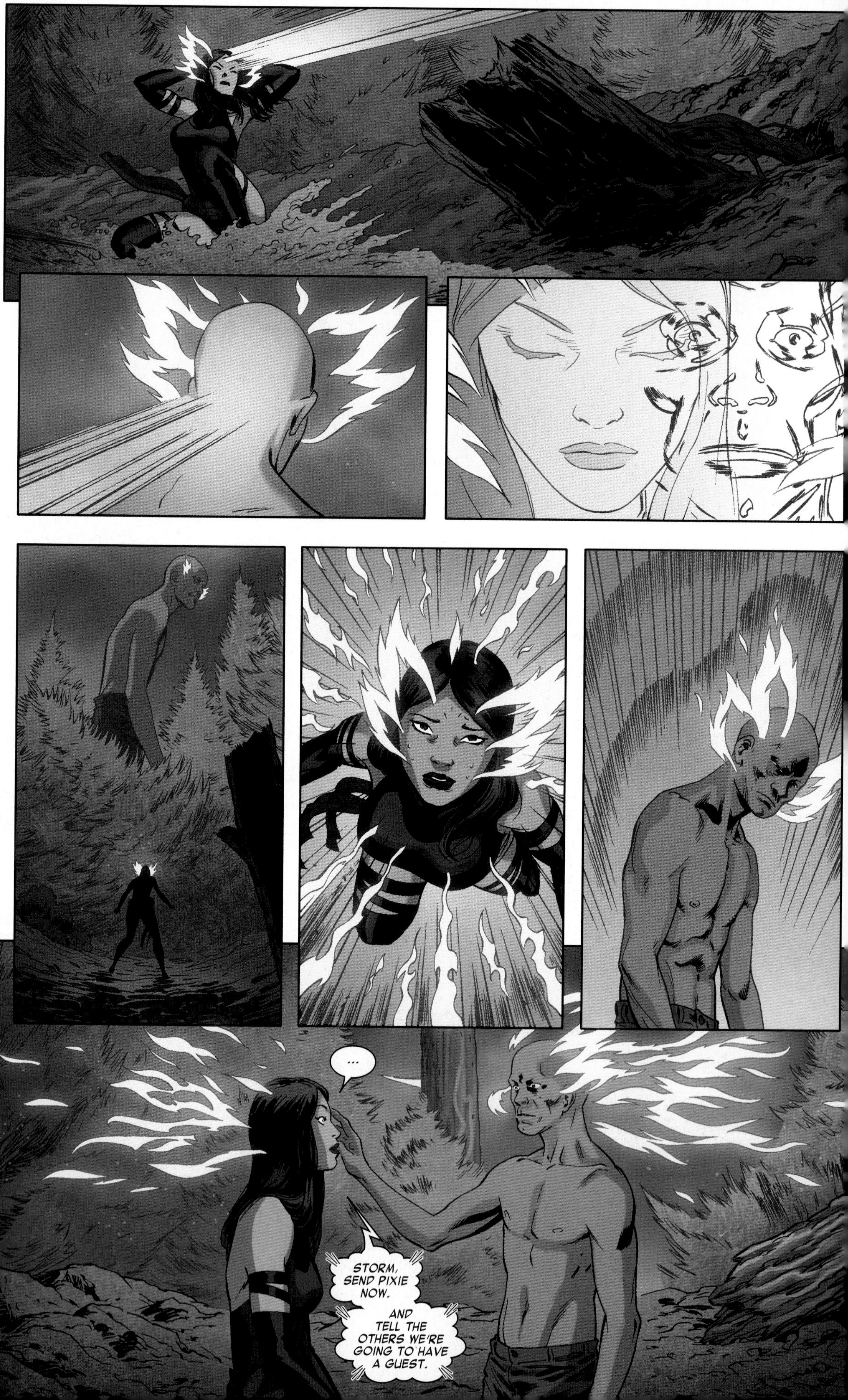
...
STORM, SEND PIXIE NOW.
AND TELL THE OTHERS WE'RE GOING TO HAVE A GUEST.

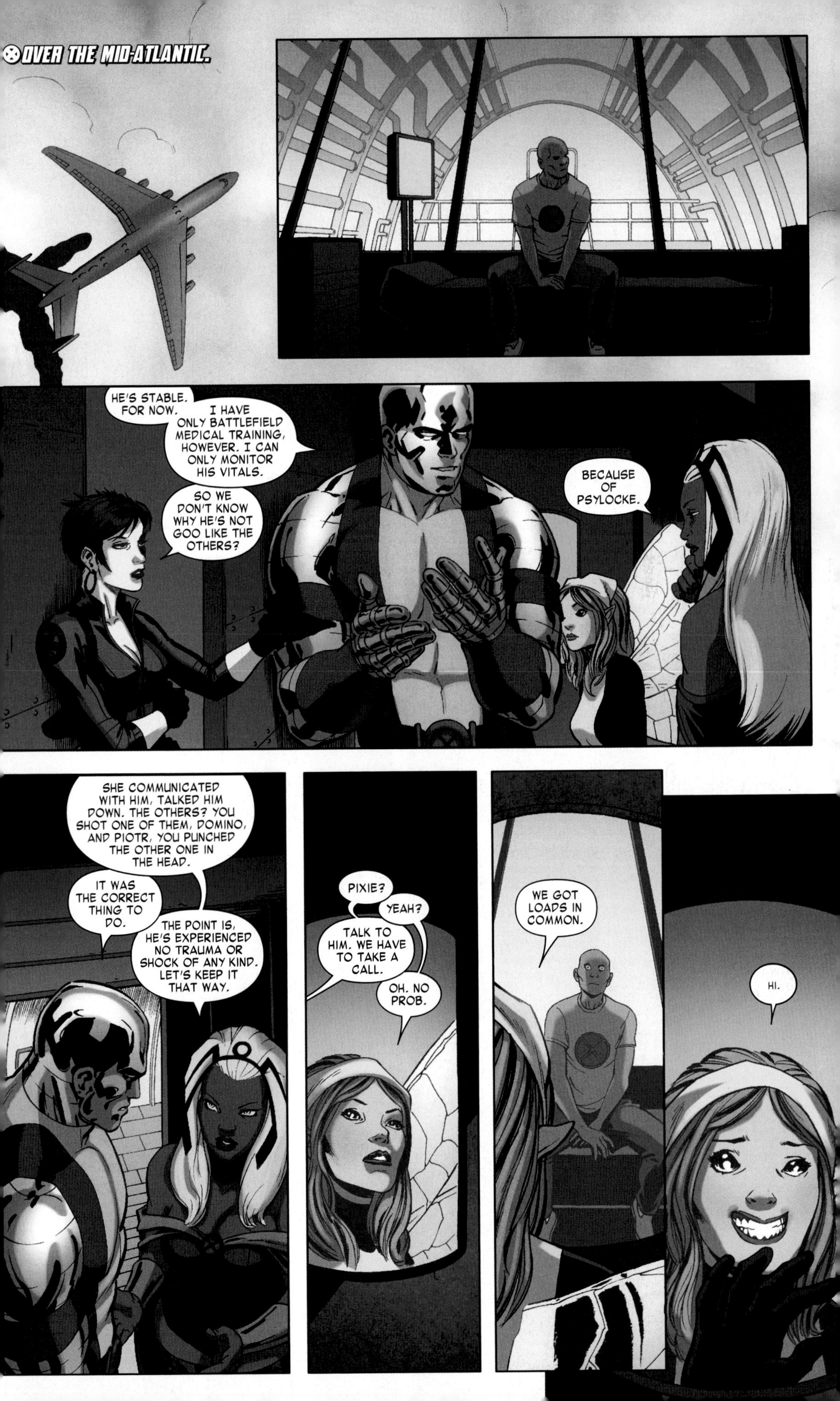

OVER THE MID-ATLANTIC.
HE'S STABLE. FOR NOW.
I HAVE ONLY BATTLEFIELD MEDICAL TRAINING, HOWEVER. I CAN ONLY MONITOR HIS VITALS.
SO WE DON'T KNOW WHY HE'S NOT GOO LIKE THE OTHERS?
BECAUSE OF PSYLOCKE.
SHE COMMUNICATED WITH HIM, TALKED HIM DOWN. THE OTHERS? YOU SHOT ONE OF THEM, DOMINO, AND PIOTR, YOU PUNCHED THE OTHER ONE IN THE HEAD.
IT WAS THE CORRECT THING TO DO.
THE POINT IS, HE'S EXPERIENCED NO TRAUMA OR SHOCK OF ANY KIND. LET'S KEEP IT THAT WAY.
PIXIE?
YEAH?
TALK TO HIM. WE HAVE TO TAKE A CALL.
OH. NO PROB.
WE GOT LOADS IN COMMON.
HI.

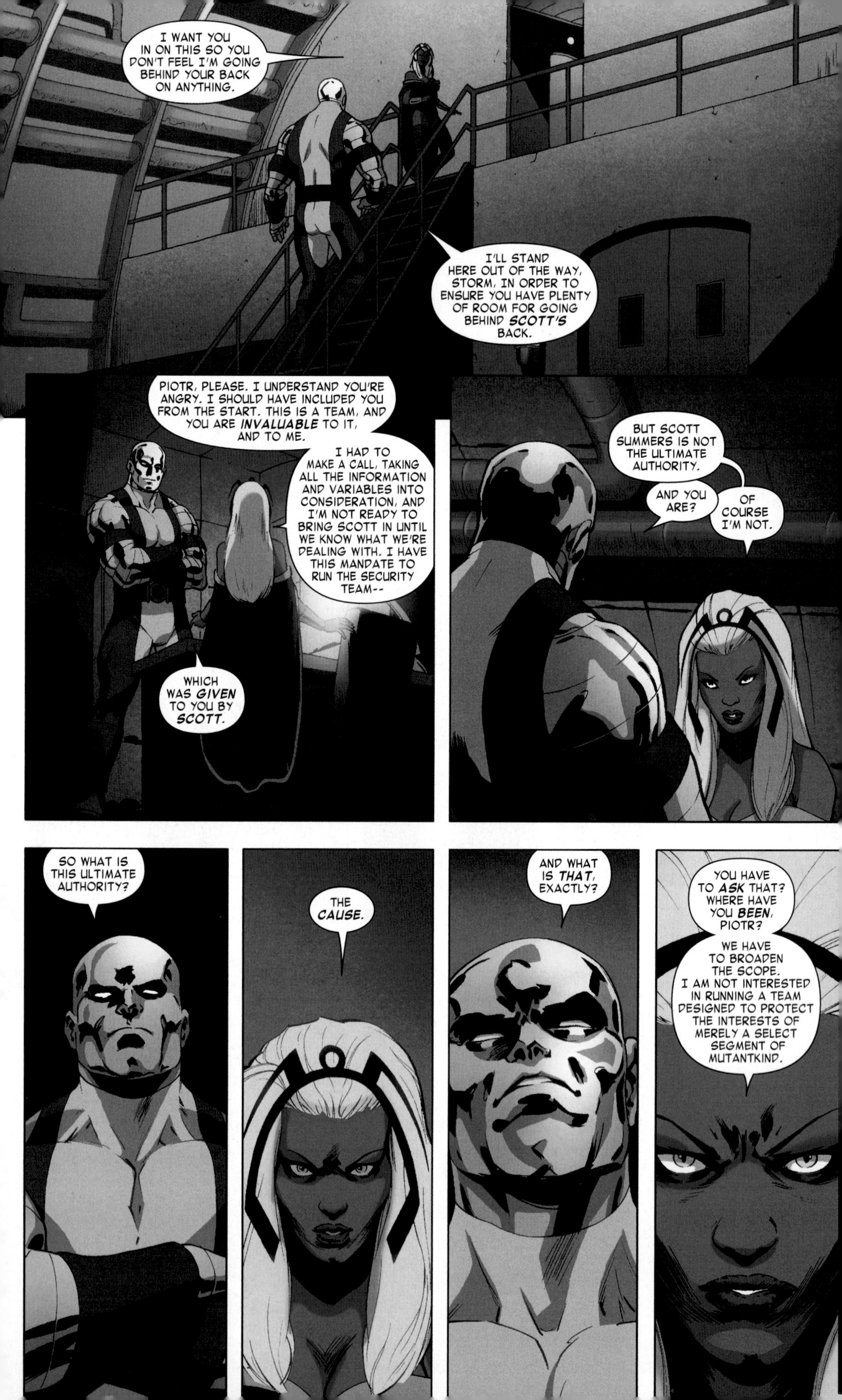
I WANT YOU IN ON THIS SO YOU DON'T FEEL I'M GOING BEHIND YOUR BACK ON ANYTHING.
I'LL STAND HERE OUT OF THE WAY, STORM, IN ORDER TO ENSURE YOU HAVE PLENTY OF ROOM FOR GOING BEHIND SCOTT'S BACK.
PIOTR, PLEASE. I UNDERSTAND YOU'RE ANGRY. I SHOULD HAVE INCLUDED YOU FROM THE START. THIS IS A TEAM, AND YOU ARE INVALUABLE TO IT, AND TO ME.
I HAD TO MAKE A CALL, TAKING ALL THE INFORMATION AND VARIABLES INTO CONSIDERATION, AND I'M NOT READY TO BRING SCOTT IN UNTIL WE KNOW WHAT WE'RE DEALING WITH. I HAVE THIS MANDATE TO RUN THE SECURITY TEAM--
WHICH WAS GIVEN TO YOU BY SCOTT.
BUT SCOTT SUMMERS IS NOT THE ULTIMATE AUTHORITY.
AND YOU ARE?
OF COURSE I'M NOT.
SO WHAT IS THIS ULTIMATE AUTHORITY?
THE CAUSE.
AND WHAT IS THAT, EXACTLY?
YOU HAVE TO ASK THAT? WHERE HAVE YOU BEEN, PIOTR?
WE HAVE TO BROADEN THE SCOPE. I AM NOT INTERESTED IN RUNNING A TEAM DESIGNED TO PROTECT THE INTERESTS OF MERELY A SELECT SEGMENT OF MUTANTKIND.

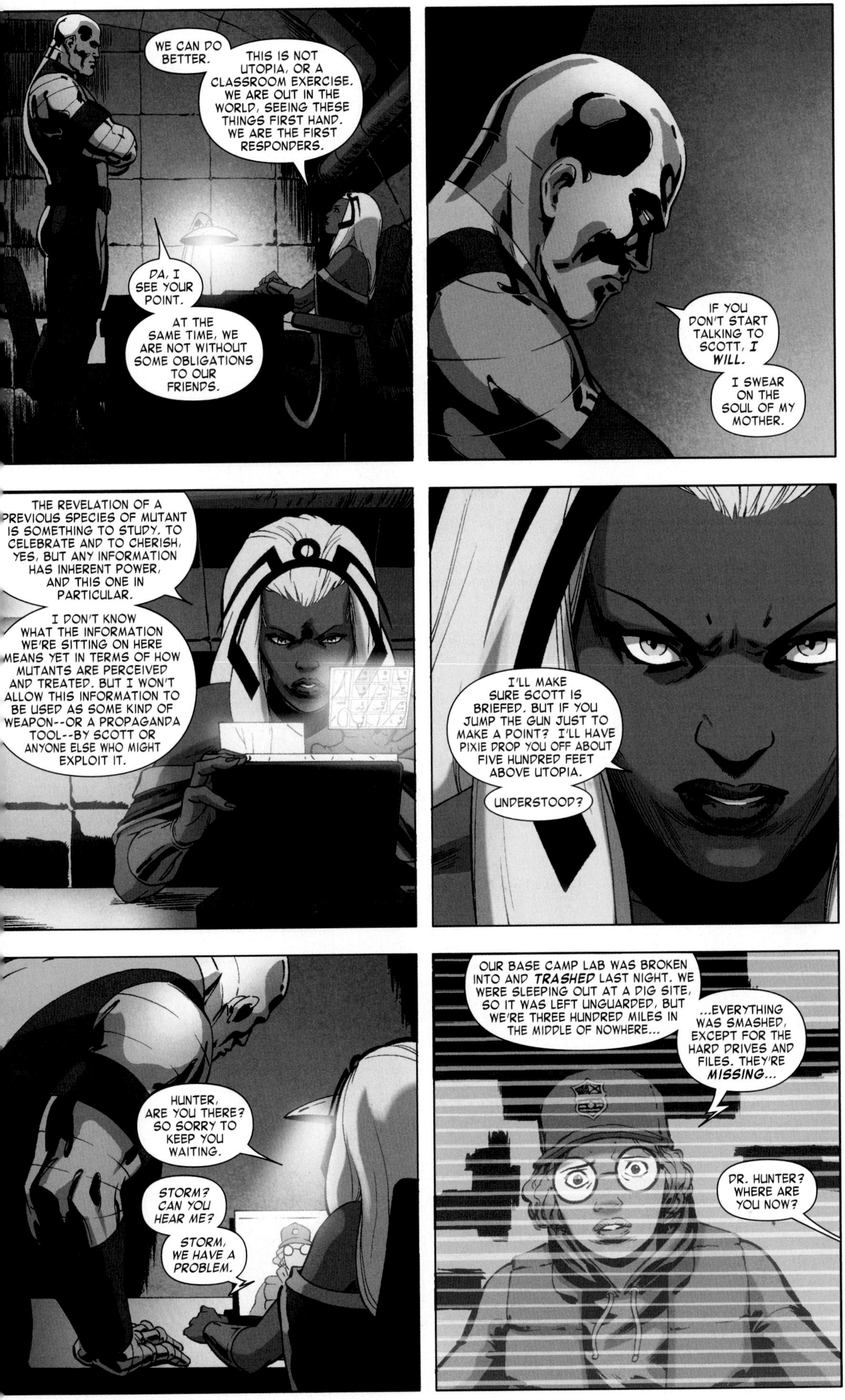

WE CAN DO BETTER.
THIS IS NOT UTOPIA, OR A CLASSROOM EXERCISE. WE ARE OUT IN THE WORLD, SEEING THESE THINGS FIRST HAND. WE ARE THE FIRST RESPONDERS.
DA, I SEE YOUR POINT.
AT THE SAME TIME, WE ARE NOT WITHOUT SOME OBLIGATIONS TO OUR FRIENDS.
IF YOU DON'T START TALKING TO SCOTT, *I WILL.*
I SWEAR ON THE SOUL OF MY MOTHER.
THE REVELATION OF A PREVIOUS SPECIES OF MUTANT IS SOMETHING TO STUDY. TO CELEBRATE AND TO CHERISH, YES, BUT ANY INFORMATION HAS INHERENT POWER, AND THIS ONE IN PARTICULAR.
I DON'T KNOW WHAT THE INFORMATION WE'RE SITTING ON HERE MEANS YET IN TERMS OF HOW MUTANTS ARE PERCEIVED AND TREATED. BUT I WON'T ALLOW THIS INFORMATION TO BE USED AS SOME KIND OF WEAPON--OR A PROPAGANDA TOOL--BY SCOTT OR ANYONE ELSE WHO MIGHT EXPLOIT IT.
I'LL MAKE SURE SCOTT IS BRIEFED. BUT IF YOU JUMP THE GUN JUST TO MAKE A POINT? I'LL HAVE PIXIE DROP YOU OFF ABOUT FIVE HUNDRED FEET ABOVE UTOPIA.
UNDERSTOOD?
HUNTER, ARE YOU THERE? SO SORRY TO KEEP YOU WAITING.
STORM? CAN YOU HEAR ME?
STORM, WE HAVE A PROBLEM.
OUR BASE CAMP LAB WAS BROKEN INTO AND *TRASHED* LAST NIGHT. WE WERE SLEEPING OUT AT A DIG SITE, SO IT WAS LEFT UNGUARDED, BUT WE'RE THREE HUNDRED MILES IN THE MIDDLE OF NOWHERE...
...EVERYTHING WAS SMASHED, EXCEPT FOR THE HARD DRIVES AND FILES. THEY'RE *MISSING...*
DR. HUNTER? WHERE ARE YOU NOW?

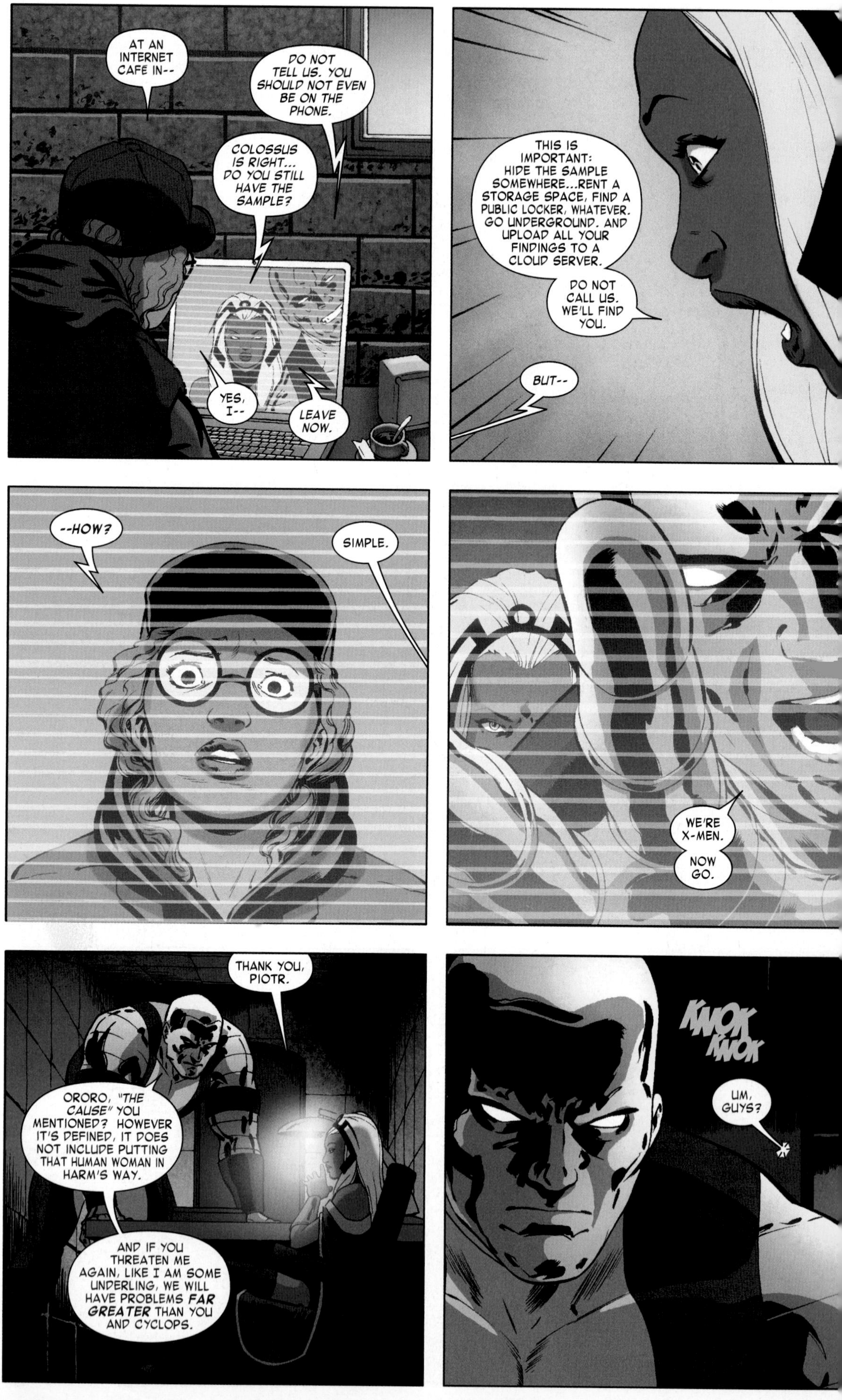

AT AN INTERNET CAFÉ IN--
DO NOT TELL US. YOU SHOULD NOT EVEN BE ON THE PHONE.
COLOSSUS IS RIGHT... DO YOU STILL HAVE THE SAMPLE?
YES, I--
LEAVE NOW.
THIS IS IMPORTANT: HIDE THE SAMPLE SOMEWHERE...RENT A STORAGE SPACE, FIND A PUBLIC LOCKER, WHATEVER. GO UNDERGROUND. AND UPLOAD ALL YOUR FINDINGS TO A CLOUD SERVER.
DO NOT CALL US. WE'LL FIND YOU.
BUT--
--HOW?
SIMPLE.
WE'RE X-MEN.
NOW GO.
THANK YOU, PIOTR.
ORORO, "THE CAUSE" YOU MENTIONED? HOWEVER IT'S DEFINED, IT DOES NOT INCLUDE PUTTING THAT HUMAN WOMAN IN HARM'S WAY.
AND IF YOU THREATEN ME AGAIN, LIKE I AM SOME UNDERLING, WE WILL HAVE PROBLEMS FAR GREATER THAN YOU AND CYCLOPS.
KNOK KNOK
UM, GUYS?

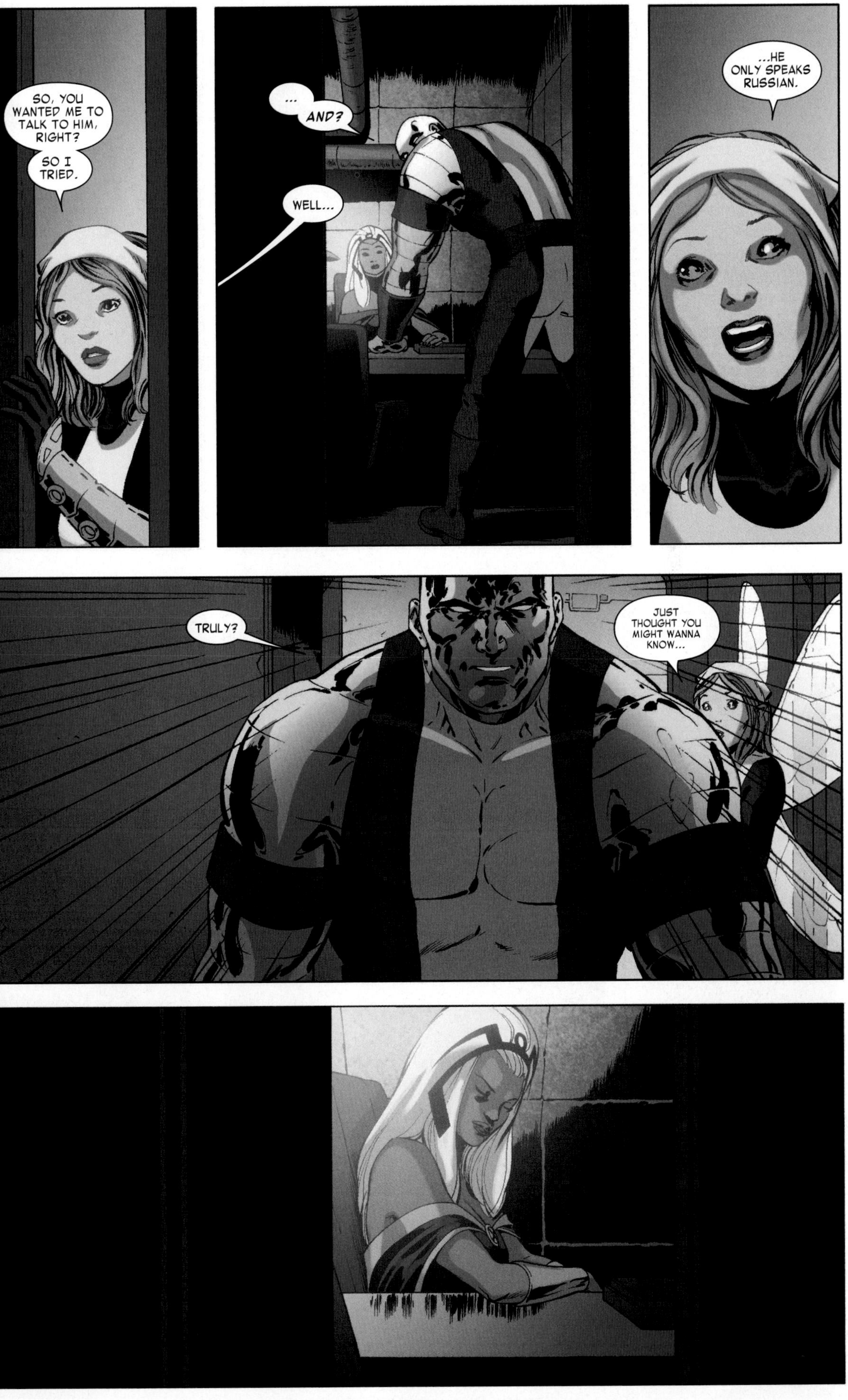
SO, YOU WANTED ME TO TALK TO HIM, RIGHT?
SO I TRIED.
... AND?
WELL...
...HE ONLY SPEAKS RUSSIAN.
TRULY?
JUST THOUGHT YOU MIGHT WANNA KNOW...

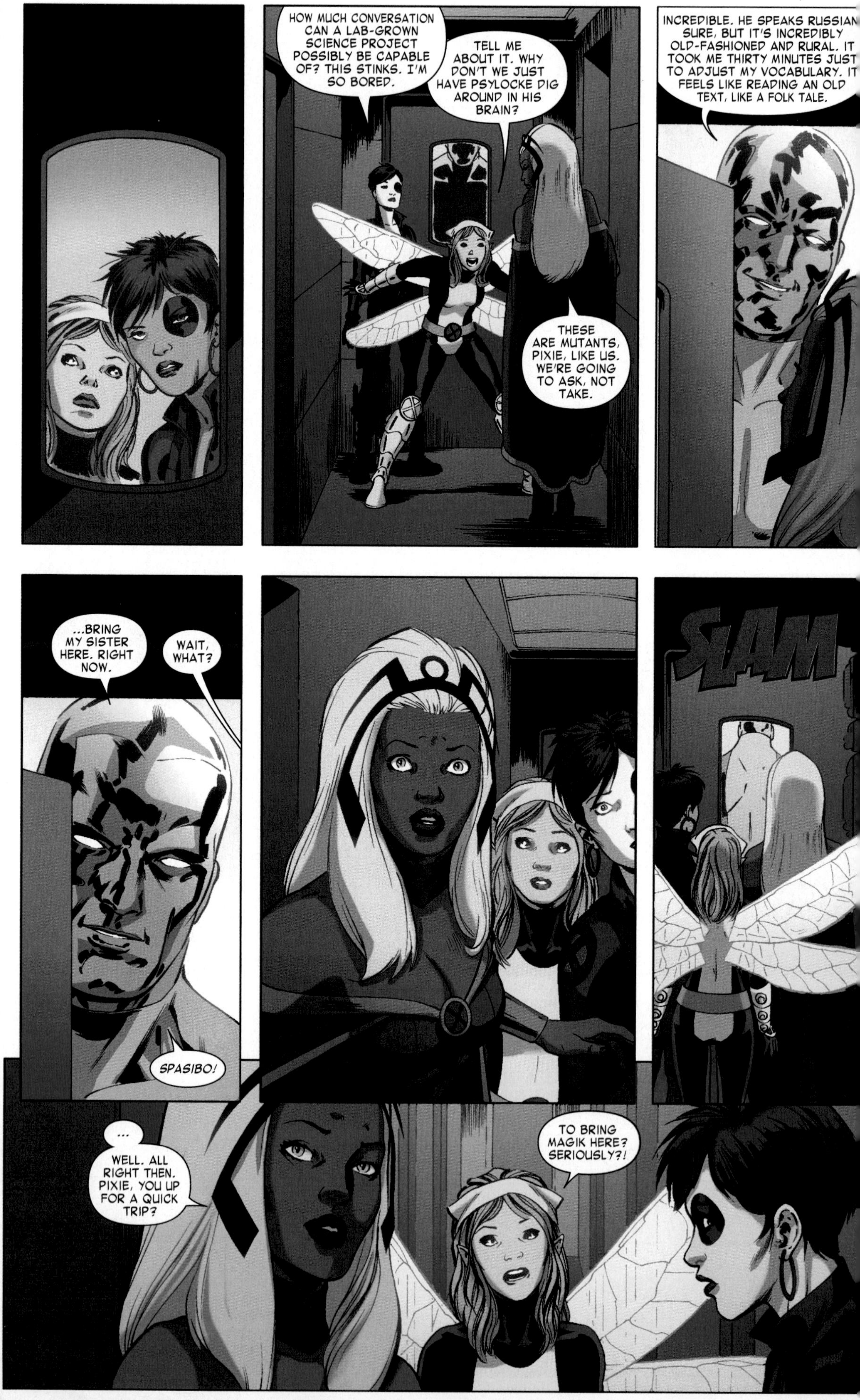
HOW MUCH CONVERSATION CAN A LAB-GROWN SCIENCE PROJECT POSSIBLY BE CAPABLE OF? THIS STINKS. I'M SO BORED.
TELL ME ABOUT IT. WHY DON'T WE JUST HAVE PSYLOCKE DIG AROUND IN HIS BRAIN?
THESE ARE MUTANTS, PIXIE, LIKE US. WE'RE GOING TO ASK, NOT TAKE.
INCREDIBLE. HE SPEAKS RUSSIAN, SURE, BUT IT'S INCREDIBLY OLD-FASHIONED AND RURAL. IT TOOK ME THIRTY MINUTES JUST TO ADJUST MY VOCABULARY. IT FEELS LIKE READING AN OLD TEXT, LIKE A FOLK TALE.
...BRING MY SISTER HERE. RIGHT NOW.
WAIT, WHAT?
SPASIBO!
SLAM
...
WELL. ALL RIGHT THEN. PIXIE, YOU UP FOR A QUICK TRIP?
TO BRING MAGIK HERE? SERIOUSLY?!

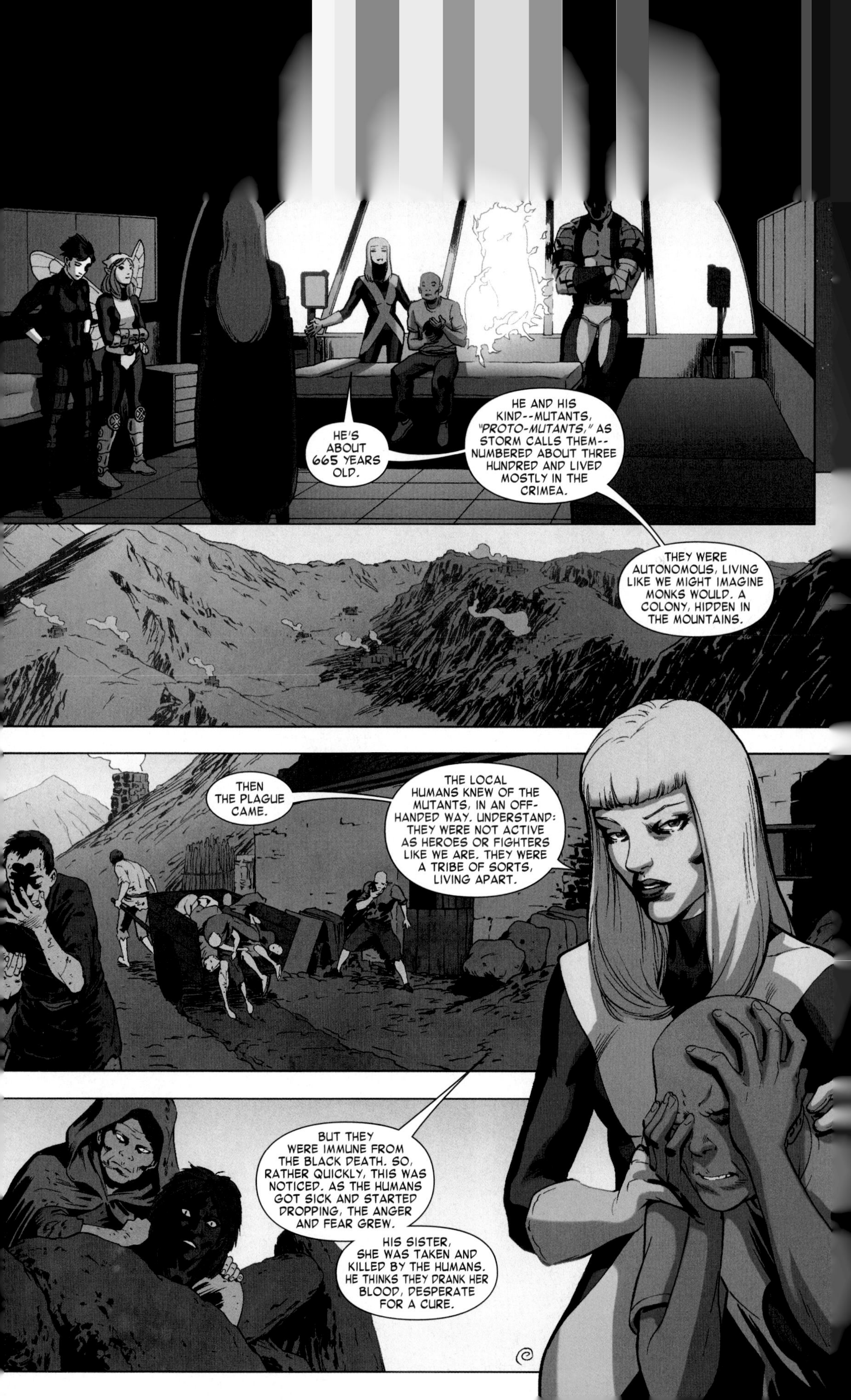
HE'S ABOUT 665 YEARS OLD.
HE AND HIS KIND--MUTANTS, "PROTO-MUTANTS," AS STORM CALLS THEM--NUMBERED ABOUT THREE HUNDRED AND LIVED MOSTLY IN THE CRIMEA.
THEY WERE AUTONOMOUS, LIVING LIKE WE MIGHT IMAGINE MONKS WOULD. A COLONY, HIDDEN IN THE MOUNTAINS.
THEN THE PLAGUE CAME.
THE LOCAL HUMANS KNEW OF THE MUTANTS, IN AN OFF-HANDED WAY. UNDERSTAND: THEY WERE NOT ACTIVE AS HEROES OR FIGHTERS LIKE WE ARE. THEY WERE A TRIBE OF SORTS, LIVING APART.
BUT THEY WERE IMMUNE FROM THE BLACK DEATH. SO, RATHER QUICKLY, THIS WAS NOTICED. AS THE HUMANS GOT SICK AND STARTED DROPPING, THE ANGER AND FEAR GREW.
HIS SISTER, SHE WAS TAKEN AND KILLED BY THE HUMANS. HE THINKS THEY DRANK HER BLOOD, DESPERATE FOR A CURE.

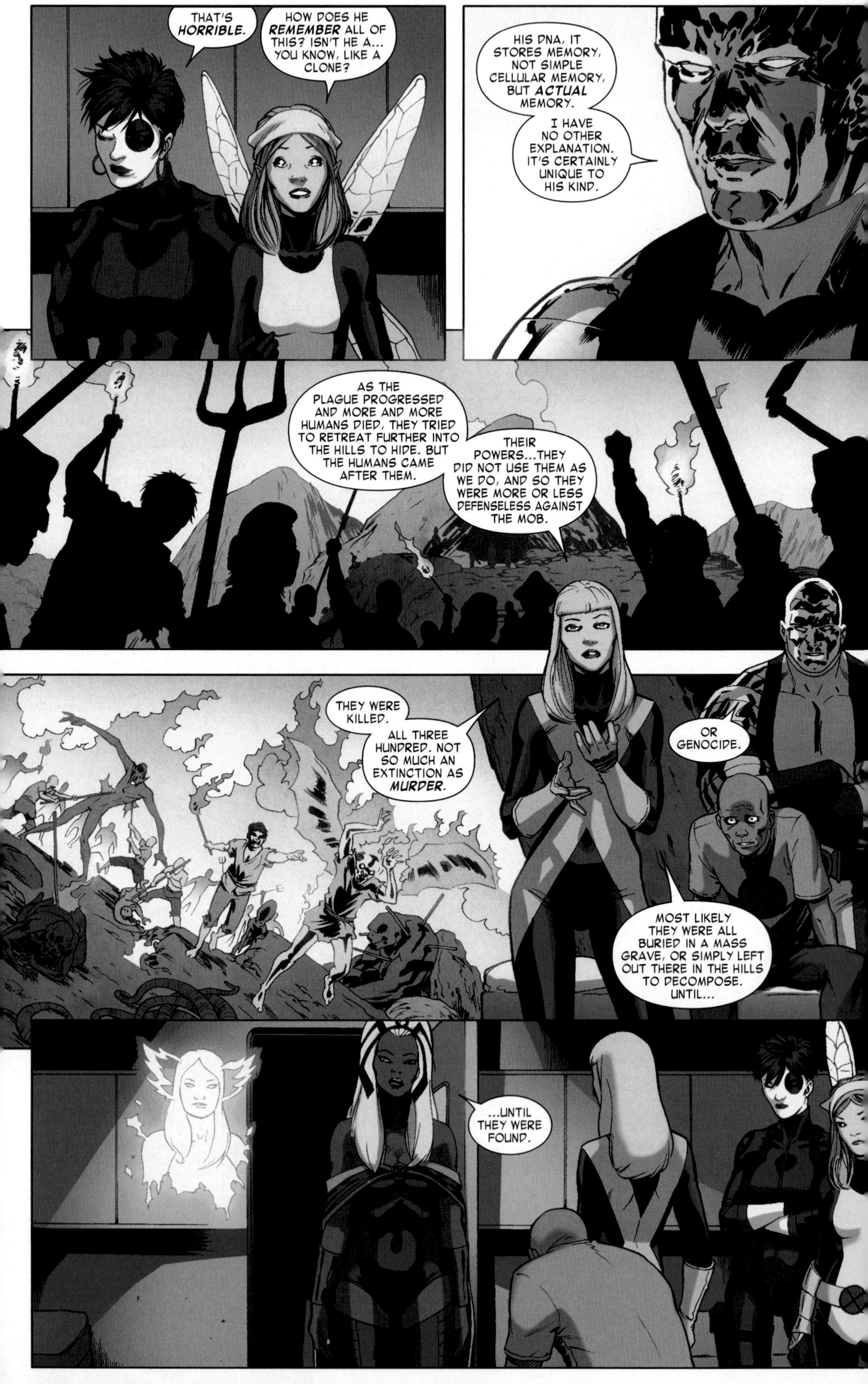
THAT'S HORRIBLE.
HOW DOES HE REMEMBER ALL OF THIS? ISN'T HE A... YOU KNOW, LIKE A CLONE?
HIS DNA, IT STORES MEMORY, NOT SIMPLE CELLULAR MEMORY, BUT ACTUAL MEMORY.
I HAVE NO OTHER EXPLANATION. IT'S CERTAINLY UNIQUE TO HIS KIND.
AS THE PLAGUE PROGRESSED AND MORE AND MORE HUMANS DIED, THEY TRIED TO RETREAT FURTHER INTO THE HILLS TO HIDE. BUT THE HUMANS CAME AFTER THEM.
THEIR POWERS...THEY DID NOT USE THEM AS WE DO, AND SO THEY WERE MORE OR LESS DEFENSELESS AGAINST THE MOB.
THEY WERE KILLED.
ALL THREE HUNDRED. NOT SO MUCH AN EXTINCTION AS MURDER.
OR GENOCIDE.
MOST LIKELY THEY WERE ALL BURIED IN A MASS GRAVE, OR SIMPLY LEFT OUT THERE IN THE HILLS TO DECOMPOSE. UNTIL...
...UNTIL THEY WERE FOUND.

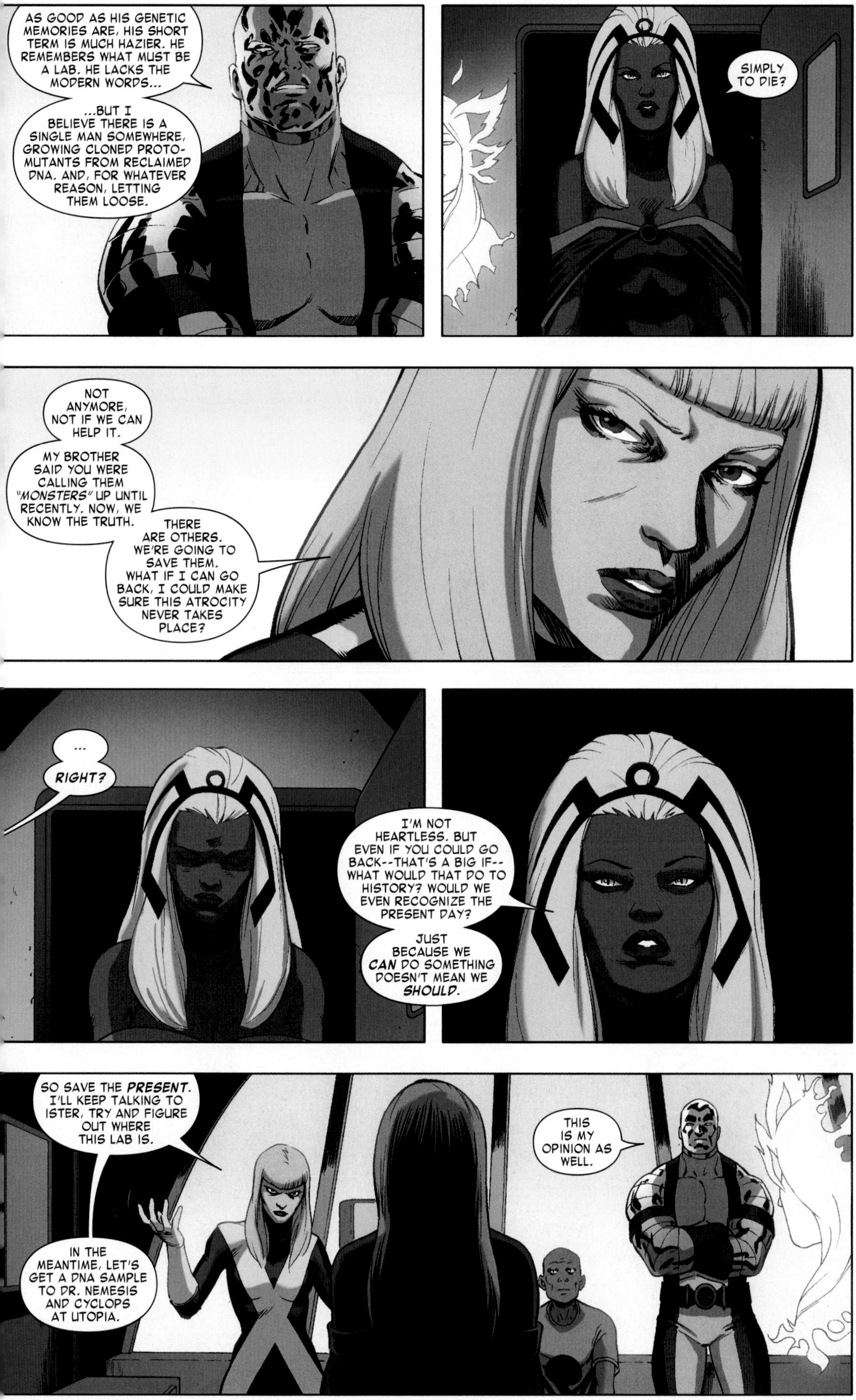
AS GOOD AS HIS GENETIC MEMORIES ARE, HIS SHORT TERM IS MUCH HAZIER. HE REMEMBERS WHAT MUST BE A LAB. HE LACKS THE MODERN WORDS...
...BUT I BELIEVE THERE IS A SINGLE MAN SOMEWHERE, GROWING CLONED PROTO-MUTANTS FROM RECLAIMED DNA. AND, FOR WHATEVER REASON, LETTING THEM LOOSE.
SIMPLY TO DIE?
NOT ANYMORE, NOT IF WE CAN HELP IT.
MY BROTHER SAID YOU WERE CALLING THEM "MONSTERS" UP UNTIL RECENTLY. NOW, WE KNOW THE TRUTH.
THERE ARE OTHERS. WE'RE GOING TO SAVE THEM. WHAT IF I CAN GO BACK, I COULD MAKE SURE THIS ATROCITY NEVER TAKES PLACE?
... RIGHT?
I'M NOT HEARTLESS. BUT EVEN IF YOU COULD GO BACK--THAT'S A BIG IF--WHAT WOULD THAT DO TO HISTORY? WOULD WE EVEN RECOGNIZE THE PRESENT DAY?
JUST BECAUSE WE CAN DO SOMETHING DOESN'T MEAN WE SHOULD.
SO SAVE THE PRESENT. I'LL KEEP TALKING TO ISTER, TRY AND FIGURE OUT WHERE THIS LAB IS.
IN THE MEANTIME, LET'S GET A DNA SAMPLE TO DR. NEMESIS AND CYCLOPS AT UTOPIA.
THIS IS MY OPINION AS WELL.

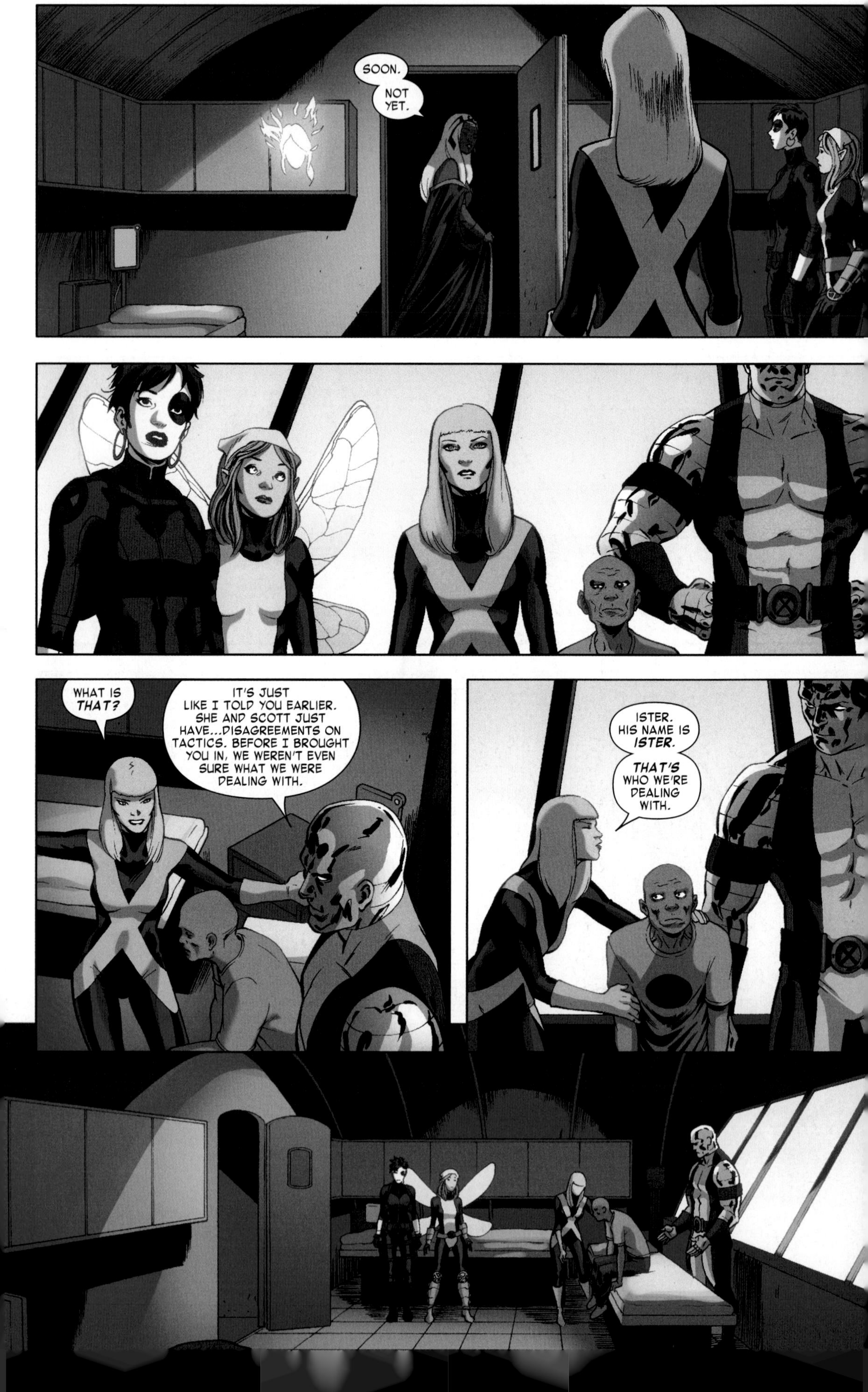
SOON.
NOT YET.
WHAT IS THAT?
IT'S JUST LIKE I TOLD YOU EARLIER. SHE AND SCOTT JUST HAVE...DISAGREEMENTS ON TACTICS. BEFORE I BROUGHT YOU IN, WE WEREN'T EVEN SURE WHAT WE WERE DEALING WITH.
ISTER. HIS NAME IS ISTER.
THAT'S WHO WE'RE DEALING WITH.

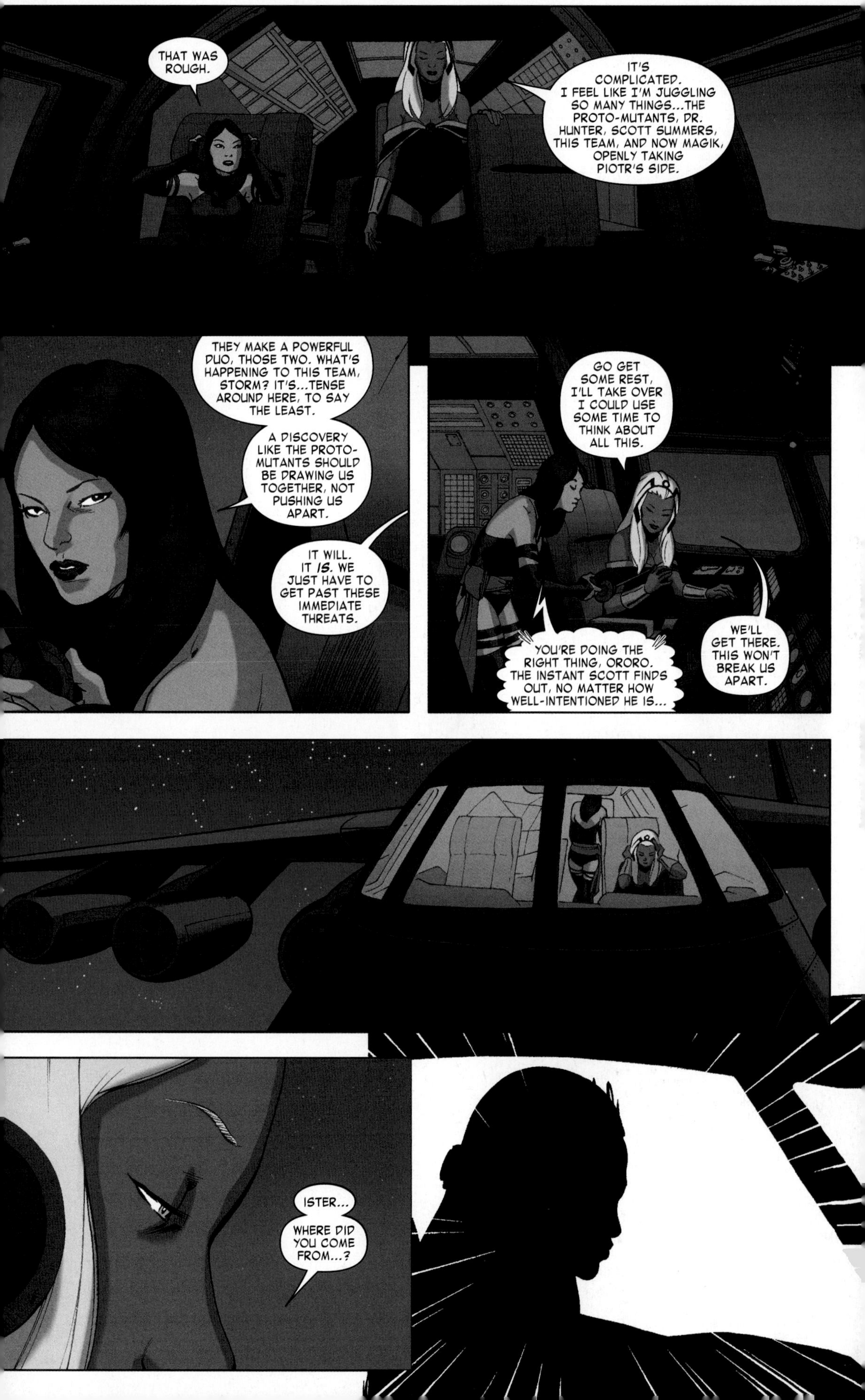
THAT WAS ROUGH.
IT'S COMPLICATED. I FEEL LIKE I'M JUGGLING SO MANY THINGS...THE PROTO-MUTANTS, DR. HUNTER, SCOTT SUMMERS, THIS TEAM, AND NOW MAGIK, OPENLY TAKING PIOTR'S SIDE.
THEY MAKE A POWERFUL DUO, THOSE TWO. WHAT'S HAPPENING TO THIS TEAM, STORM? IT'S...TENSE AROUND HERE, TO SAY THE LEAST.
A DISCOVERY LIKE THE PROTO-MUTANTS SHOULD BE DRAWING US TOGETHER, NOT PUSHING US APART.
IT WILL. IT IS. WE JUST HAVE TO GET PAST THESE IMMEDIATE THREATS.
GO GET SOME REST, I'LL TAKE OVER I COULD USE SOME TIME TO THINK ABOUT ALL THIS.
YOU'RE DOING THE RIGHT THING, ORORO. THE INSTANT SCOTT FINDS OUT, NO MATTER HOW WELL-INTENTIONED HE IS...
WE'LL GET THERE. THIS WON'T BREAK US APART.
ISTER...
WHERE DID YOU COME FROM...?

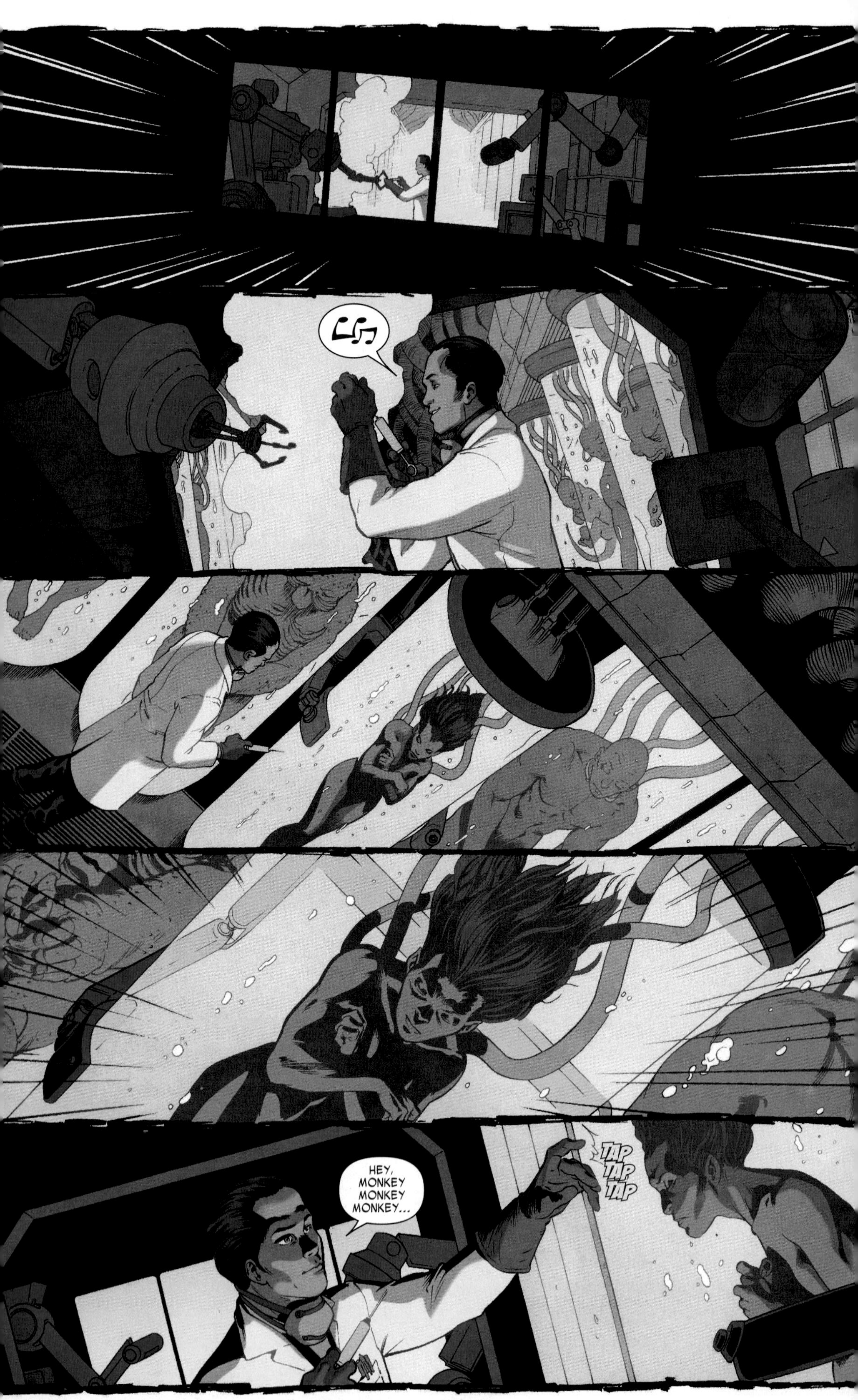
HEY, MONKEY MONKEY MONKEY...
TAP TAP TAP

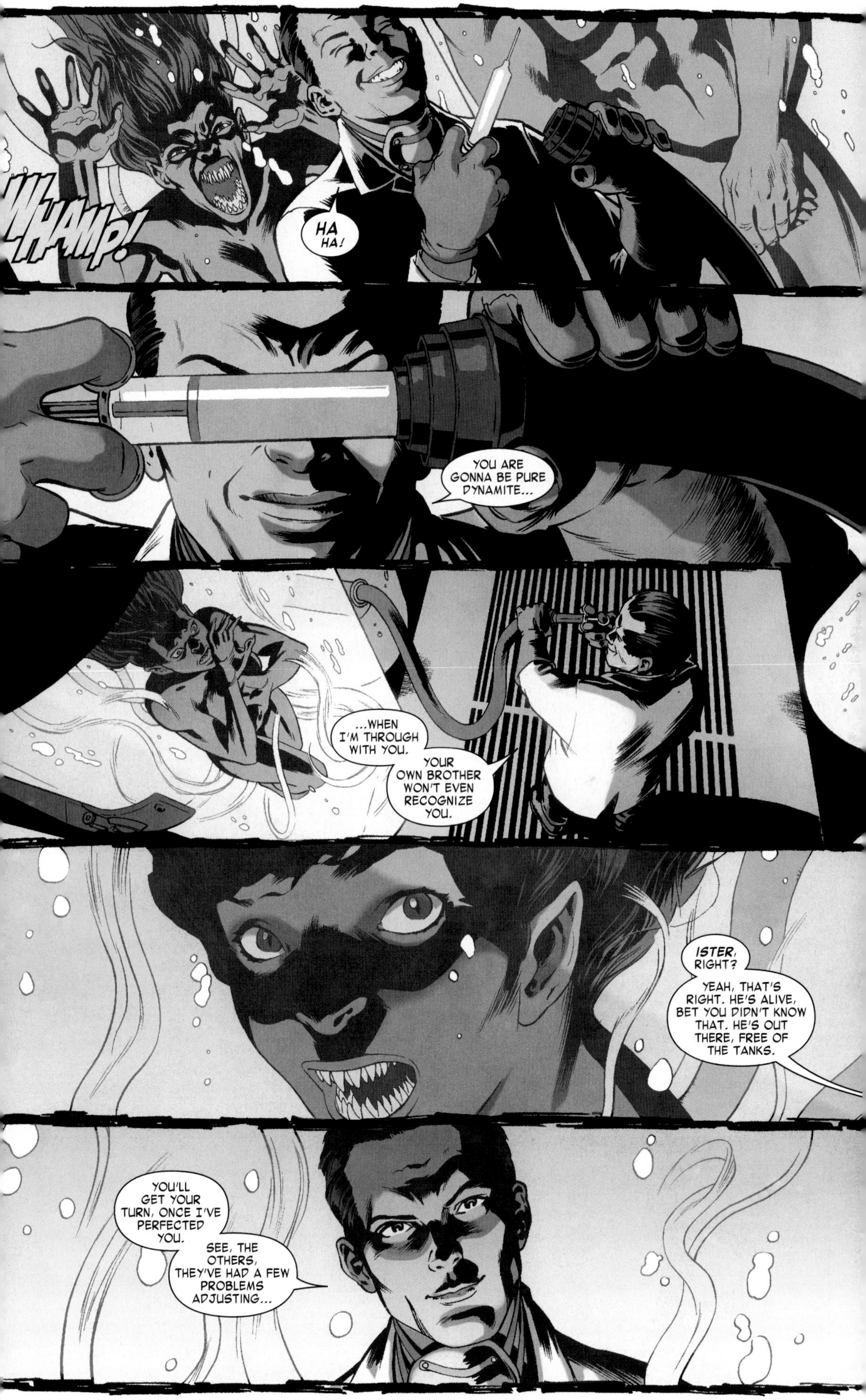
WHAMP!
HA HA!
YOU ARE GONNA BE PURE DYNAMITE...
...WHEN I'M THROUGH WITH YOU.
YOUR OWN BROTHER WON'T EVEN RECOGNIZE YOU.
ISTER, RIGHT?
YEAH, THAT'S RIGHT. HE'S ALIVE, BET YOU DIDN'T KNOW THAT. HE'S OUT THERE, FREE OF THE TANKS.
YOU'LL GET YOUR TURN, ONCE I'VE PERFECTED YOU.
SEE, THE OTHERS, THEY'VE HAD A FEW PROBLEMS ADJUSTING...

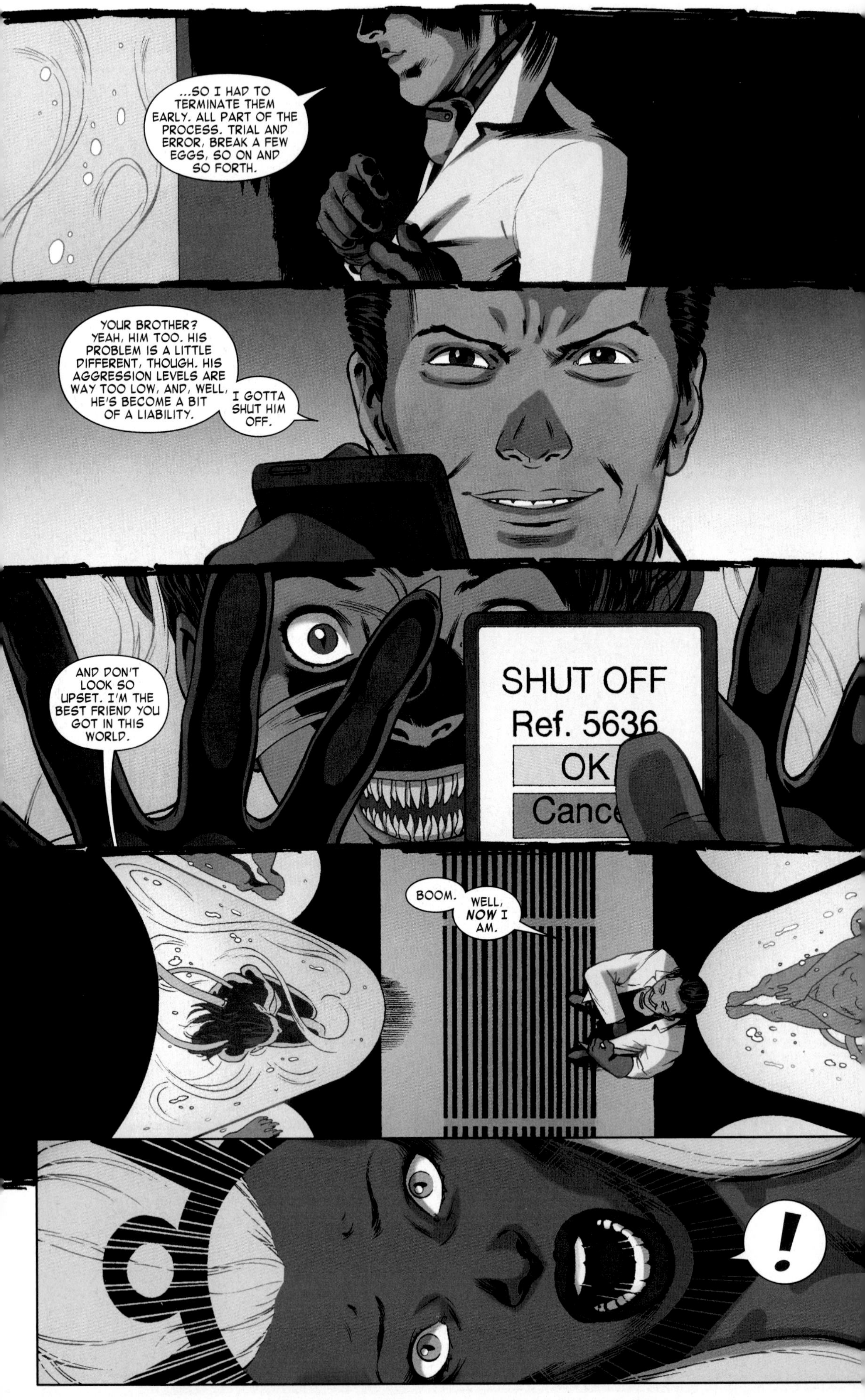
...SO I HAD TO TERMINATE THEM EARLY. ALL PART OF THE PROCESS. TRIAL AND ERROR, BREAK A FEW EGGS, SO ON AND SO FORTH.
YOUR BROTHER? YEAH, HIM TOO. HIS PROBLEM IS A LITTLE DIFFERENT, THOUGH. HIS AGGRESSION LEVELS ARE WAY TOO LOW, AND, WELL, HE'S BECOME A BIT OF A LIABILITY.
I GOTTA SHUT HIM OFF.
AND DON'T LOOK SO UPSET. I'M THE BEST FRIEND YOU GOT IN THIS WORLD.
SHUT OFF
Ref. 5636
OK
Cance
BOOM.
WELL, NOW I AM.
!

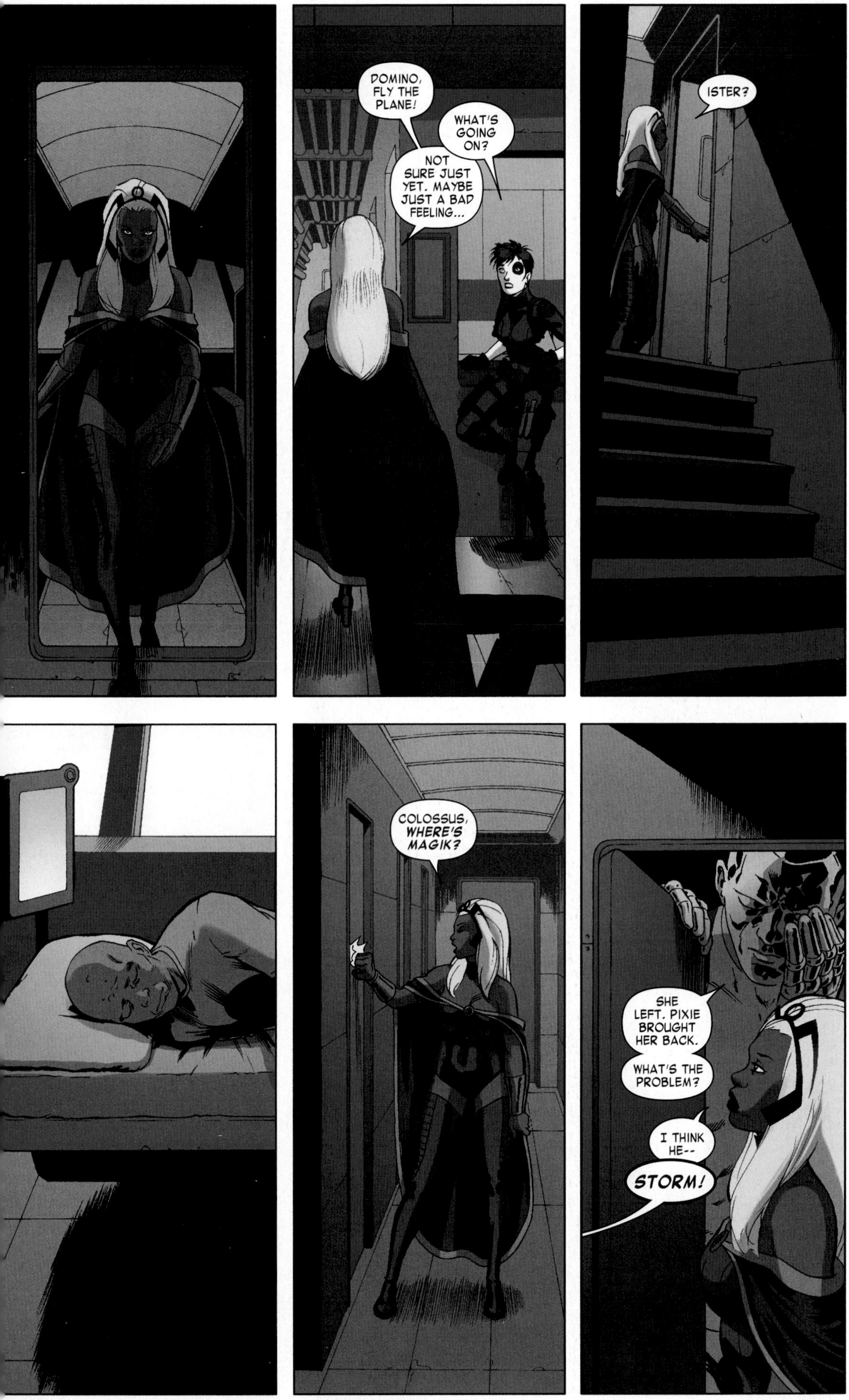
DOMINO, FLY THE PLANE!
WHAT'S GOING ON?
NOT SURE JUST YET. MAYBE JUST A BAD FEELING...
ISTER?
COLOSSUS, WHERE'S MAGIK?
SHE LEFT. PIXIE BROUGHT HER BACK.
WHAT'S THE PROBLEM?
I THINK HE--
STORM!

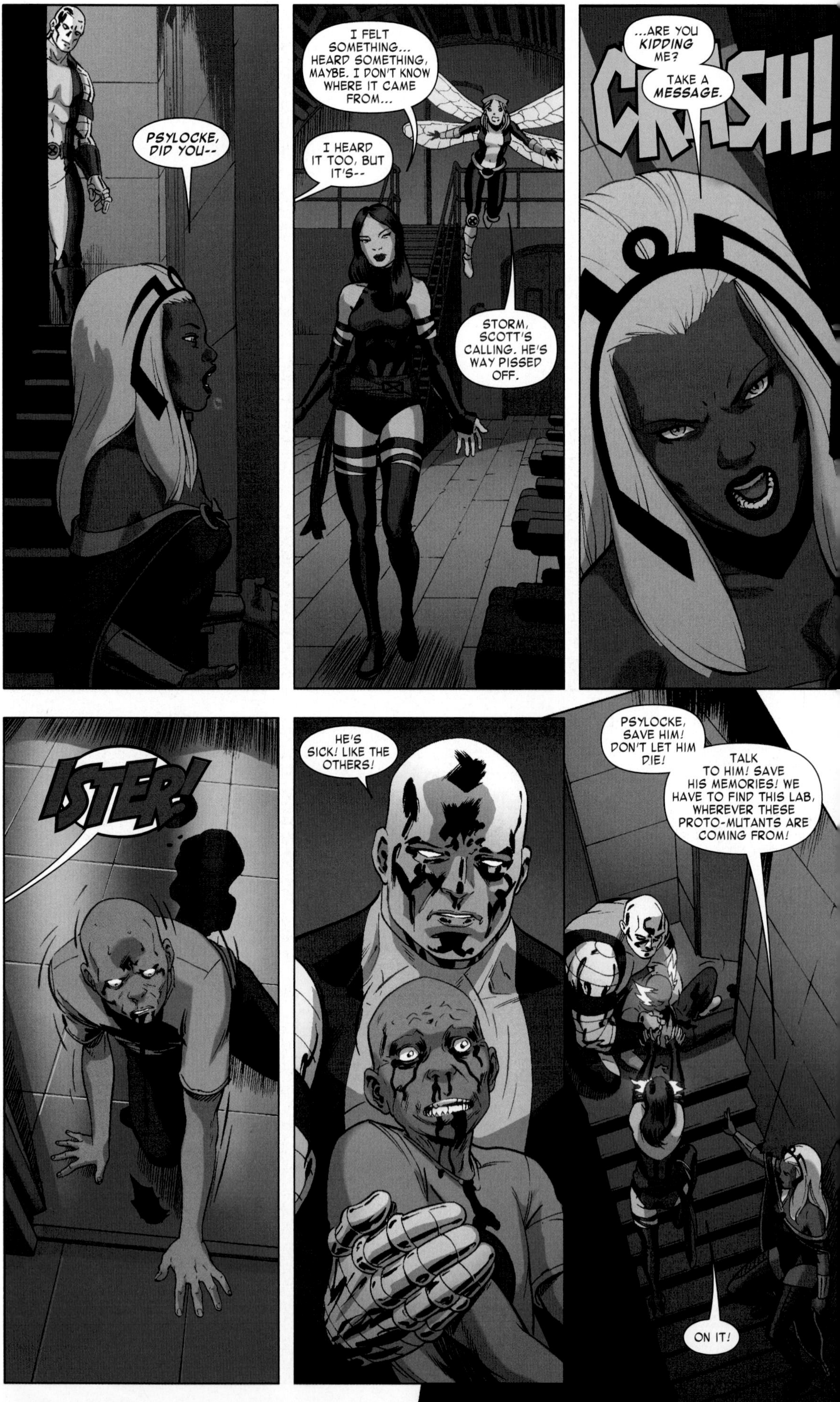
PSYLOCKE, DID YOU--
I FELT SOMETHING... HEARD SOMETHING, MAYBE. I DON'T KNOW WHERE IT CAME FROM...
I HEARD IT TOO, BUT IT'S--
STORM, SCOTT'S CALLING. HE'S WAY PISSED OFF.
...ARE YOU KIDDING ME?
TAKE A MESSAGE.
CRASH!
ISTER!
HE'S SICK! LIKE THE OTHERS!
PSYLOCKE, SAVE HIM! DON'T LET HIM DIE!
TALK TO HIM! SAVE HIS MEMORIES! WE HAVE TO FIND THIS LAB, WHEREVER THESE PROTO-MUTANTS ARE COMING FROM!
ON IT!

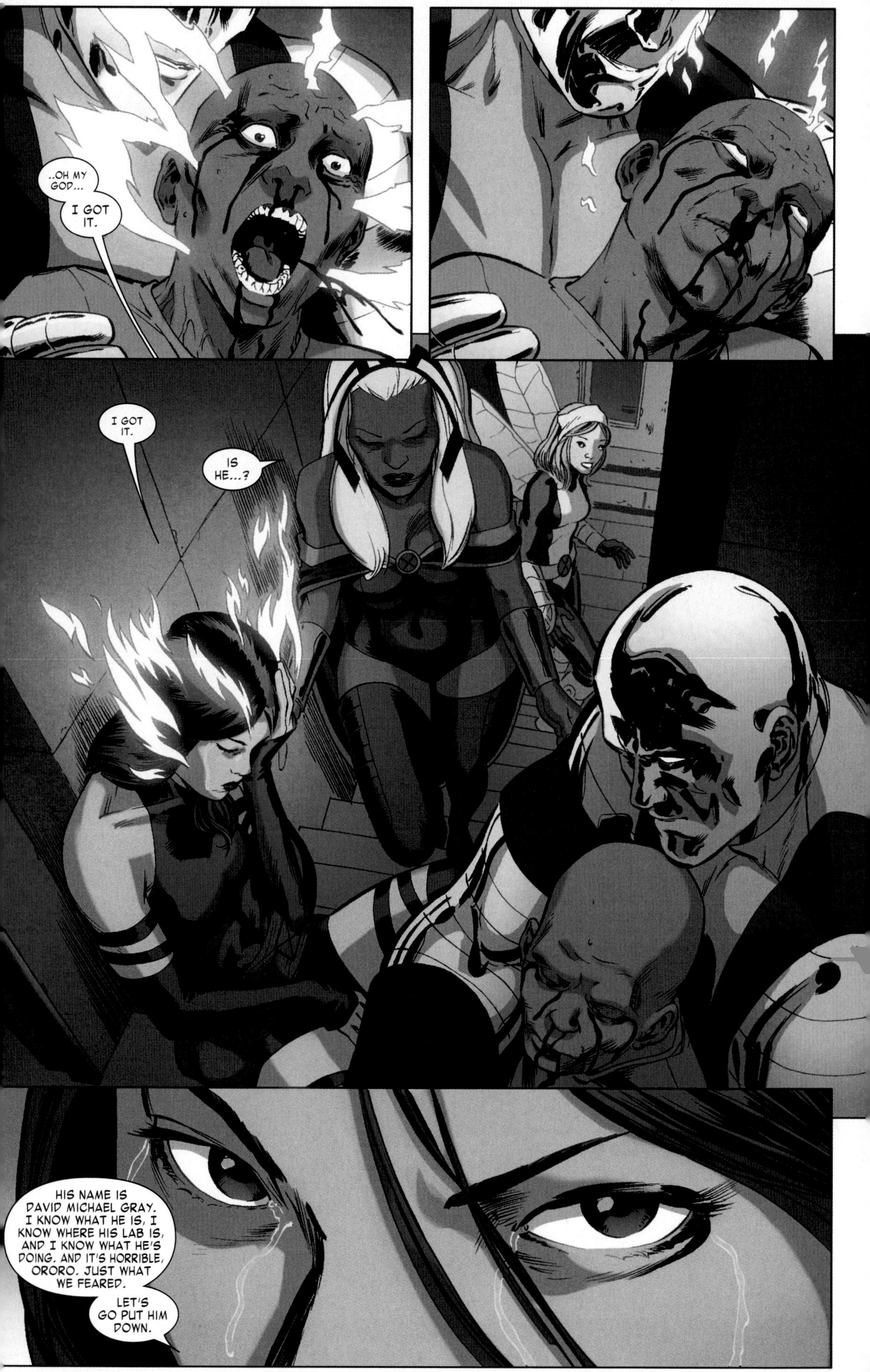
..OH MY GOD...
I GOT IT.
I GOT IT.
IS HE...?
HIS NAME IS DAVID MICHAEL GRAY. I KNOW WHAT HE IS, I KNOW WHERE HIS LAB IS, AND I KNOW WHAT HE'S DOING. AND IT'S HORRIBLE, ORORO. JUST WHAT WE FEARED.
LET'S GO PUT HIM DOWN.

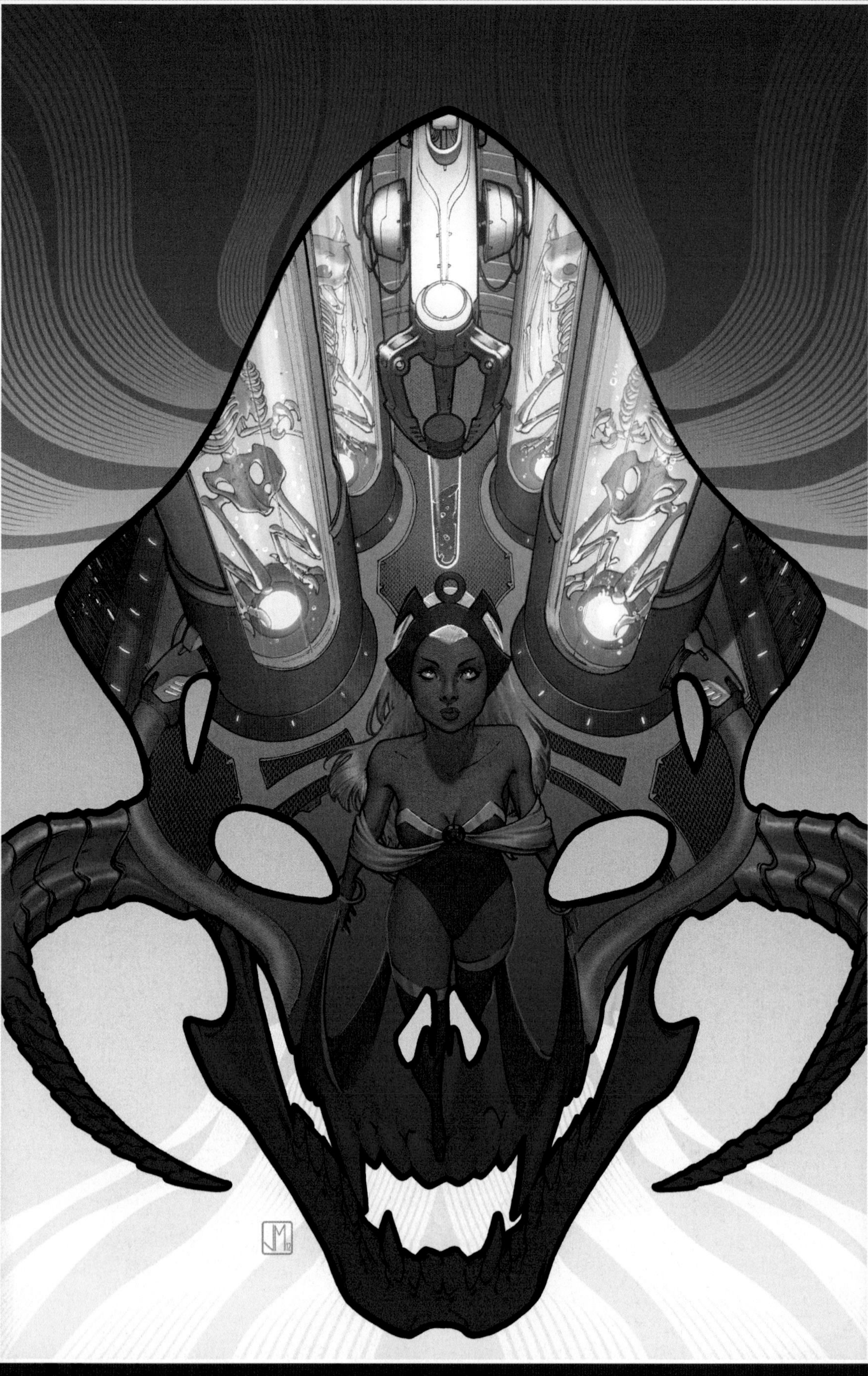

THIRTY-THREE

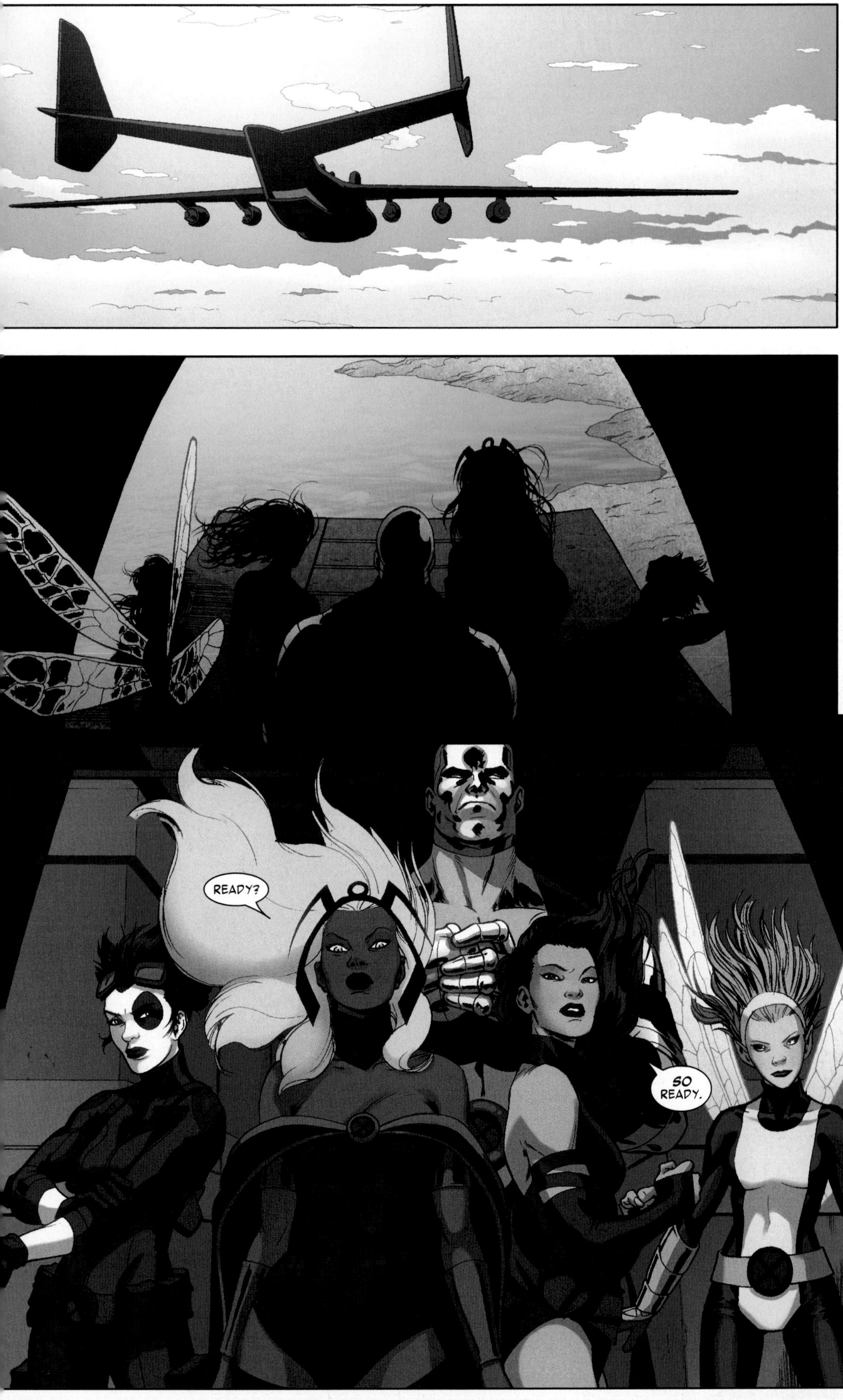
READY?
SO READY.

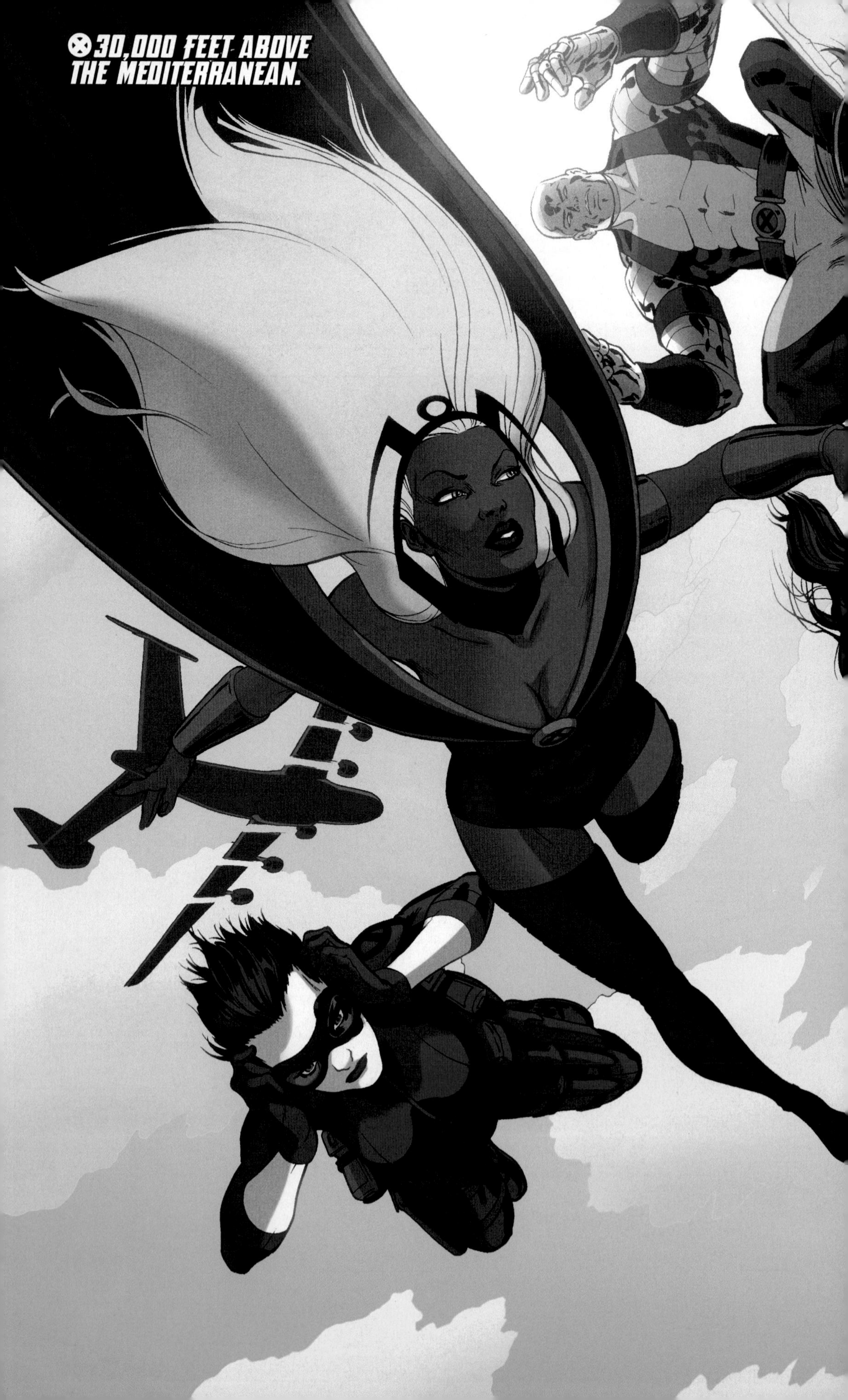
30,000 FEET ABOVE THE MEDITERRANEAN.

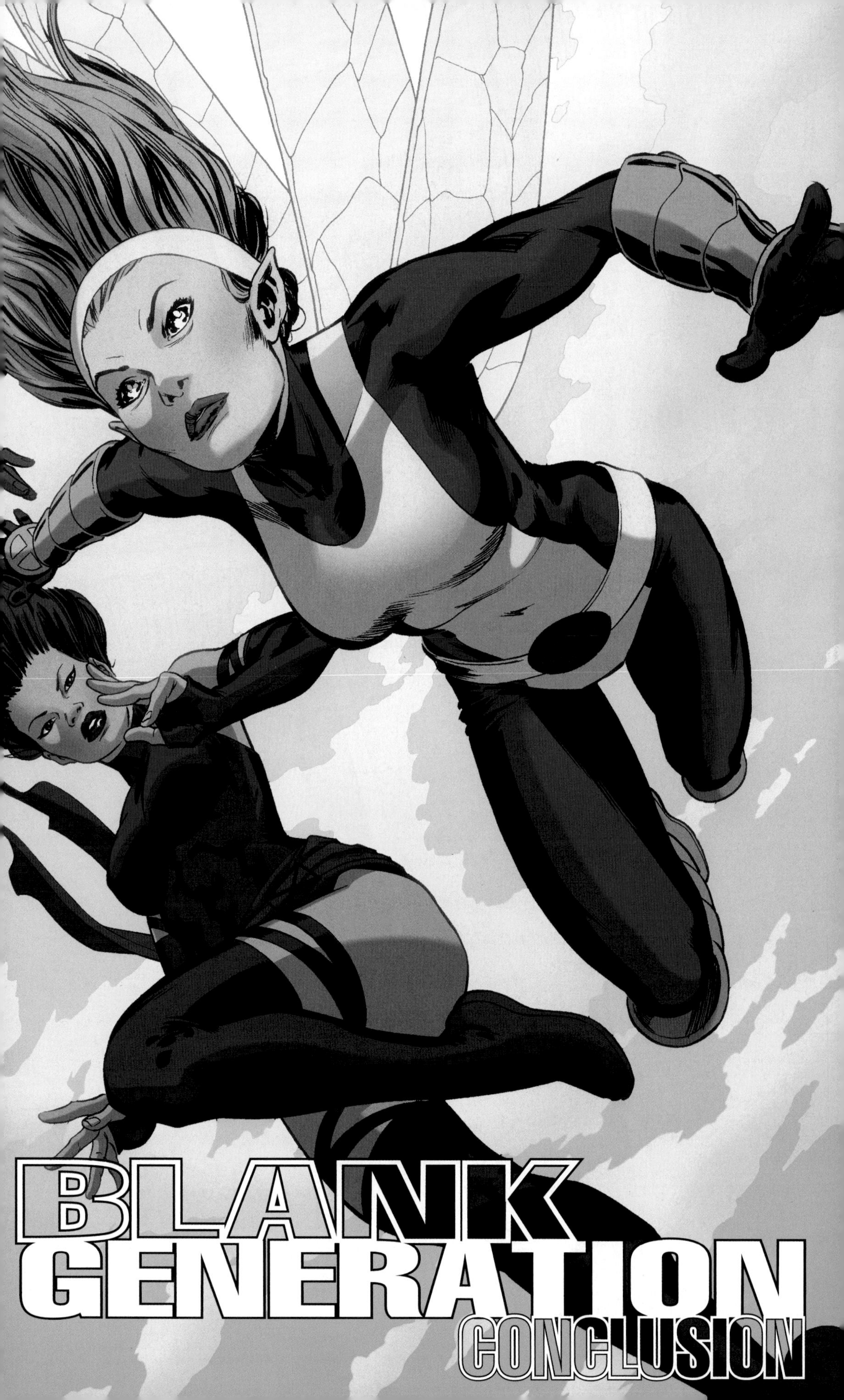
BLANK
GENERATION
CONCLUSION

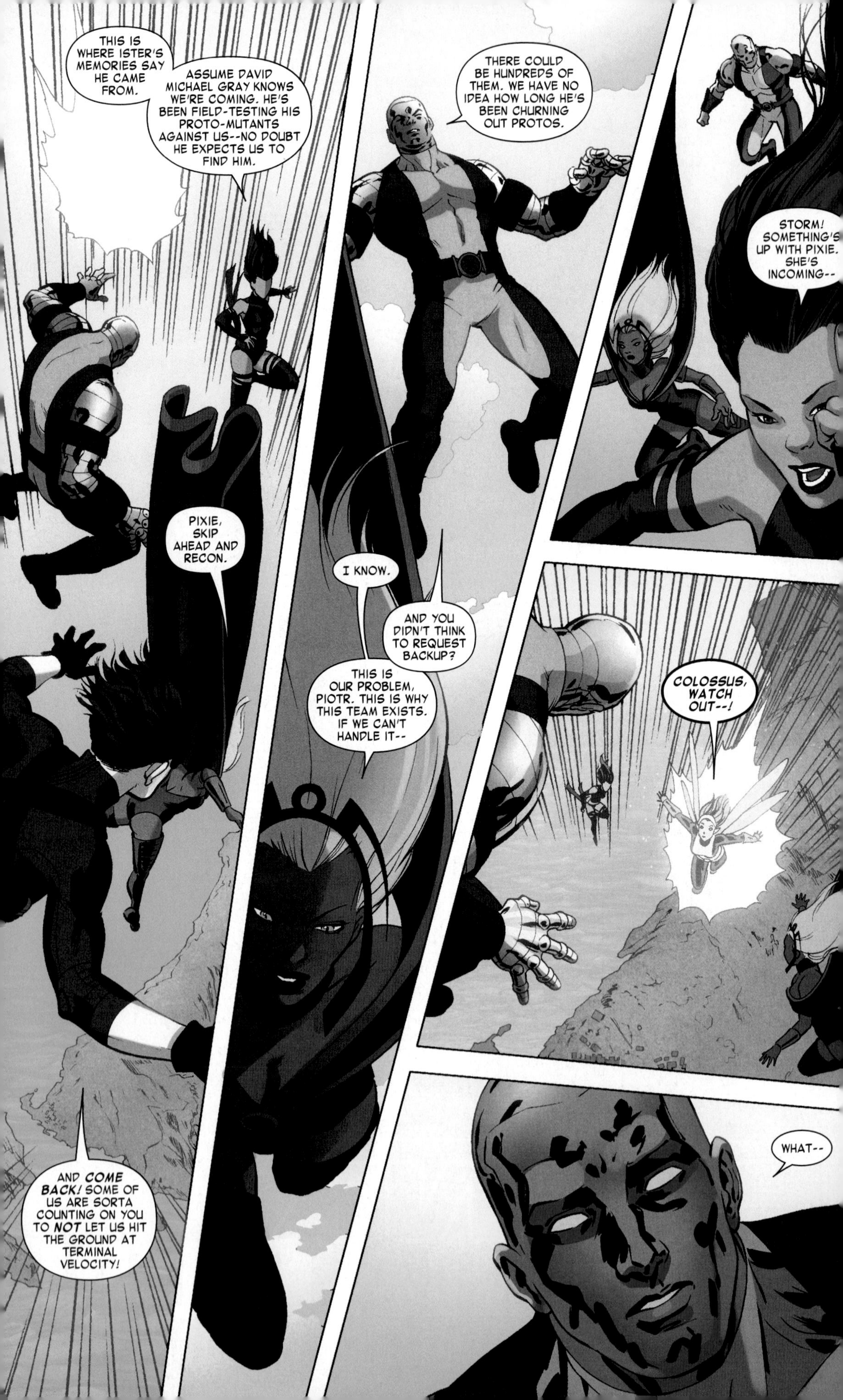
THIS IS WHERE ISTER'S MEMORIES SAY HE CAME FROM.
ASSUME DAVID MICHAEL GRAY KNOWS WE'RE COMING. HE'S BEEN FIELD-TESTING HIS PROTO-MUTANTS AGAINST US--NO DOUBT HE EXPECTS US TO FIND HIM.
PIXIE, SKIP AHEAD AND RECON.
AND COME BACK! SOME OF US ARE SORTA COUNTING ON YOU TO NOT LET US HIT THE GROUND AT TERMINAL VELOCITY!
THERE COULD BE HUNDREDS OF THEM. WE HAVE NO IDEA HOW LONG HE'S BEEN CHURNING OUT PROTOS.
I KNOW.
AND YOU DIDN'T THINK TO REQUEST BACKUP?
THIS IS OUR PROBLEM, PIOTR. THIS IS WHY THIS TEAM EXISTS. IF WE CAN'T HANDLE IT--
STORM! SOMETHING'S UP WITH PIXIE. SHE'S INCOMING--
COLOSSUS, WATCH OUT--!
WHAT--

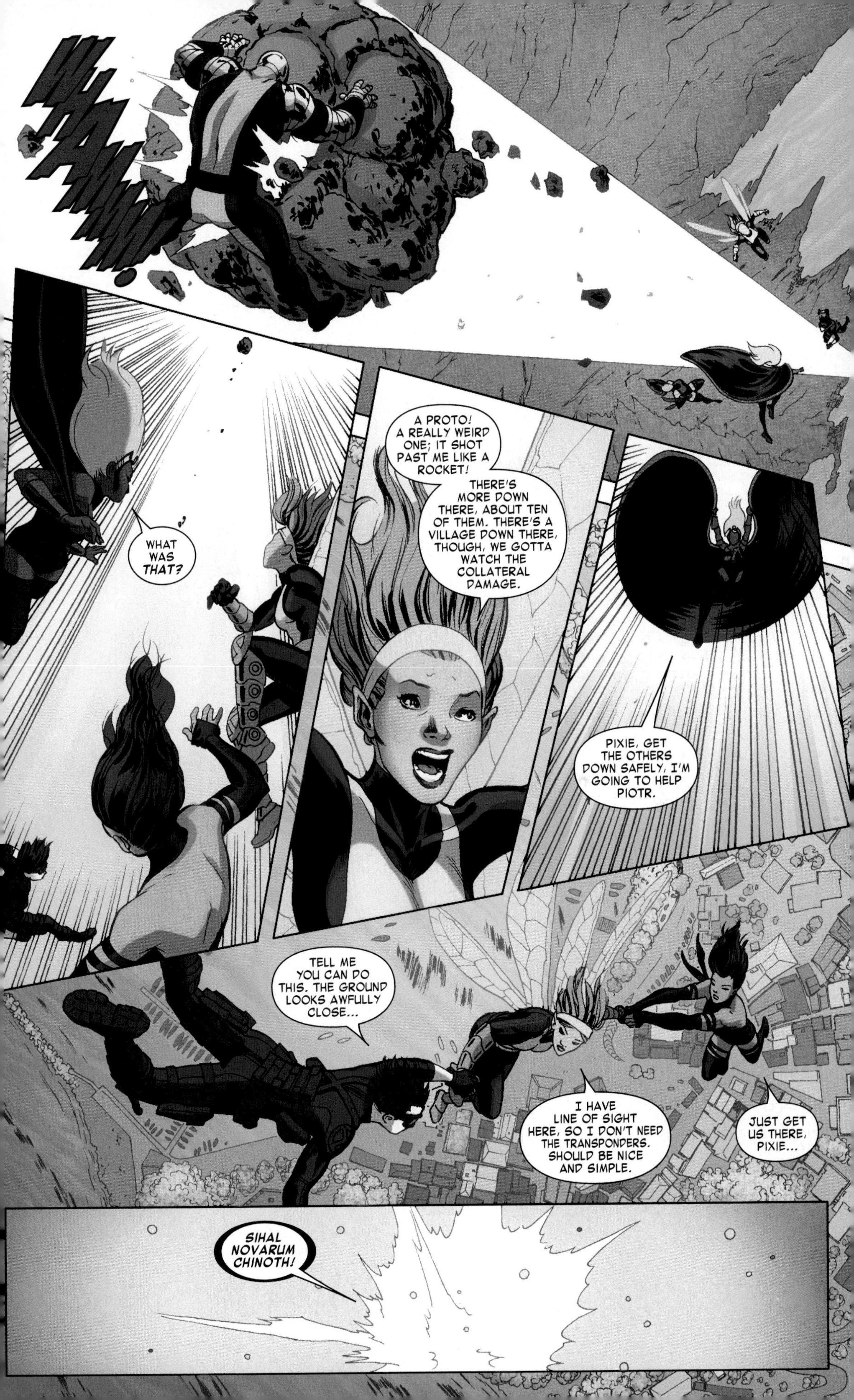
WHAAMM!
WHAT WAS THAT?
A PROTO! A REALLY WEIRD ONE; IT SHOT PAST ME LIKE A ROCKET!
THERE'S MORE DOWN THERE, ABOUT TEN OF THEM. THERE'S A VILLAGE DOWN THERE, THOUGH, WE GOTTA WATCH THE COLLATERAL DAMAGE.
PIXIE, GET THE OTHERS DOWN SAFELY, I'M GOING TO HELP PIOTR.
TELL ME YOU CAN DO THIS. THE GROUND LOOKS AWFULLY CLOSE...
I HAVE LINE OF SIGHT HERE, SO I DON'T NEED THE TRANSPONDERS. SHOULD BE NICE AND SIMPLE.
JUST GET US THERE, PIXIE...
SIHAL NOVARUM CHINOTH!

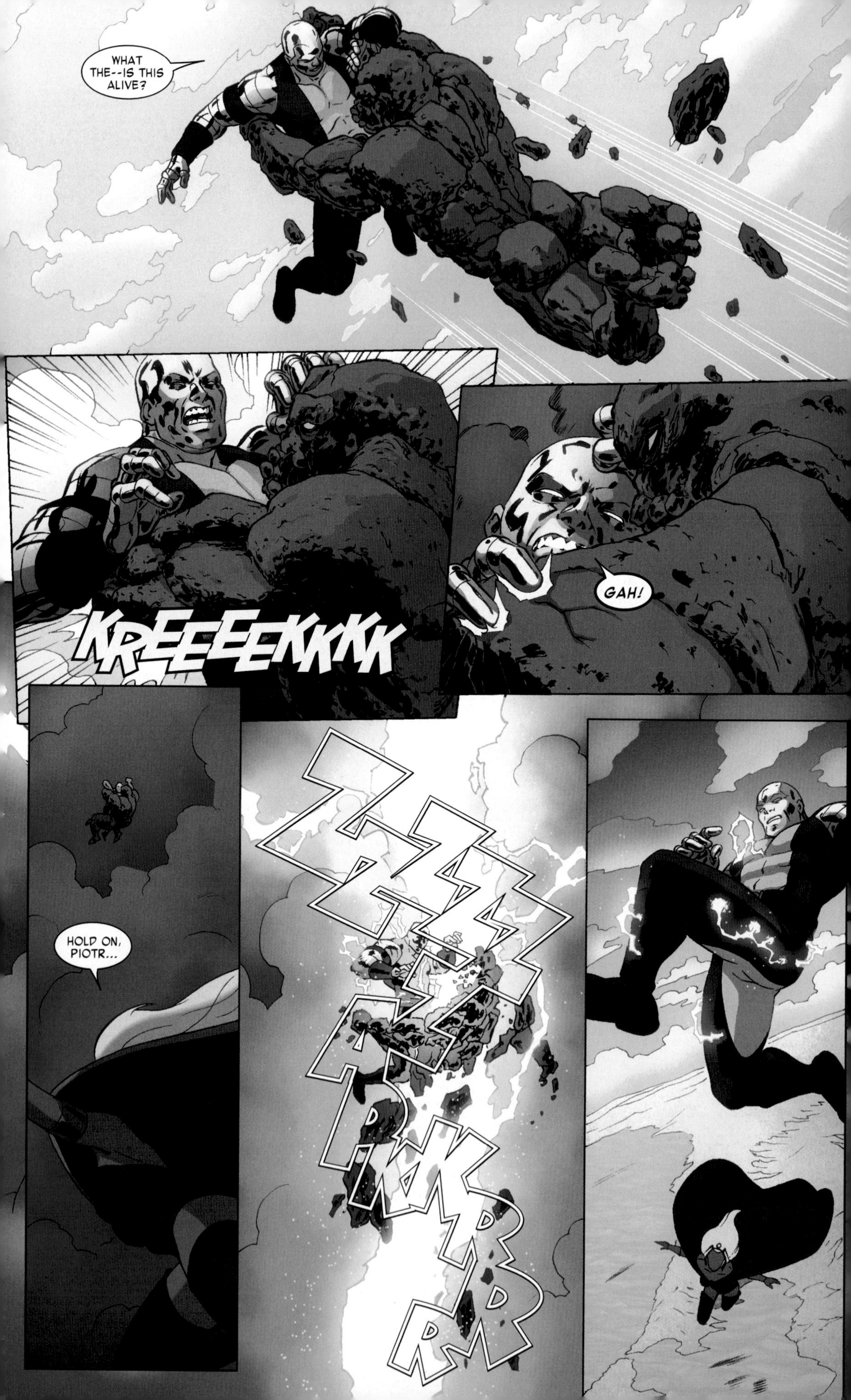
WHAT THE--IS THIS ALIVE?
KREEEEEKKKK
GAH!
HOLD ON, PIOTR...
ZZZZAKADOOM
DRRRRR

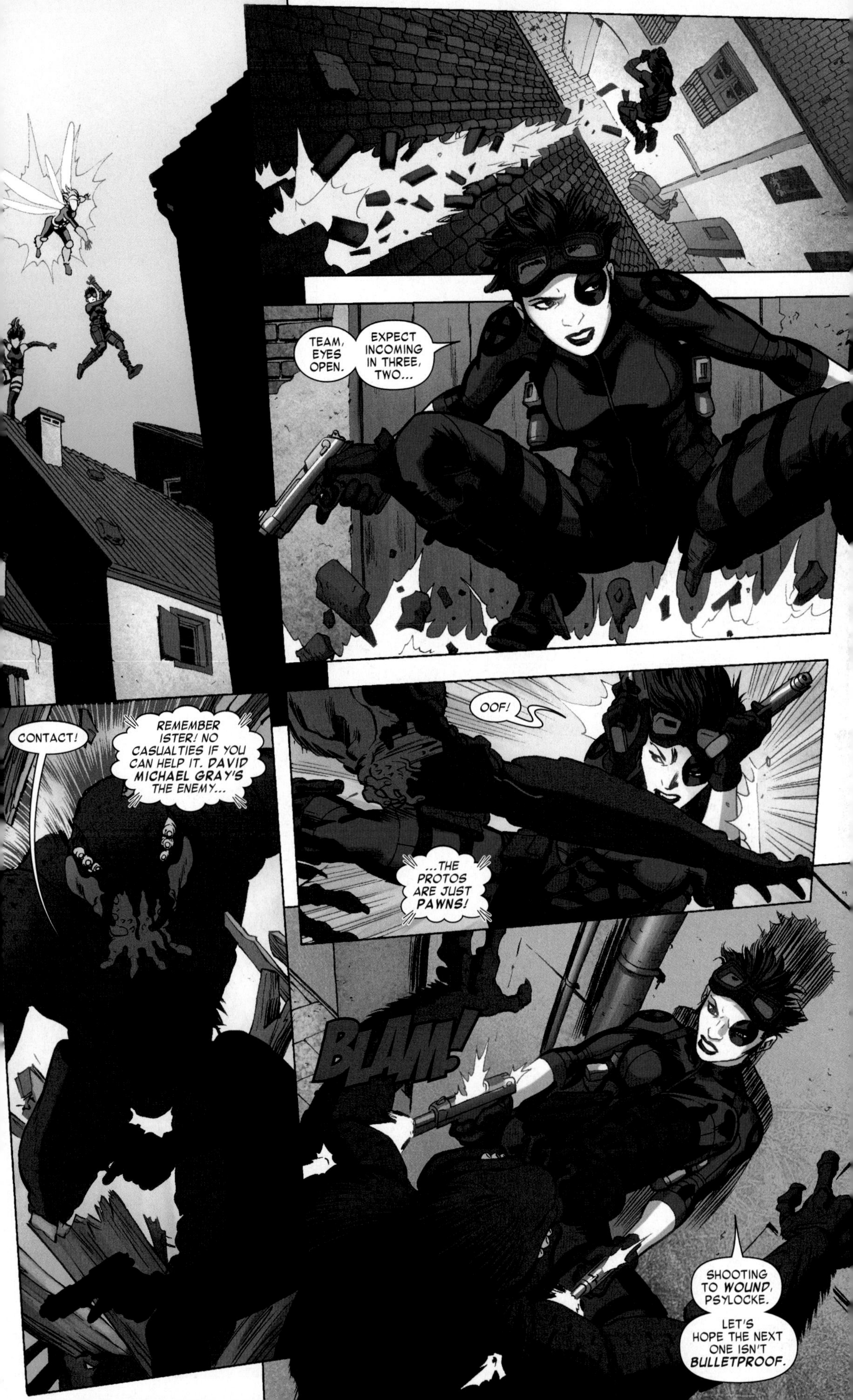
TEAM, EYES OPEN.
EXPECT INCOMING IN THREE, TWO...
CONTACT!
REMEMBER ISTER! NO CASUALTIES IF YOU CAN HELP IT. DAVID MICHAEL GRAY'S THE ENEMY...
OOF!
...THE PROTOS ARE JUST PAWNS!
BLAM!
SHOOTING TO WOUND, PSYLOCKE.
LET'S HOPE THE NEXT ONE ISN'T BULLETPROOF.

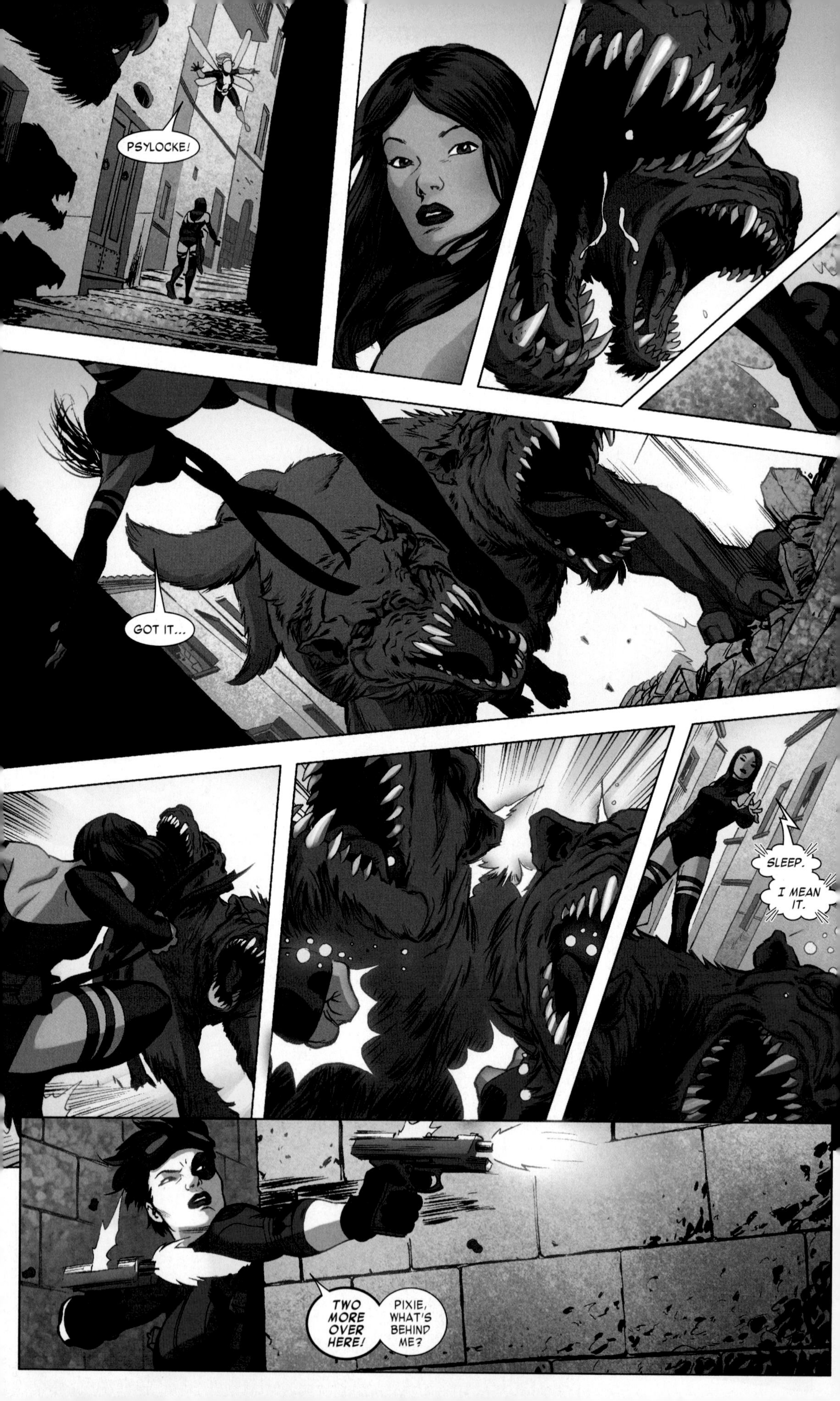
PSYLOCKE!
GOT IT...
SLEEP.
I MEAN IT.
TWO MORE OVER HERE!
PIXIE, WHAT'S BEHIND ME?

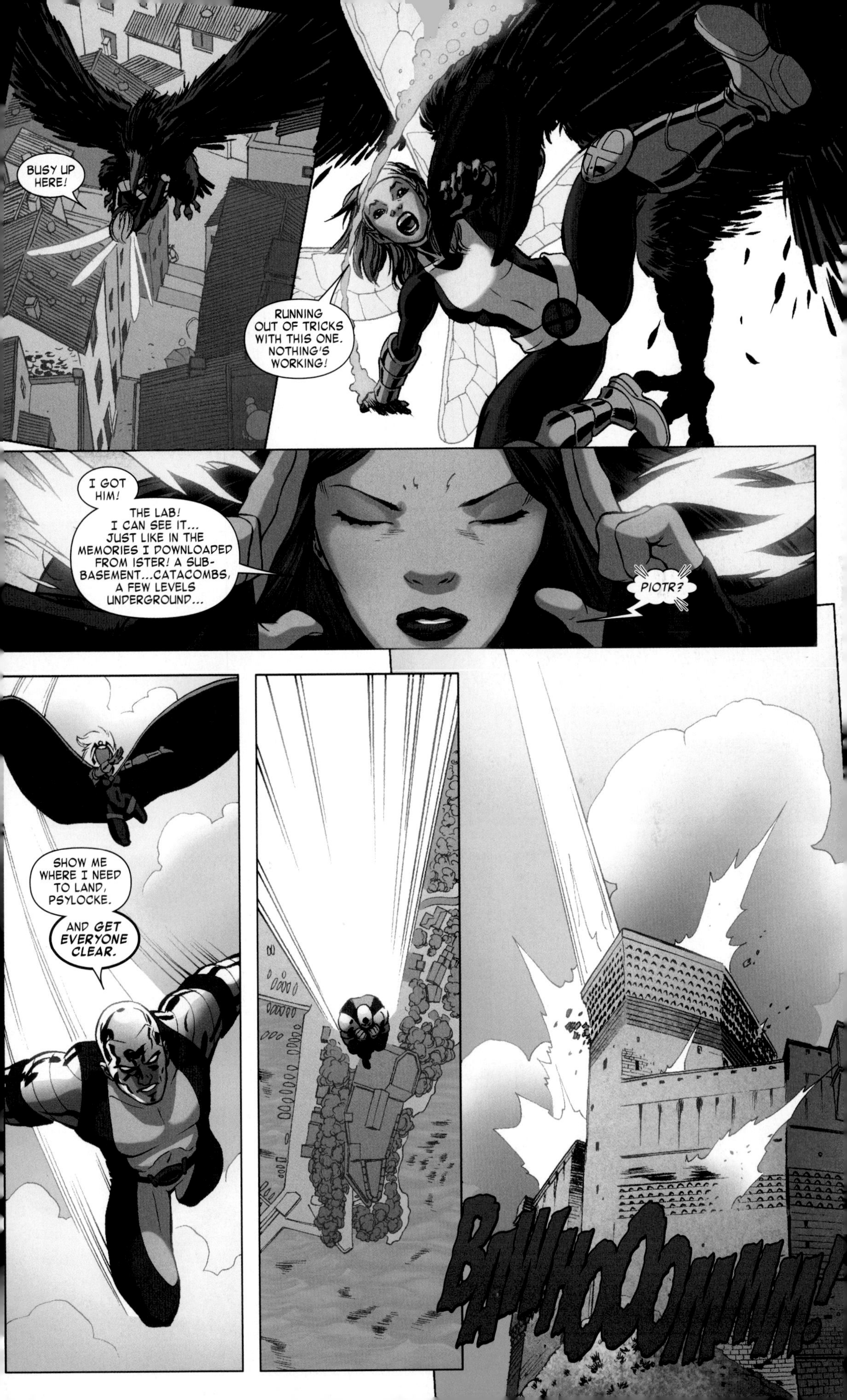
BUSY UP HERE!
RUNNING OUT OF TRICKS WITH THIS ONE. NOTHING'S WORKING!
I GOT HIM!
THE LAB! I CAN SEE IT... JUST LIKE IN THE MEMORIES I DOWNLOADED FROM ISTER! A SUB-BASEMENT...CATACOMBS, A FEW LEVELS UNDERGROUND...
PIOTR?
SHOW ME WHERE I NEED TO LAND, PSYLOCKE.
AND GET EVERYONE CLEAR.
BAWHOOOMMM!

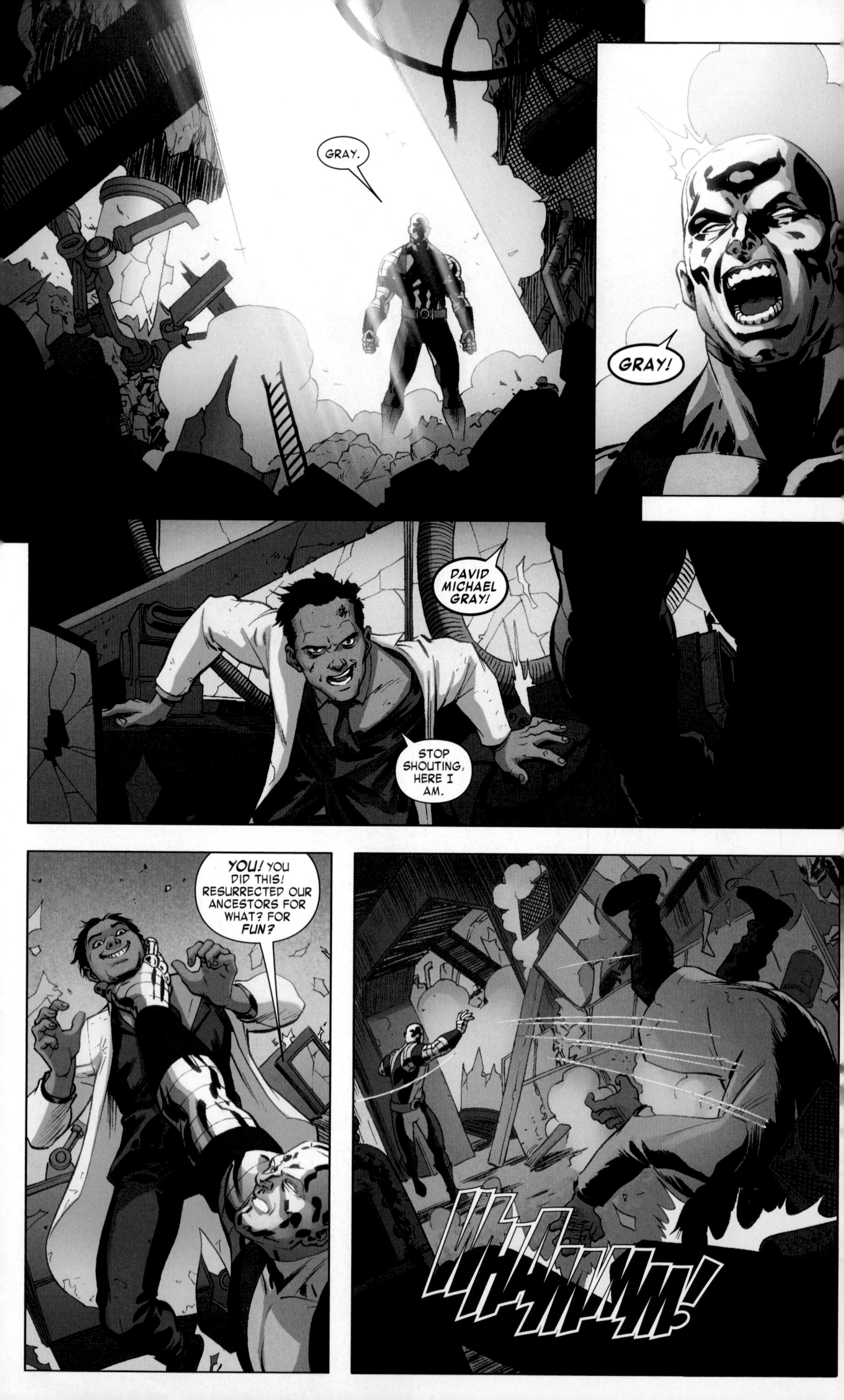
GRAY.
GRAY!
DAVID MICHAEL GRAY!
STOP SHOUTING, HERE I AM.
YOU! YOU DID THIS! RESURRECTED OUR ANCESTORS FOR WHAT? FOR FUN?
WHAMMMM!

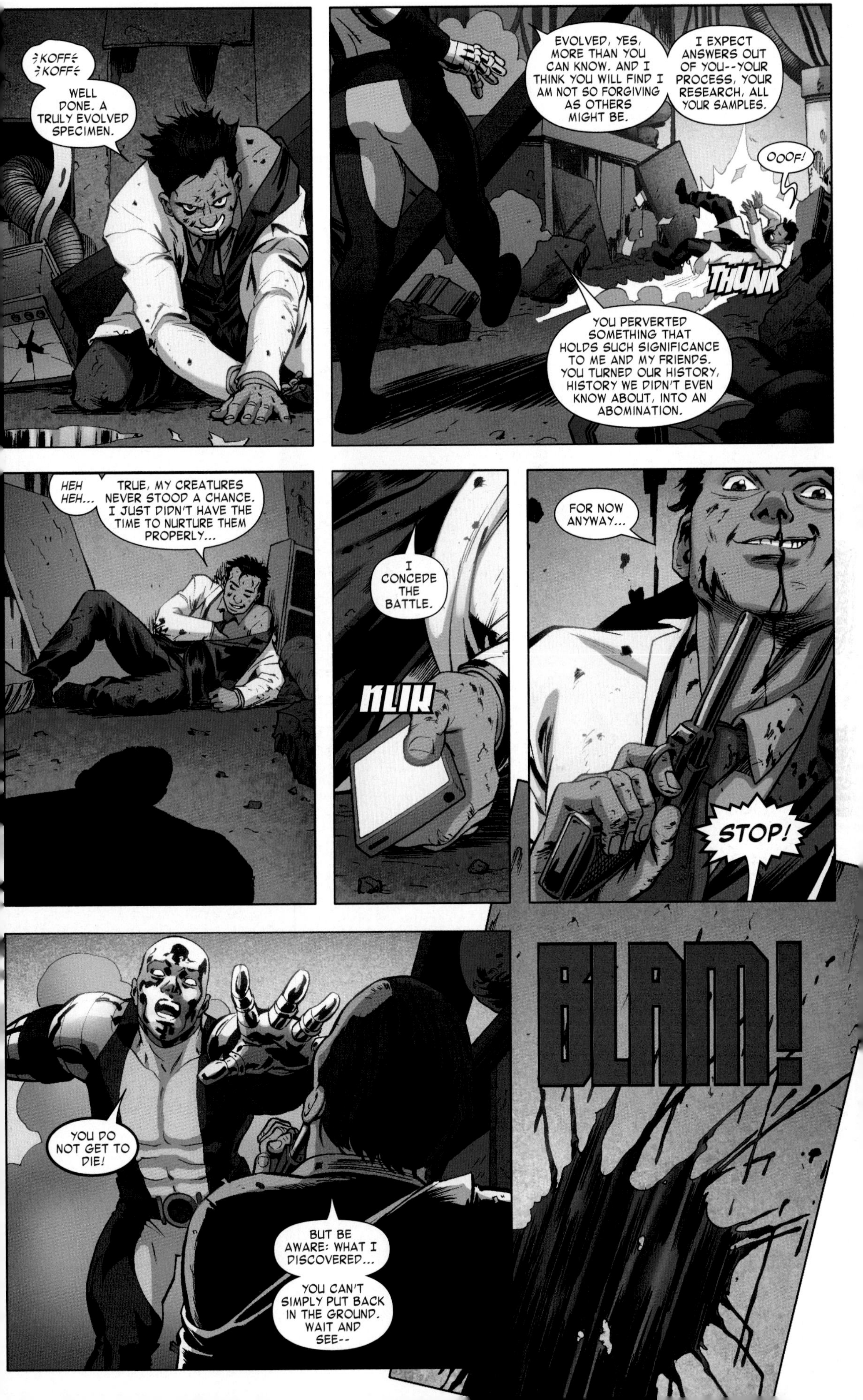

KOFF KOFF
WELL DONE. A TRULY EVOLVED SPECIMEN.
EVOLVED, YES, MORE THAN YOU CAN KNOW. AND I THINK YOU WILL FIND I AM NOT SO FORGIVING AS OTHERS MIGHT BE.
I EXPECT ANSWERS OUT OF YOU--YOUR PROCESS, YOUR RESEARCH, ALL YOUR SAMPLES.
OOOF!
THUNK
YOU PERVERTED SOMETHING THAT HOLDS SUCH SIGNIFICANCE TO ME AND MY FRIENDS. YOU TURNED OUR HISTORY, HISTORY WE DIDN'T EVEN KNOW ABOUT, INTO AN ABOMINATION.
HEH HEH...
TRUE, MY CREATURES NEVER STOOD A CHANCE. I JUST DIDN'T HAVE THE TIME TO NURTURE THEM PROPERLY...
I CONCEDE THE BATTLE.
KLIK
FOR NOW ANYWAY...
STOP!
YOU DO NOT GET TO DIE!
BUT BE AWARE: WHAT I DISCOVERED...
YOU CAN'T SIMPLY PUT BACK IN THE GROUND. WAIT AND SEE--
BLAM!

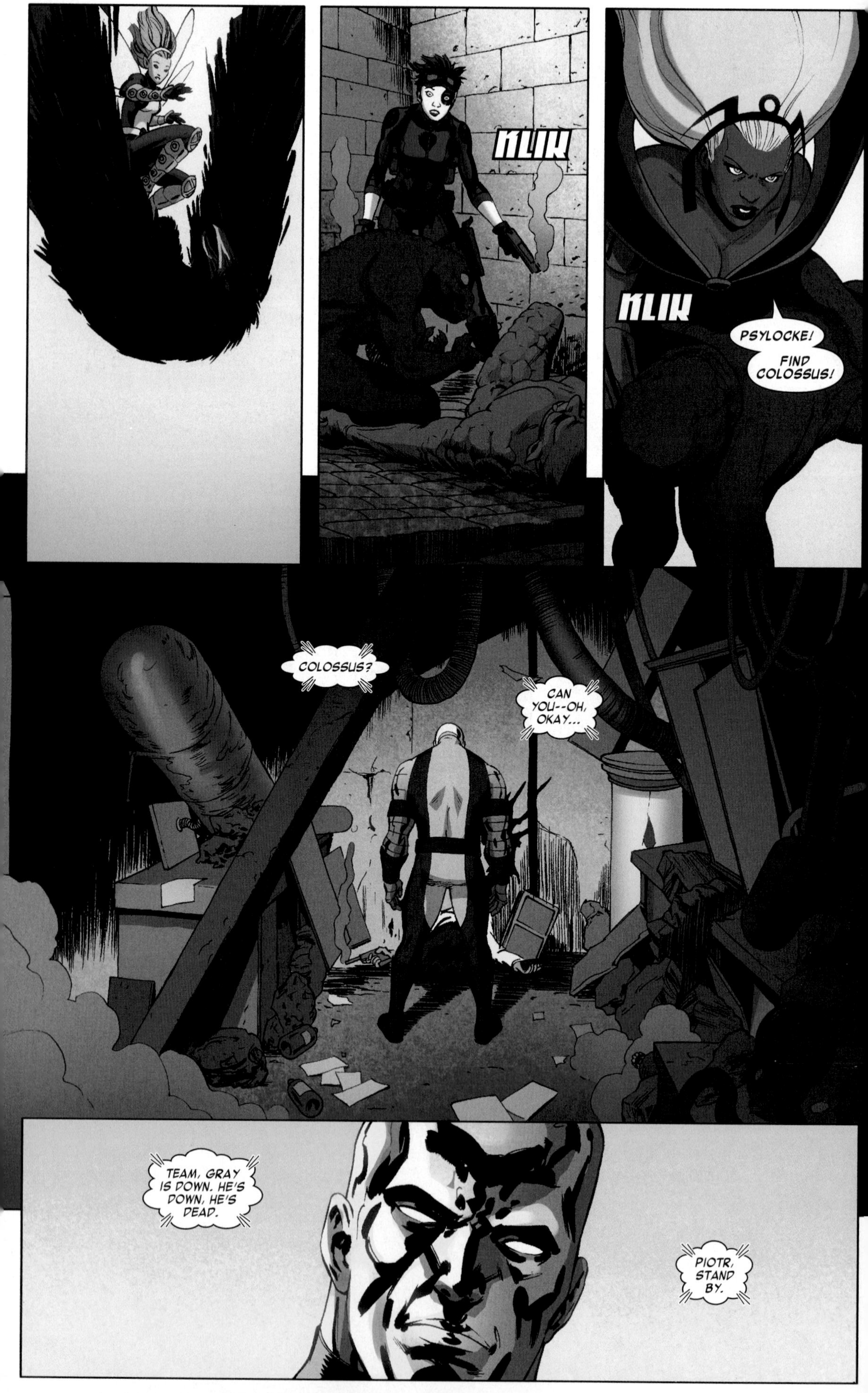
KLIK
KLIK
PSYLOCKE! FIND COLOSSUS!
COLOSSUS?
CAN YOU--OH, OKAY...
TEAM, GRAY IS DOWN. HE'S DOWN, HE'S DEAD.
PIOTR, STAND BY.

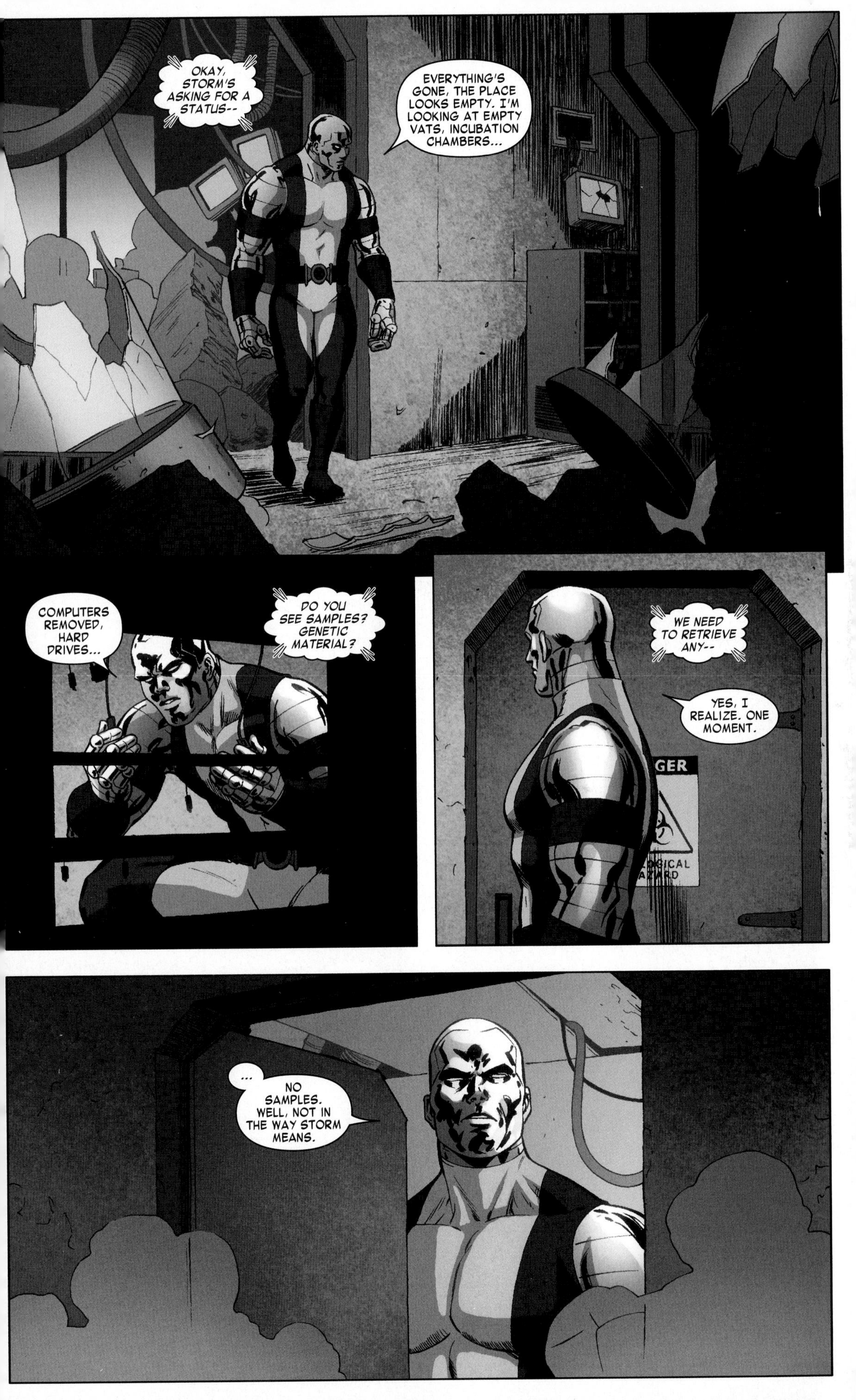
OKAY, STORM'S ASKING FOR A STATUS--
EVERYTHING'S GONE, THE PLACE LOOKS EMPTY. I'M LOOKING AT EMPTY VATS, INCUBATION CHAMBERS...
COMPUTERS REMOVED, HARD DRIVES...
DO YOU SEE SAMPLES? GENETIC MATERIAL?
WE NEED TO RETRIEVE ANY--
YES, I REALIZE. ONE MOMENT.
... NO SAMPLES. WELL, NOT IN THE WAY STORM MEANS.

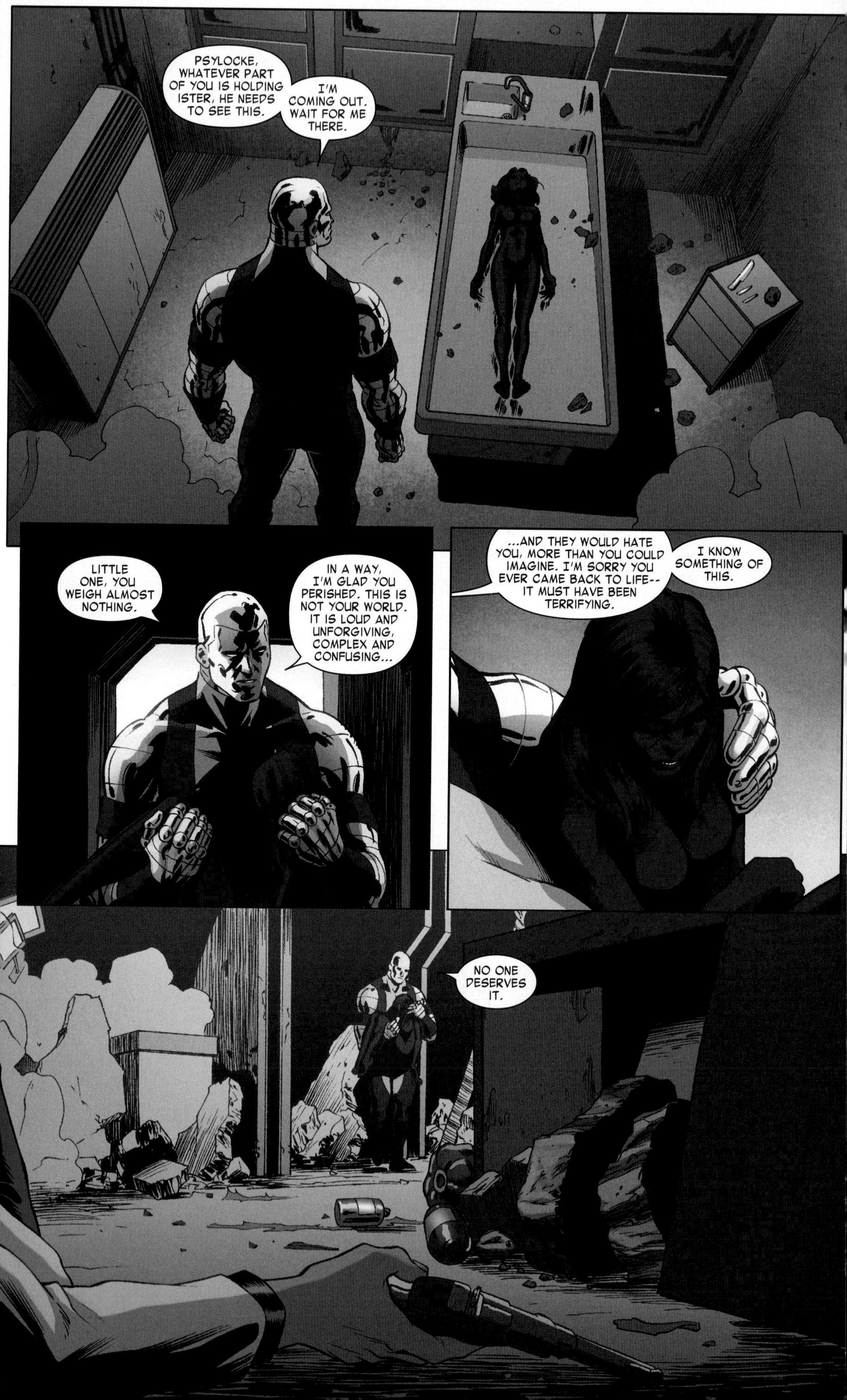

PSYLOCKE, WHATEVER PART OF YOU IS HOLDING ISTER, HE NEEDS TO SEE THIS.
I'M COMING OUT. WAIT FOR ME THERE.
LITTLE ONE, YOU WEIGH ALMOST NOTHING.
IN A WAY, I'M GLAD YOU PERISHED. THIS IS NOT YOUR WORLD. IT IS LOUD AND UNFORGIVING, COMPLEX AND CONFUSING...
...AND THEY WOULD HATE YOU, MORE THAN YOU COULD IMAGINE. I'M SORRY YOU EVER CAME BACK TO LIFE-- IT MUST HAVE BEEN TERRIFYING.
I KNOW SOMETHING OF THIS.
NO ONE DESERVES IT.

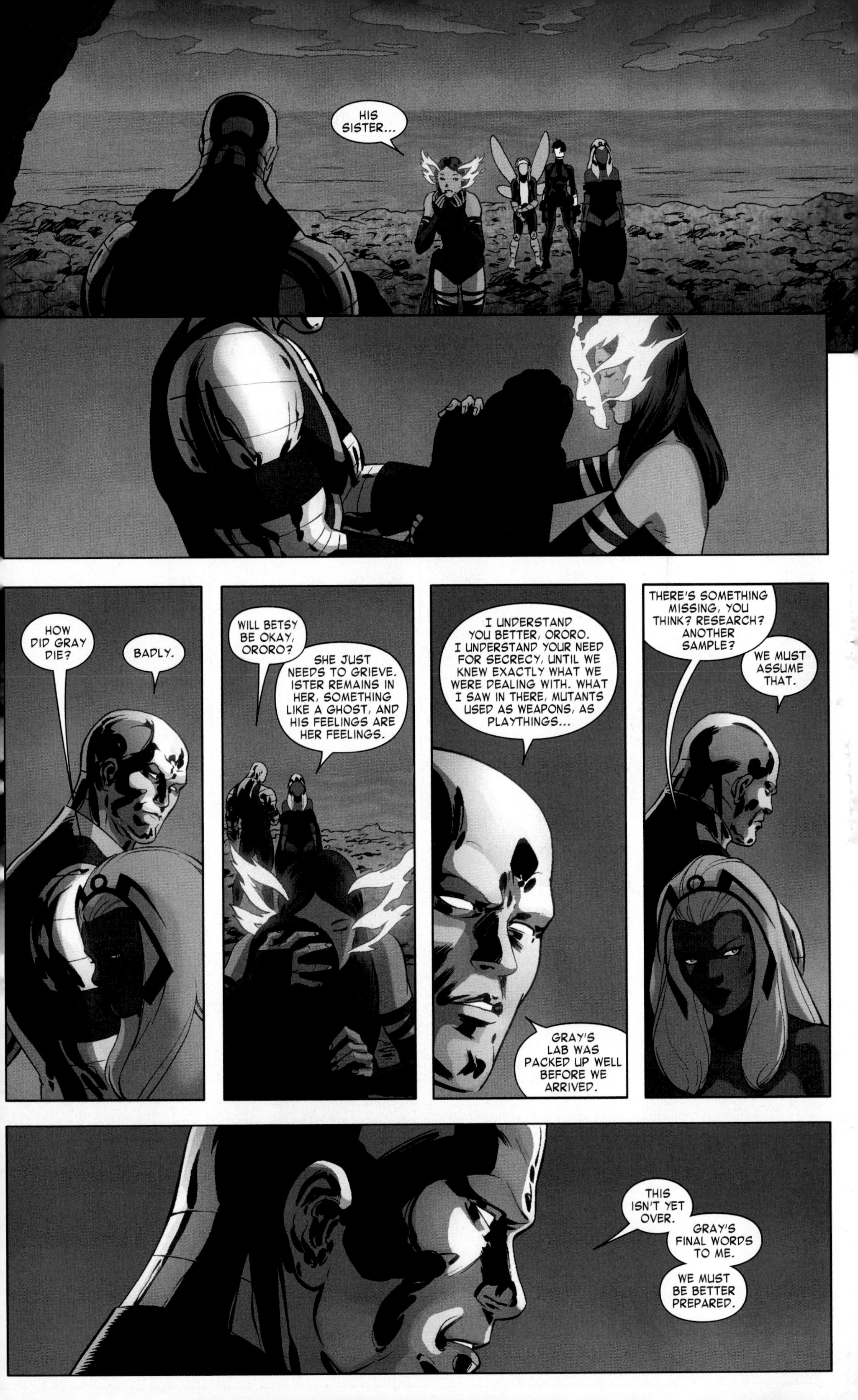
HIS SISTER...
HOW DID GRAY DIE?
BADLY.
WILL BETSY BE OKAY, ORORO?
SHE JUST NEEDS TO GRIEVE. ISTER REMAINS IN HER, SOMETHING LIKE A GHOST, AND HIS FEELINGS ARE HER FEELINGS.
I UNDERSTAND YOU BETTER, ORORO. I UNDERSTAND YOUR NEED FOR SECRECY, UNTIL WE KNEW EXACTLY WHAT WE WERE DEALING WITH. WHAT I SAW IN THERE, MUTANTS USED AS WEAPONS, AS PLAYTHINGS...
GRAY'S LAB WAS PACKED UP WELL BEFORE WE ARRIVED.
THERE'S SOMETHING MISSING, YOU THINK? RESEARCH? ANOTHER SAMPLE?
WE MUST ASSUME THAT.
THIS ISN'T YET OVER.
GRAY'S FINAL WORDS TO ME.
WE MUST BE BETTER PREPARED.

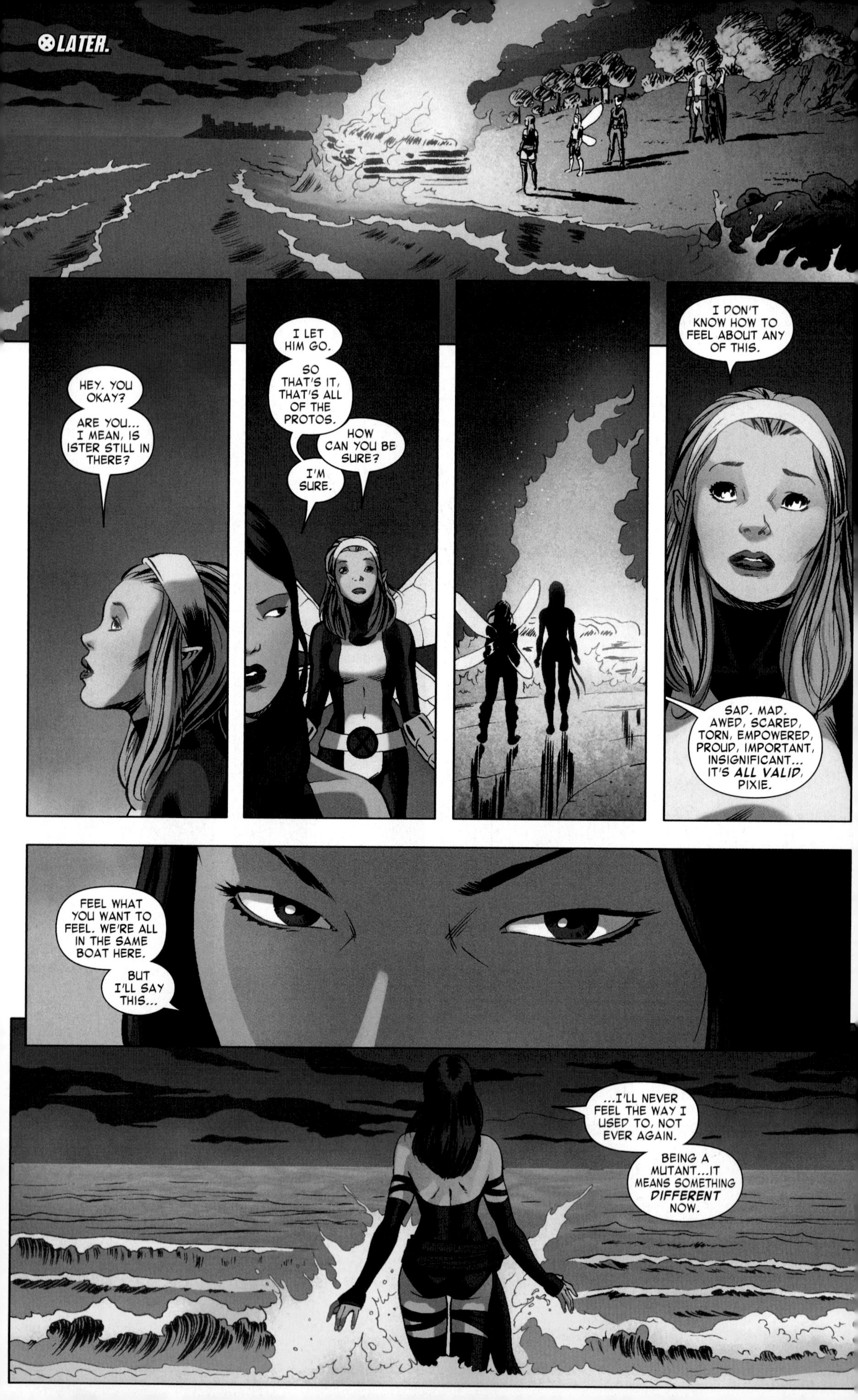
LATER.
HEY. YOU OKAY?
ARE YOU... I MEAN, IS ISTER STILL IN THERE?
I LET HIM GO.
SO THAT'S IT, THAT'S ALL OF THE PROTOS.
HOW CAN YOU BE SURE?
I'M SURE.
I DON'T KNOW HOW TO FEEL ABOUT ANY OF THIS.
SAD. MAD. AWED, SCARED, TORN, EMPOWERED, PROUD, IMPORTANT, INSIGNIFICANT... IT'S ALL VALID, PIXIE.
FEEL WHAT YOU WANT TO FEEL. WE'RE ALL IN THE SAME BOAT HERE.
BUT I'LL SAY THIS...
...I'LL NEVER FEEL THE WAY I USED TO, NOT EVER AGAIN.
BEING A MUTANT...IT MEANS SOMETHING DIFFERENT NOW.

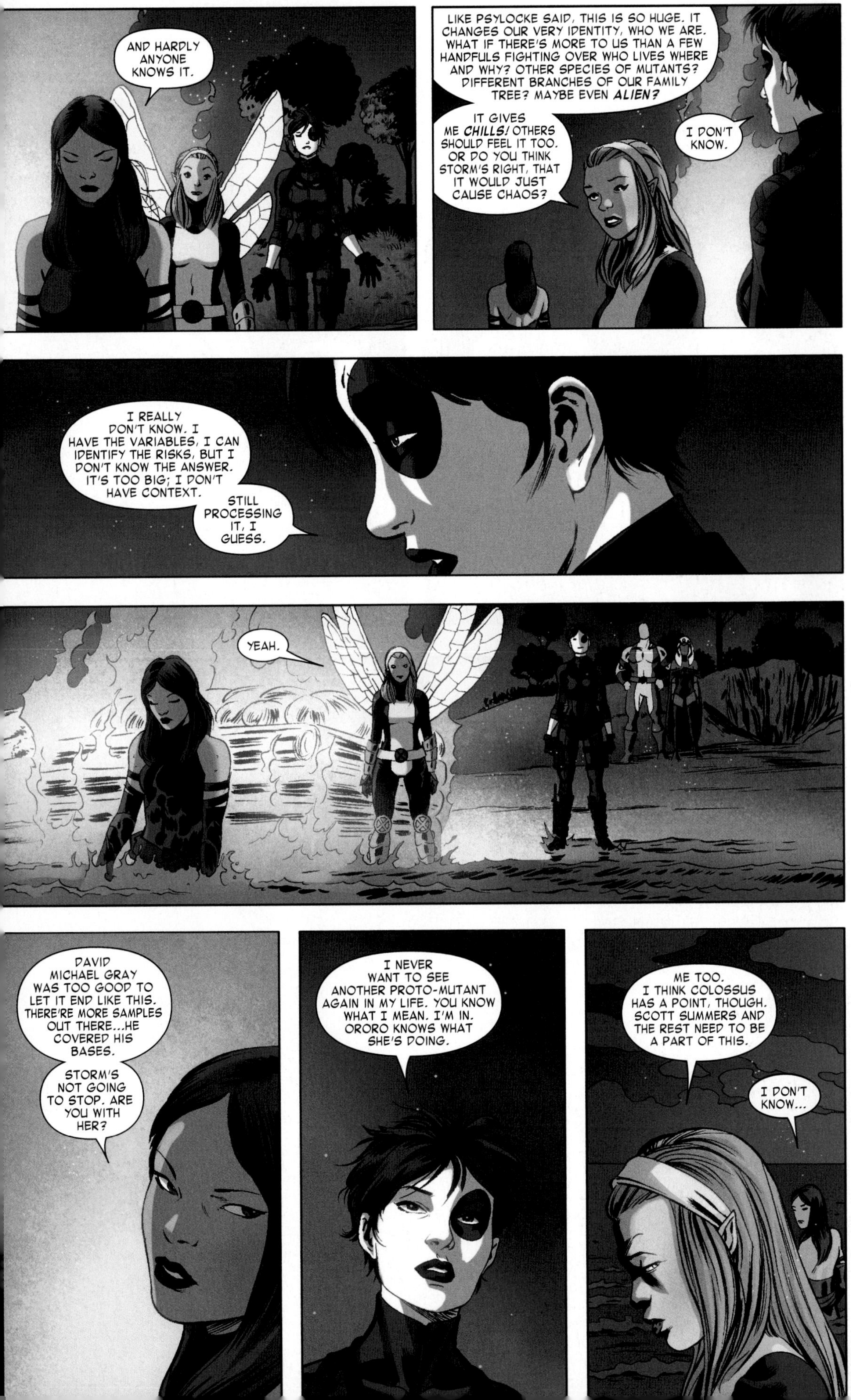
AND HARDLY ANYONE KNOWS IT.
LIKE PSYLOCKE SAID, THIS IS SO HUGE. IT CHANGES OUR VERY IDENTITY, WHO WE ARE. WHAT IF THERE'S MORE TO US THAN A FEW HANDFULS FIGHTING OVER WHO LIVES WHERE AND WHY? OTHER SPECIES OF MUTANTS? DIFFERENT BRANCHES OF OUR FAMILY TREE? MAYBE EVEN ALIEN?
IT GIVES ME CHILLS! OTHERS SHOULD FEEL IT TOO. OR DO YOU THINK STORM'S RIGHT, THAT IT WOULD JUST CAUSE CHAOS?
I DON'T KNOW.
I REALLY DON'T KNOW. I HAVE THE VARIABLES, I CAN IDENTIFY THE RISKS, BUT I DON'T KNOW THE ANSWER. IT'S TOO BIG; I DON'T HAVE CONTEXT.
STILL PROCESSING IT, I GUESS.
YEAH.
DAVID MICHAEL GRAY WAS TOO GOOD TO LET IT END LIKE THIS. THERE'RE MORE SAMPLES OUT THERE...HE COVERED HIS BASES.
STORM'S NOT GOING TO STOP. ARE YOU WITH HER?
I NEVER WANT TO SEE ANOTHER PROTO-MUTANT AGAIN IN MY LIFE. YOU KNOW WHAT I MEAN. I'M IN. ORORO KNOWS WHAT SHE'S DOING.
ME TOO. I THINK COLOSSUS HAS A POINT, THOUGH. SCOTT SUMMERS AND THE REST NEED TO BE A PART OF THIS.
I DON'T KNOW...

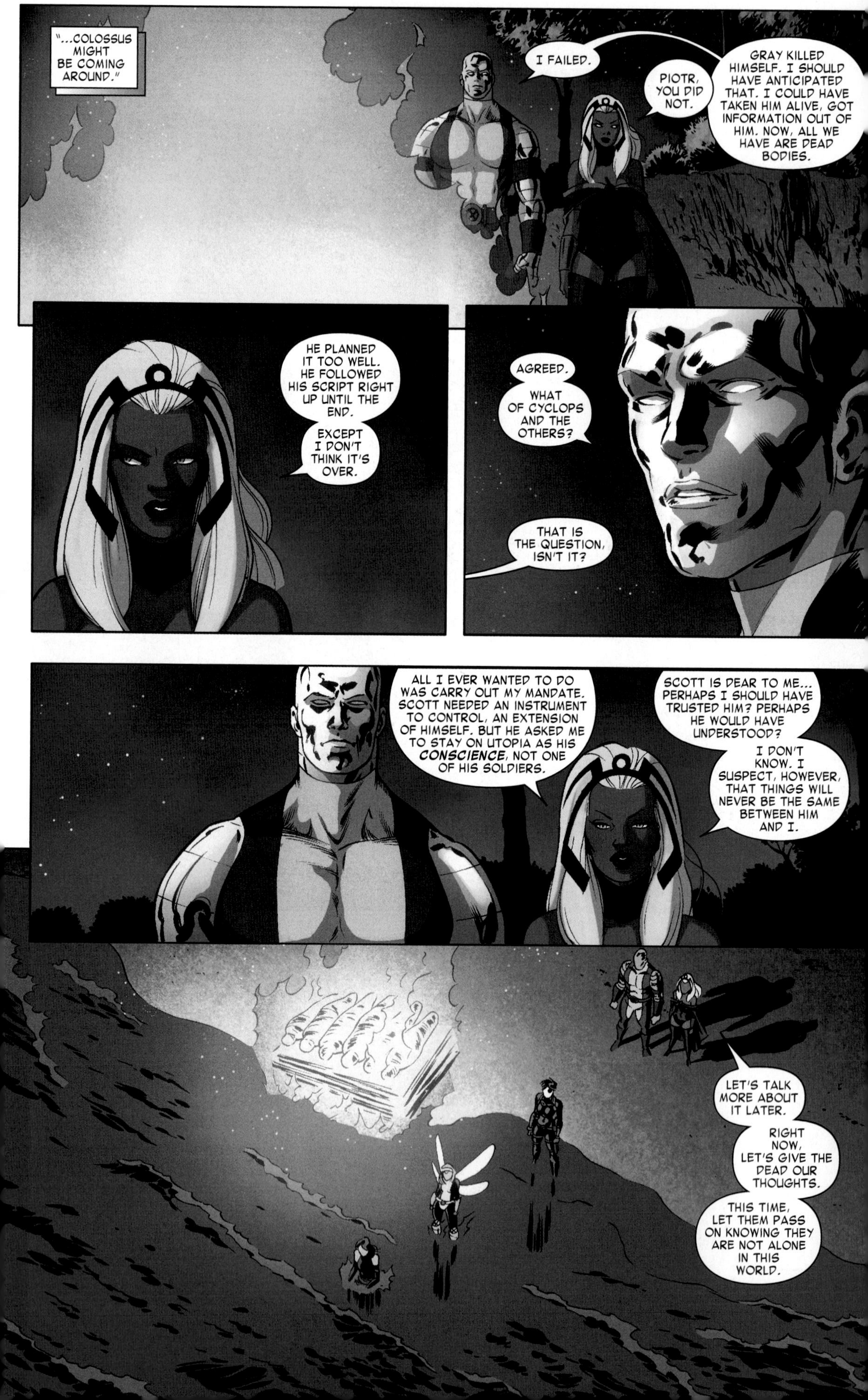
"...COLOSSUS MIGHT BE COMING AROUND."
I FAILED.
GRAY KILLED HIMSELF. I SHOULD HAVE ANTICIPATED THAT. I COULD HAVE TAKEN HIM ALIVE, GOT INFORMATION OUT OF HIM. NOW, ALL WE HAVE ARE DEAD BODIES.
PIOTR, YOU DID NOT.
HE PLANNED IT TOO WELL. HE FOLLOWED HIS SCRIPT RIGHT UP UNTIL THE END.
EXCEPT I DON'T THINK IT'S OVER.
AGREED.
WHAT OF CYCLOPS AND THE OTHERS?
THAT IS THE QUESTION, ISN'T IT?
ALL I EVER WANTED TO DO WAS CARRY OUT MY MANDATE. SCOTT NEEDED AN INSTRUMENT TO CONTROL, AN EXTENSION OF HIMSELF. BUT HE ASKED ME TO STAY ON UTOPIA AS HIS *CONSCIENCE*, NOT ONE OF HIS SOLDIERS.
SCOTT IS DEAR TO ME... PERHAPS I SHOULD HAVE TRUSTED HIM? PERHAPS HE WOULD HAVE UNDERSTOOD?
I DON'T KNOW. I SUSPECT, HOWEVER, THAT THINGS WILL NEVER BE THE SAME BETWEEN HIM AND I.
LET'S TALK MORE ABOUT IT LATER.
RIGHT NOW, LET'S GIVE THE DEAD OUR THOUGHTS.
THIS TIME, LET THEM PASS ON KNOWING THEY ARE NOT ALONE IN THIS WORLD.

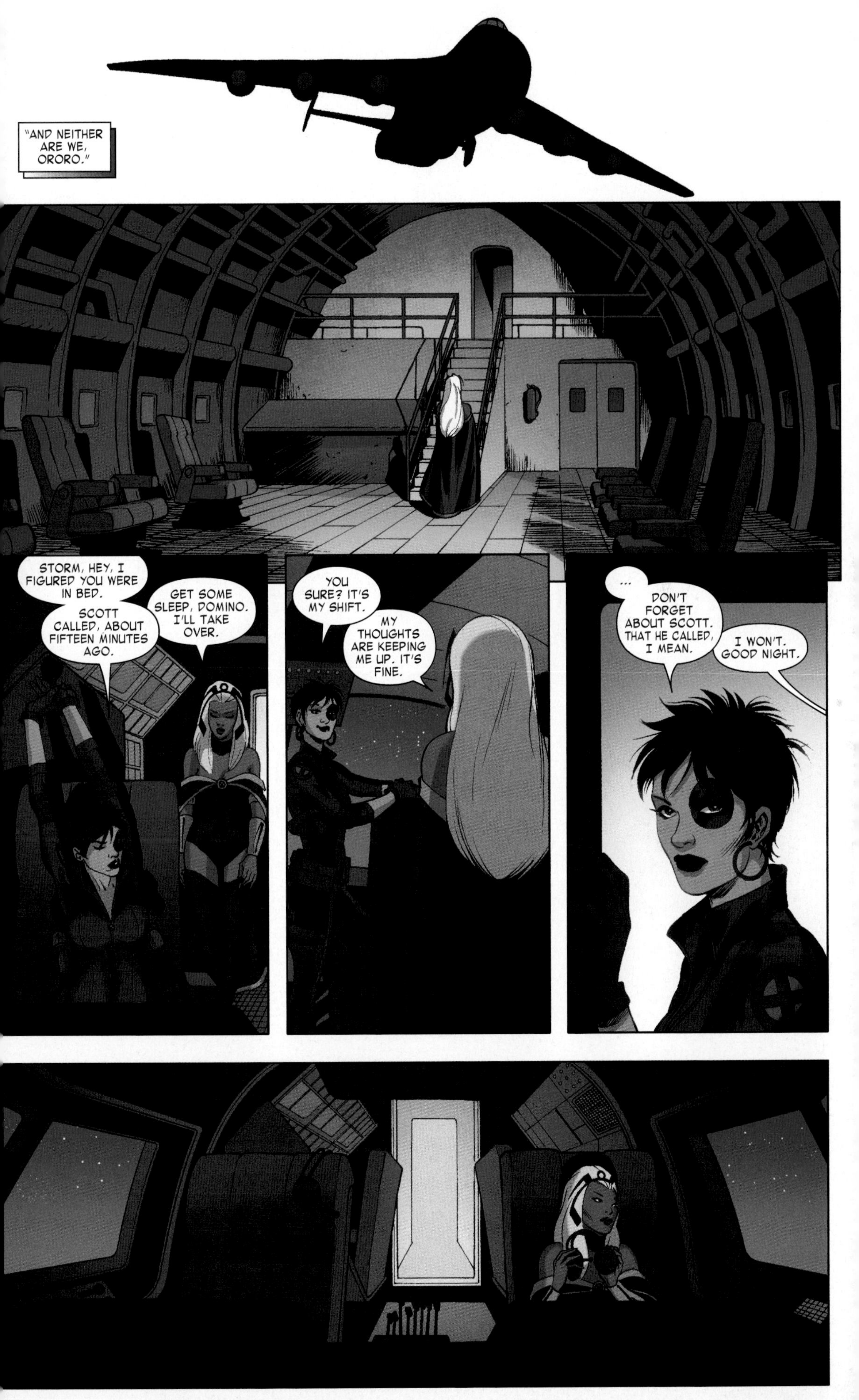
"AND NEITHER ARE WE, ORORO."
STORM, HEY, I FIGURED YOU WERE IN BED.
SCOTT CALLED, ABOUT FIFTEEN MINUTES AGO.
GET SOME SLEEP, DOMINO. I'LL TAKE OVER.
YOU SURE? IT'S MY SHIFT.
MY THOUGHTS ARE KEEPING ME UP. IT'S FINE.
...
DON'T FORGET ABOUT SCOTT. THAT HE CALLED, I MEAN.
I WON'T. GOOD NIGHT.

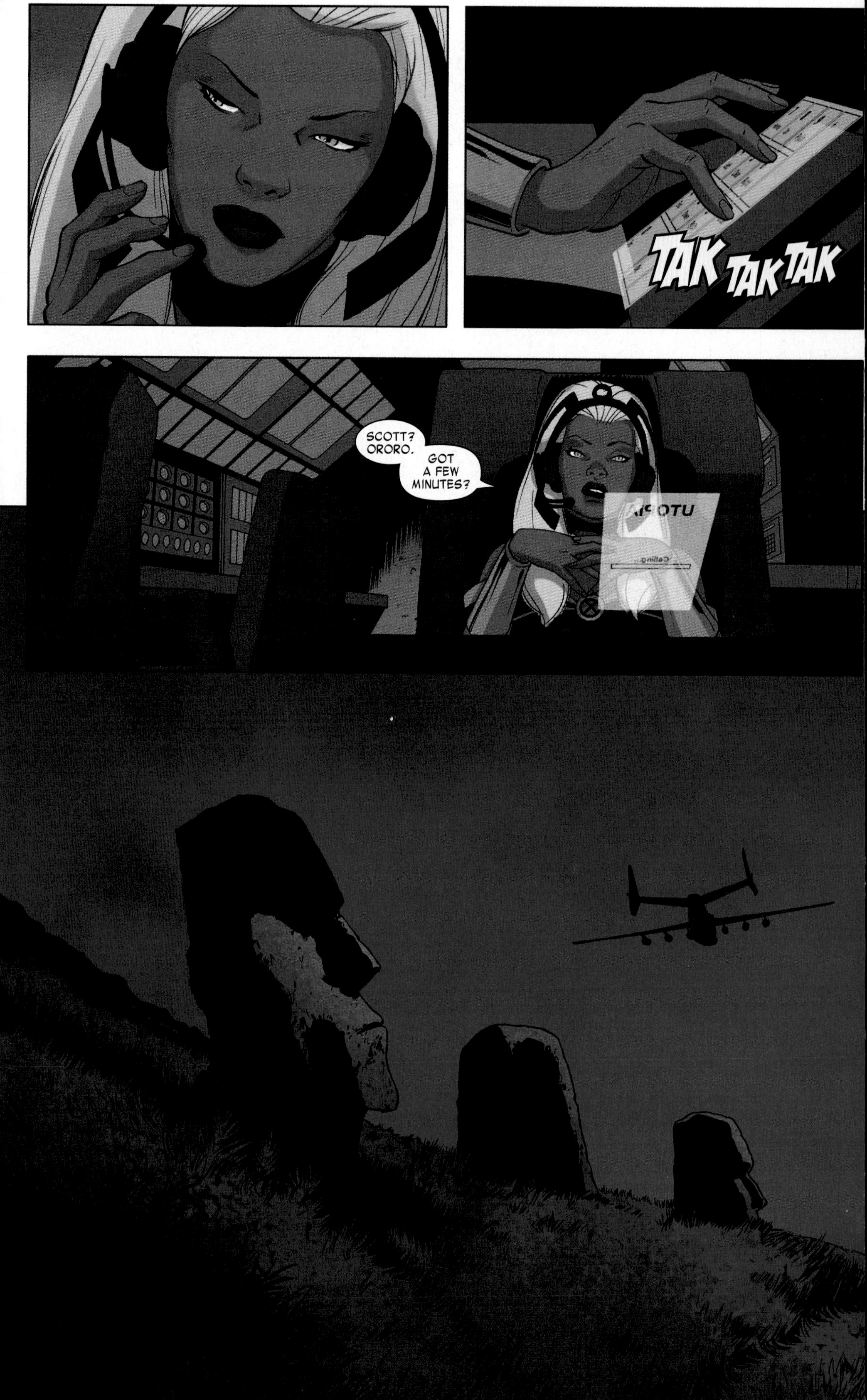
TAK TAK TAK
SCOTT? ORORO.
GOT A FEW MINUTES?
UTOPIA
Calling...

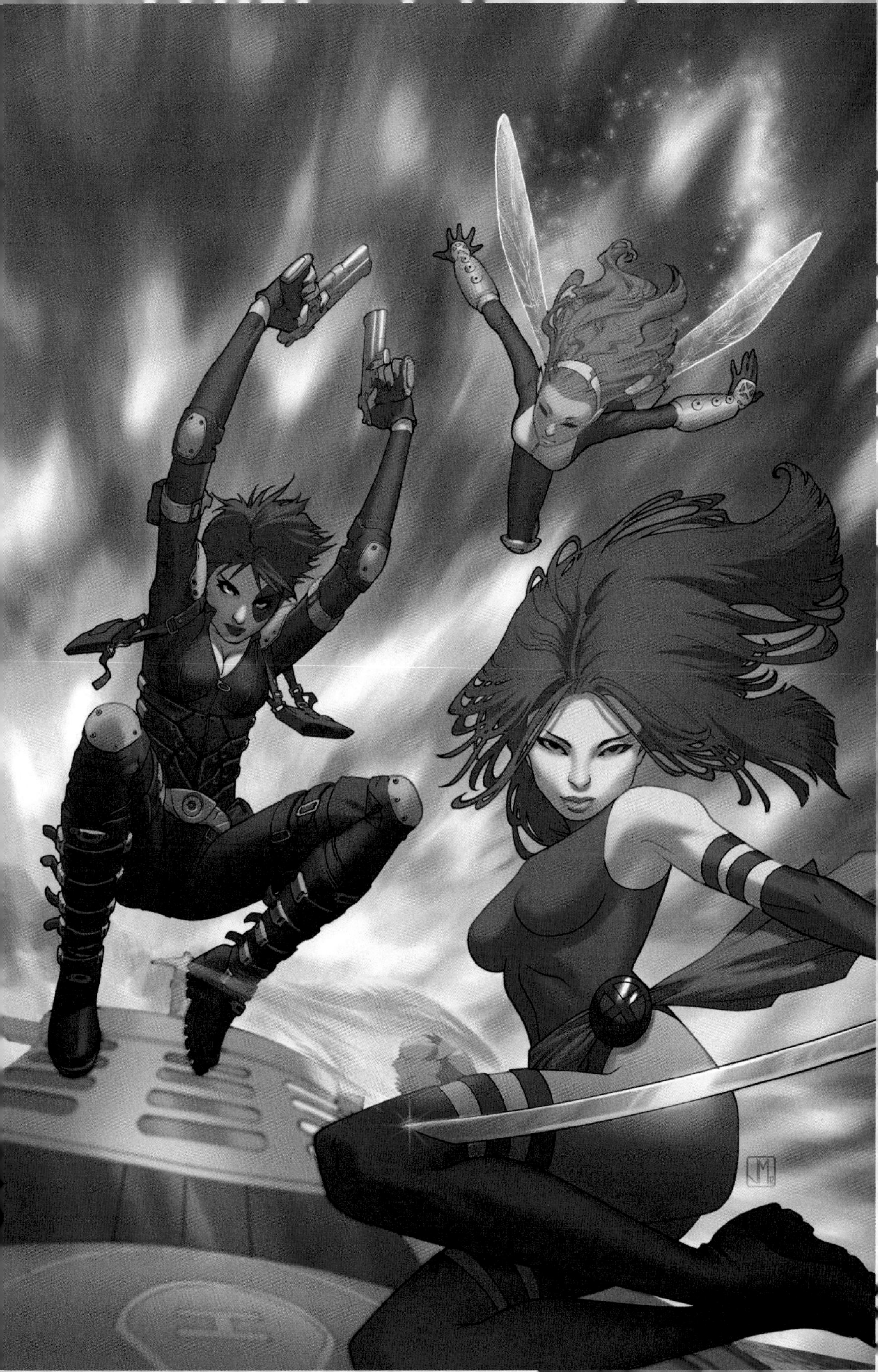

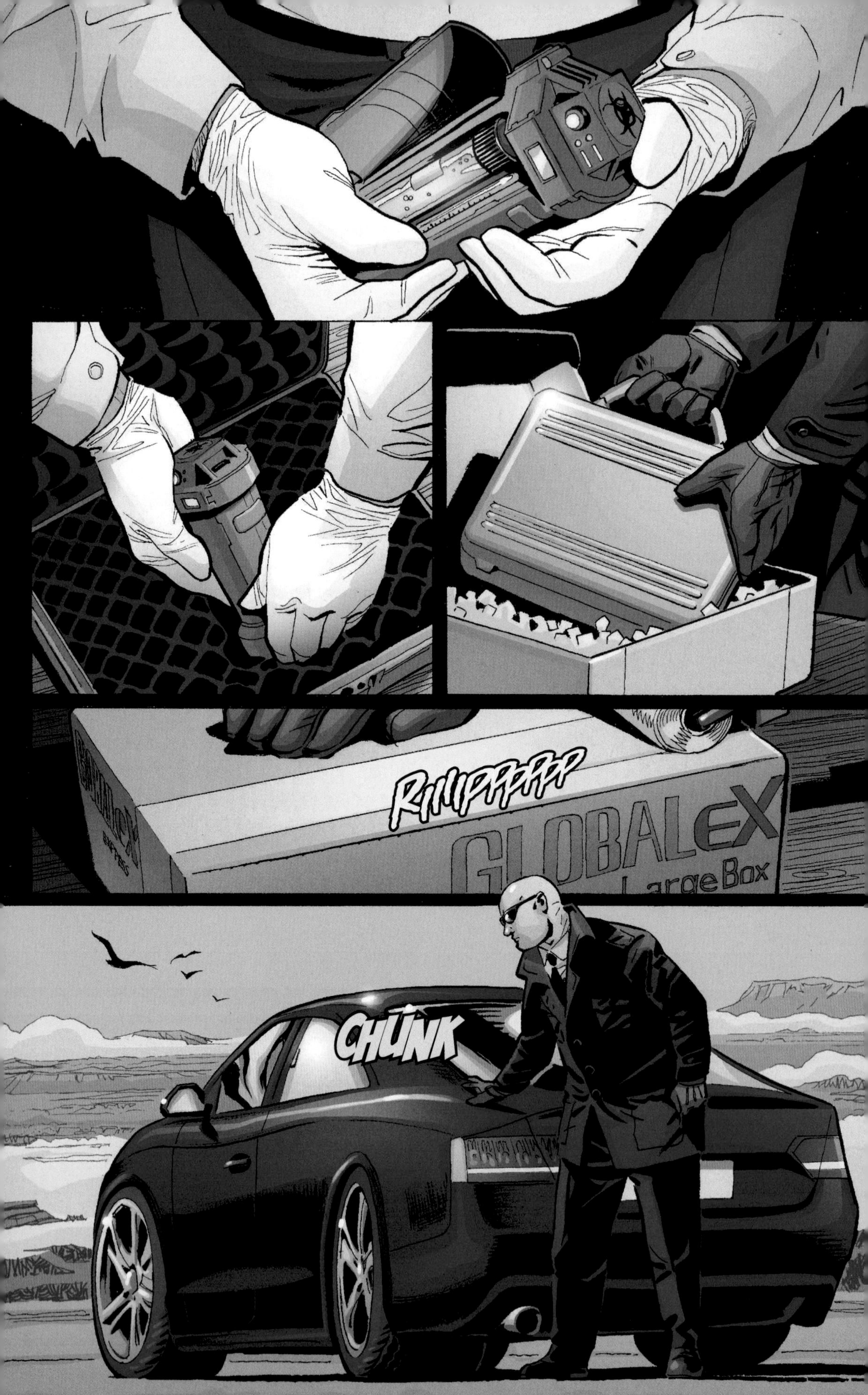
RIIIIPPPPPP
GLOBALEX
Large Box
CHUNK

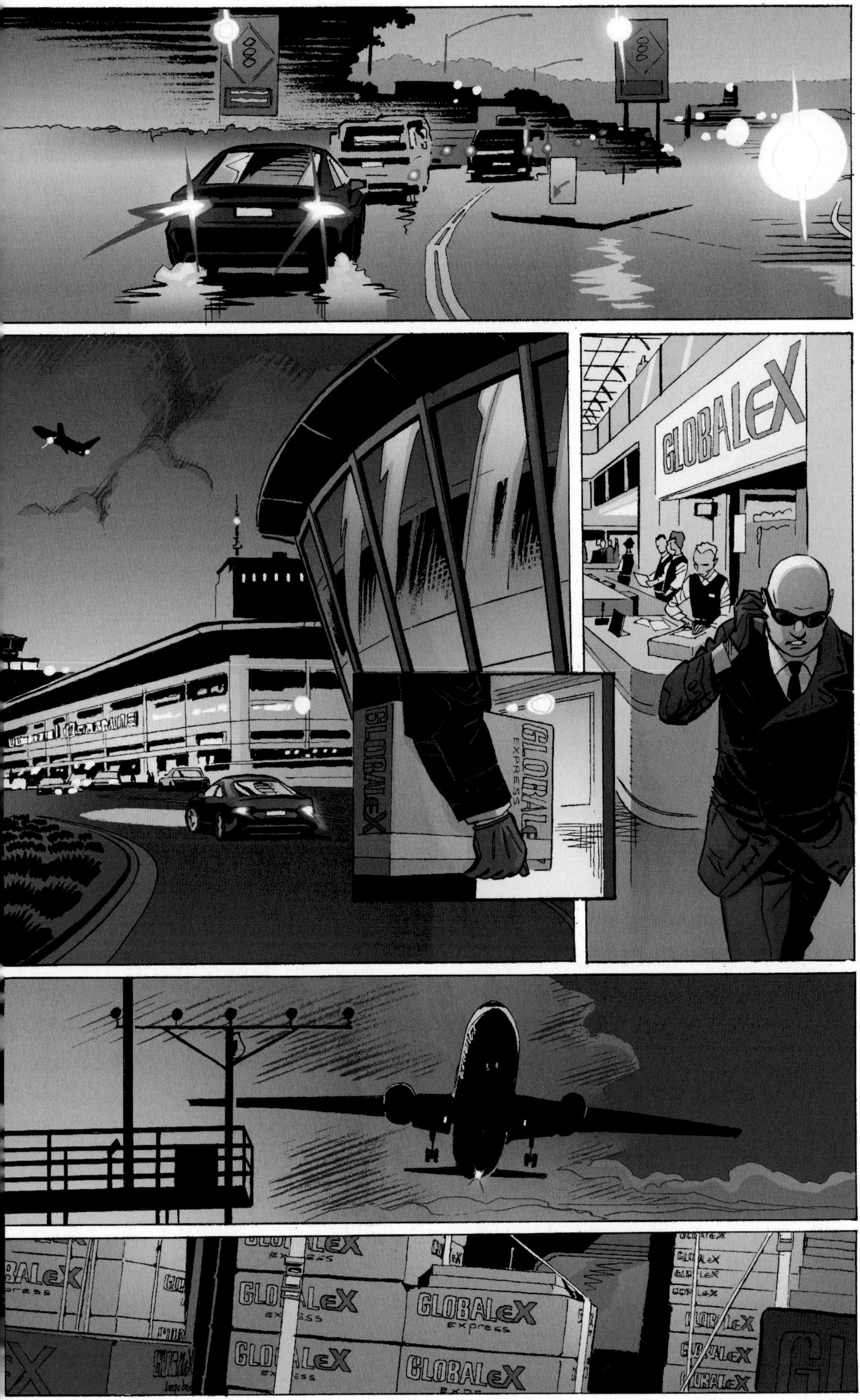
GLOBALEX
GLOBALEX EXPRESS
GLOBALEX EXPRESS
GLOBALEX EXPRESS
GLOBALEX

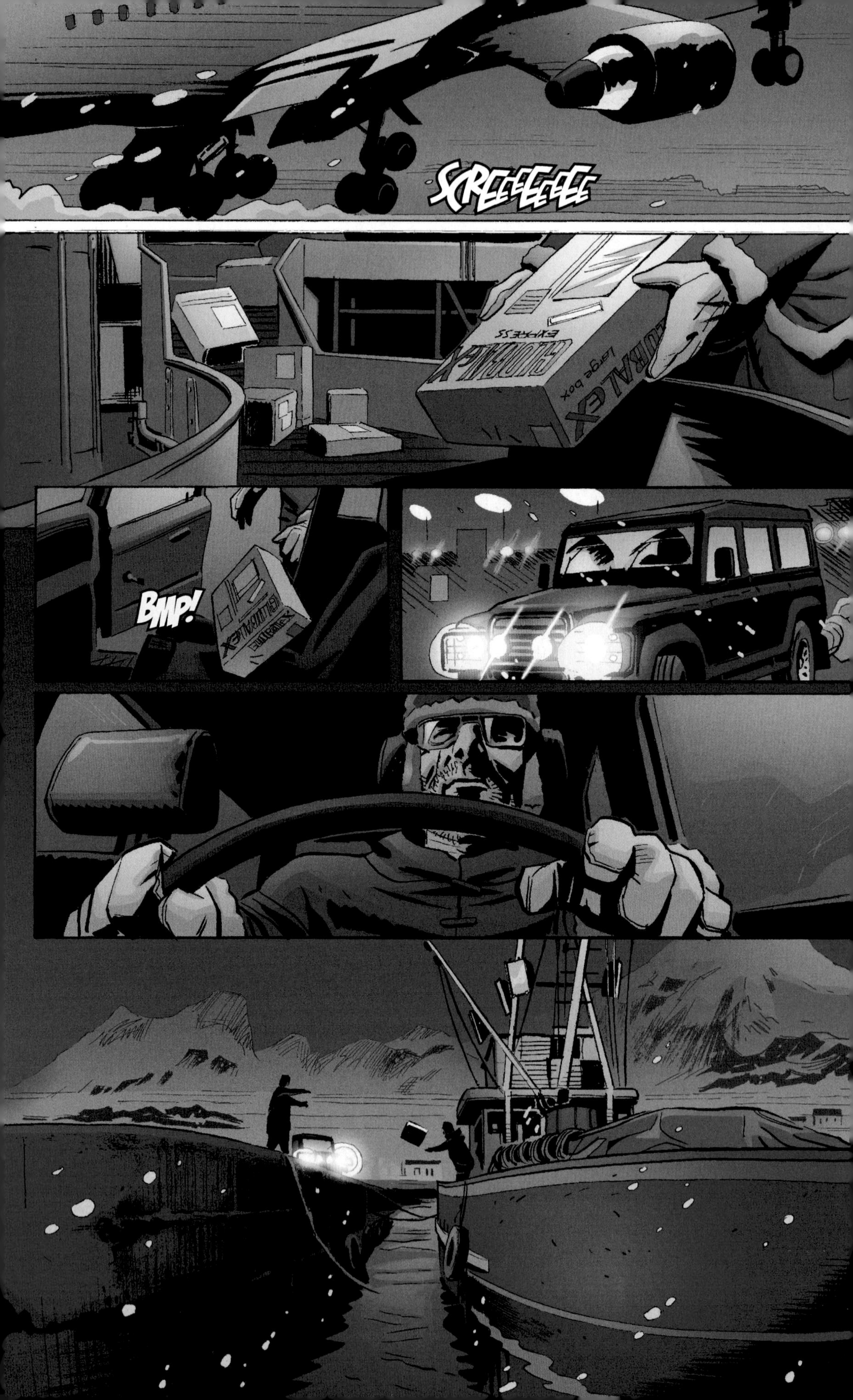
SCREEEEEEEE
GLOBAL-EX
large box
EXPRESS
BMP!

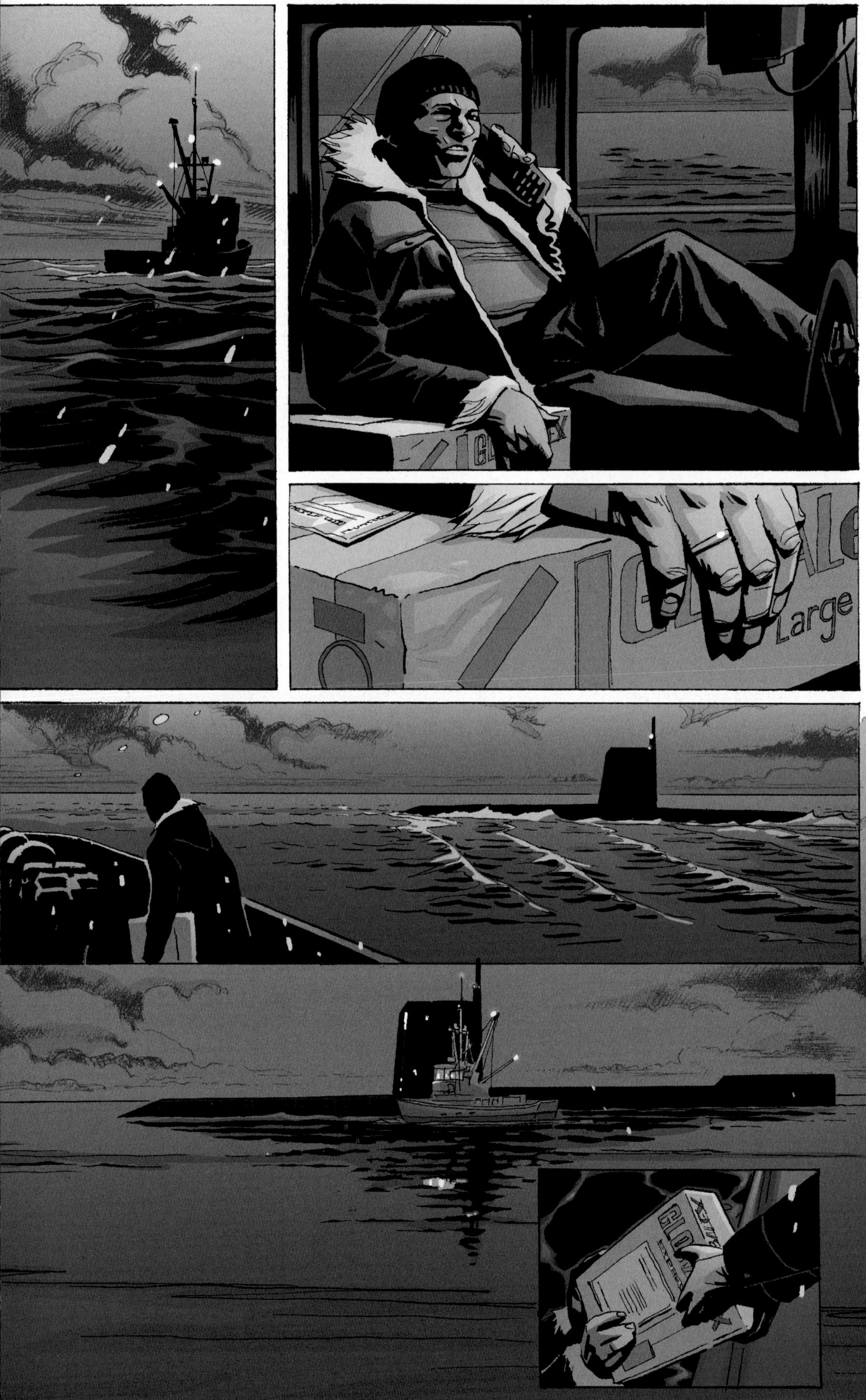
Large

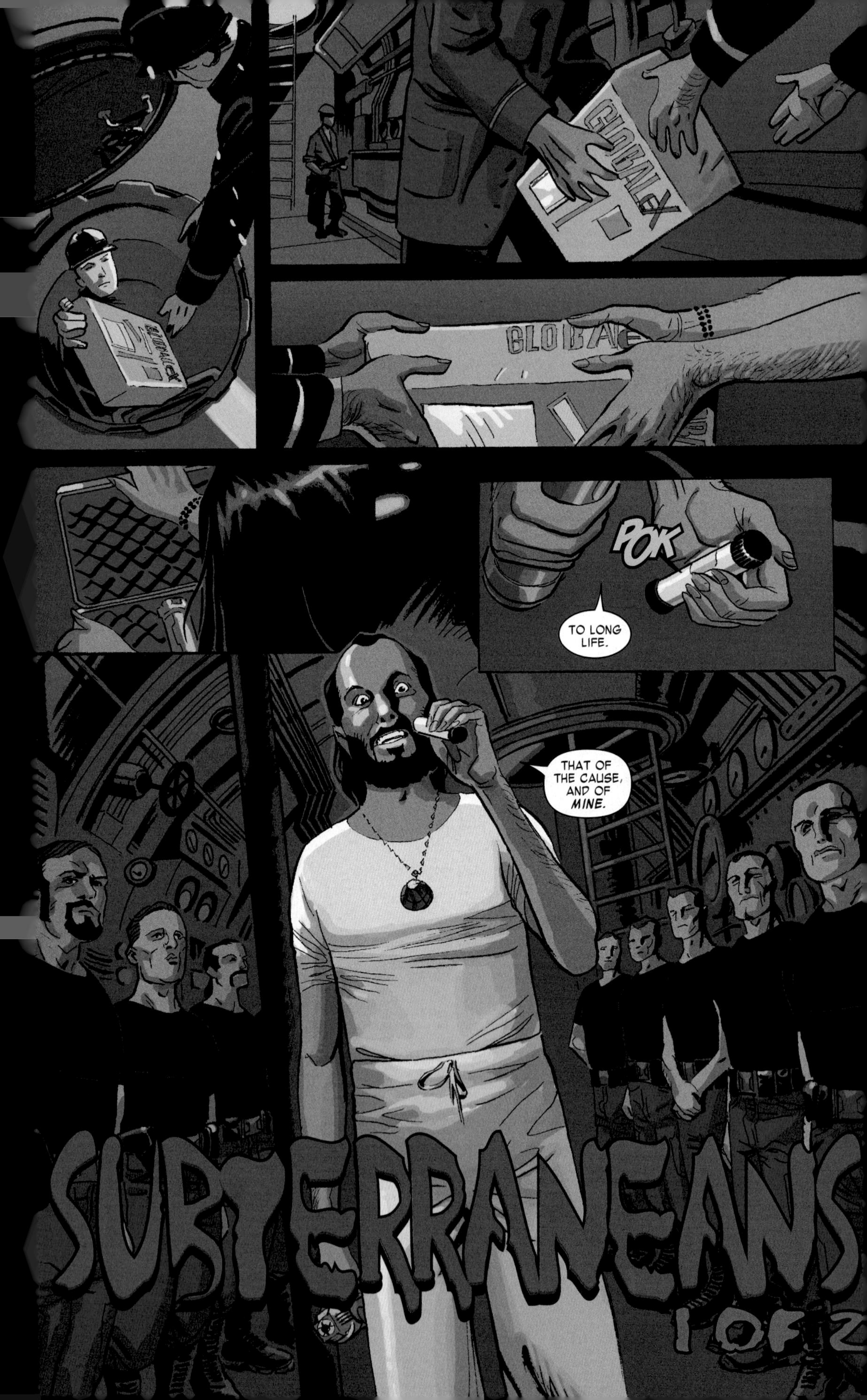

GLOBALEX
GLOBALEX
GLOBALEX
POK
TO LONG LIFE.
THAT OF THE CAUSE, AND OF *MINE.*
SUBTERRANEANS
1 OF 2

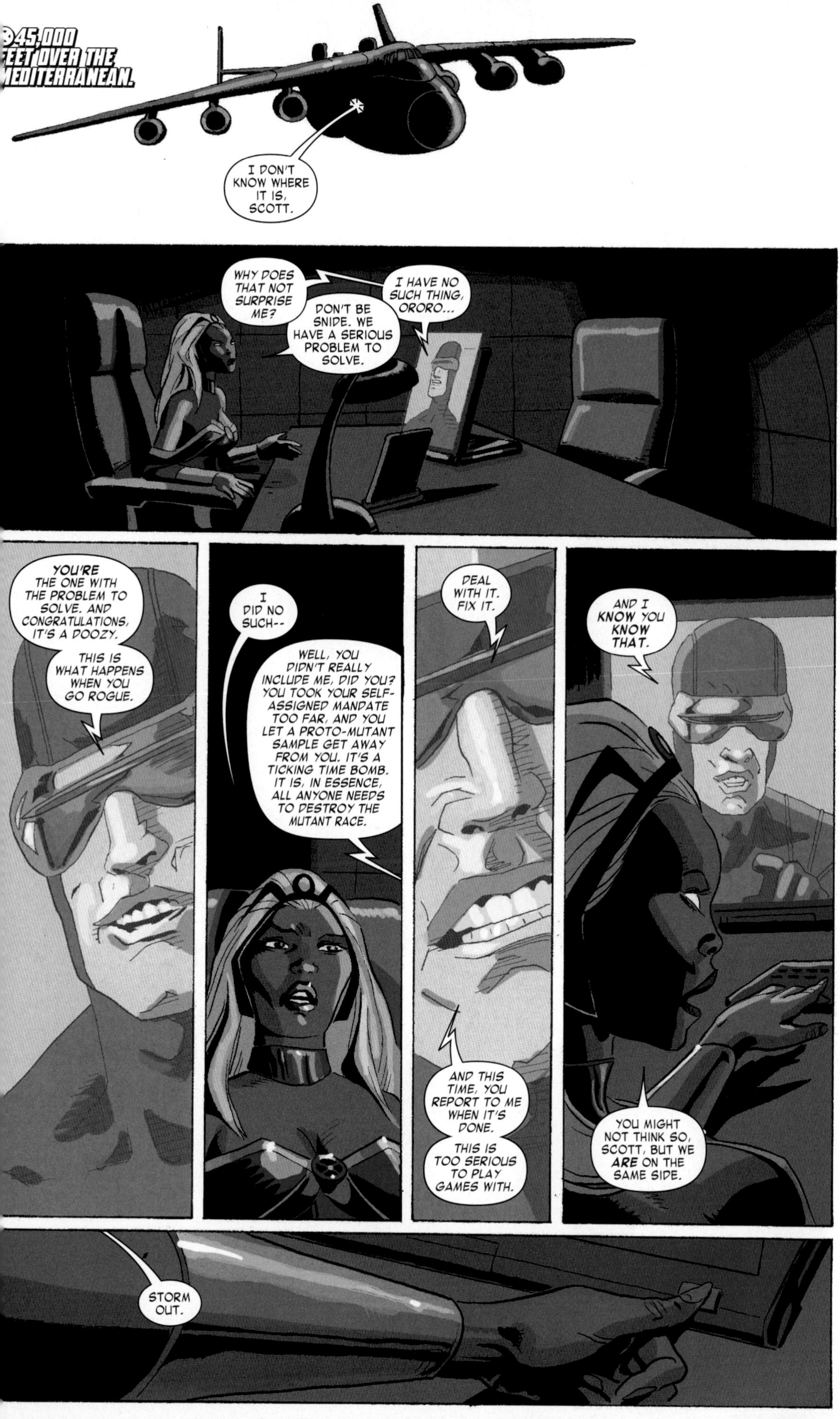
45,000 FEET OVER THE MEDITERRANEAN.
I DON'T KNOW WHERE IT IS, SCOTT.
WHY DOES THAT NOT SURPRISE ME?
I HAVE NO SUCH THING, ORORO...
DON'T BE SNIDE. WE HAVE A SERIOUS PROBLEM TO SOLVE.
YOU'RE THE ONE WITH THE PROBLEM TO SOLVE. AND CONGRATULATIONS, IT'S A DOOZY.
THIS IS WHAT HAPPENS WHEN YOU GO ROGUE.
I DID NO SUCH--
WELL, YOU DIDN'T REALLY INCLUDE ME, DID YOU? YOU TOOK YOUR SELF-ASSIGNED MANDATE TOO FAR, AND YOU LET A PROTO-MUTANT SAMPLE GET AWAY FROM YOU. IT'S A TICKING TIME BOMB. IT IS, IN ESSENCE, ALL ANYONE NEEDS TO DESTROY THE MUTANT RACE.
DEAL WITH IT. FIX IT.
AND THIS TIME, YOU REPORT TO ME WHEN IT'S DONE.
THIS IS TOO SERIOUS TO PLAY GAMES WITH.
AND I KNOW YOU KNOW THAT.
YOU MIGHT NOT THINK SO, SCOTT, BUT WE ARE ON THE SAME SIDE.
STORM OUT.

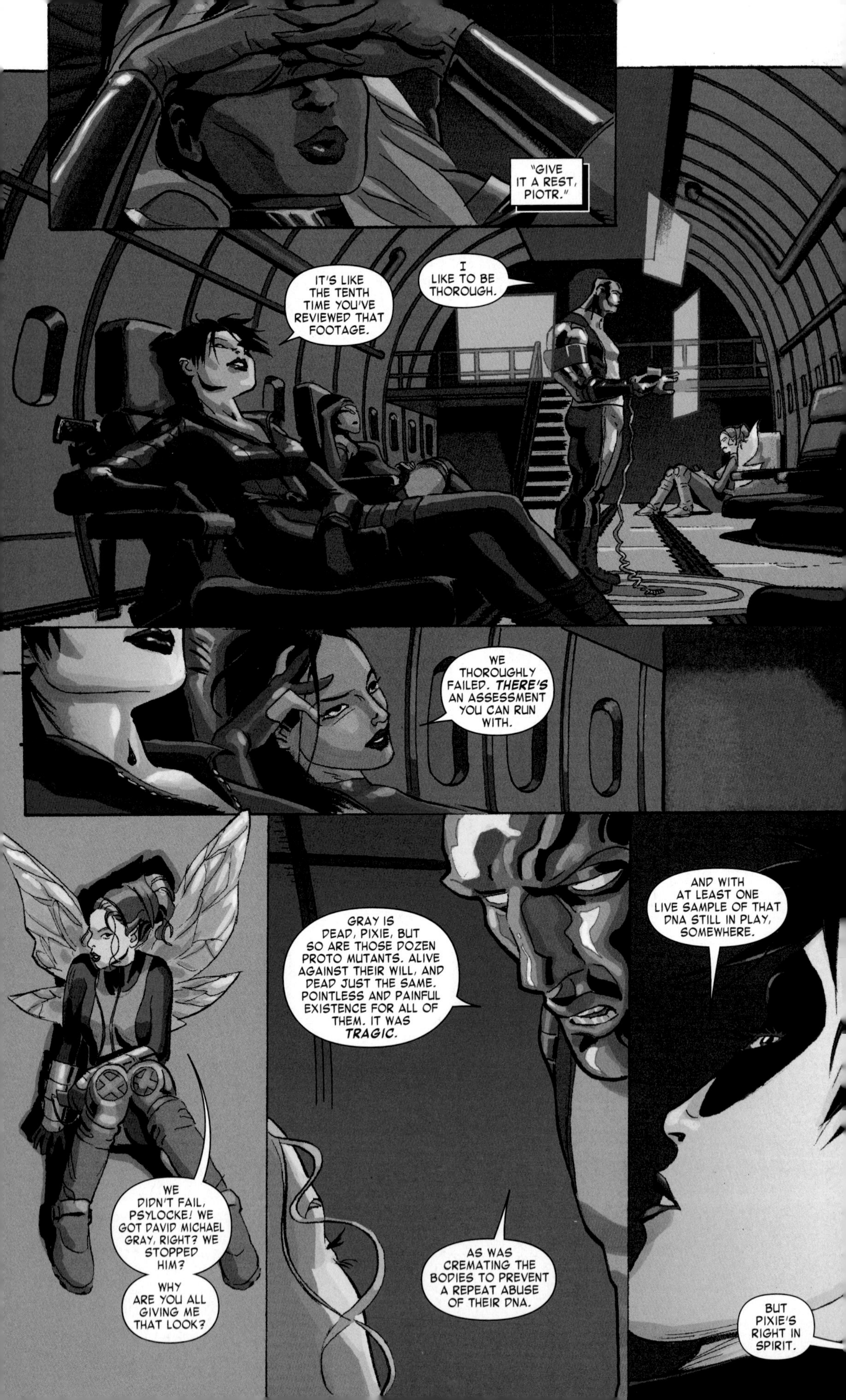
"GIVE IT A REST, PIOTR."
IT'S LIKE THE TENTH TIME YOU'VE REVIEWED THAT FOOTAGE.
I LIKE TO BE THOROUGH.
WE THOROUGHLY FAILED. THERE'S AN ASSESSMENT YOU CAN RUN WITH.
WE DIDN'T FAIL, PSYLOCKE! WE GOT DAVID MICHAEL GRAY, RIGHT? WE STOPPED HIM?
WHY ARE YOU ALL GIVING ME THAT LOOK?
GRAY IS DEAD, PIXIE, BUT SO ARE THOSE DOZEN PROTO MUTANTS. ALIVE AGAINST THEIR WILL, AND DEAD JUST THE SAME. POINTLESS AND PAINFUL EXISTENCE FOR ALL OF THEM. IT WAS TRAGIC.
AS WAS CREMATING THE BODIES TO PREVENT A REPEAT ABUSE OF THEIR DNA.
AND WITH AT LEAST ONE LIVE SAMPLE OF THAT DNA STILL IN PLAY, SOMEWHERE.
BUT PIXIE'S RIGHT IN SPIRIT.

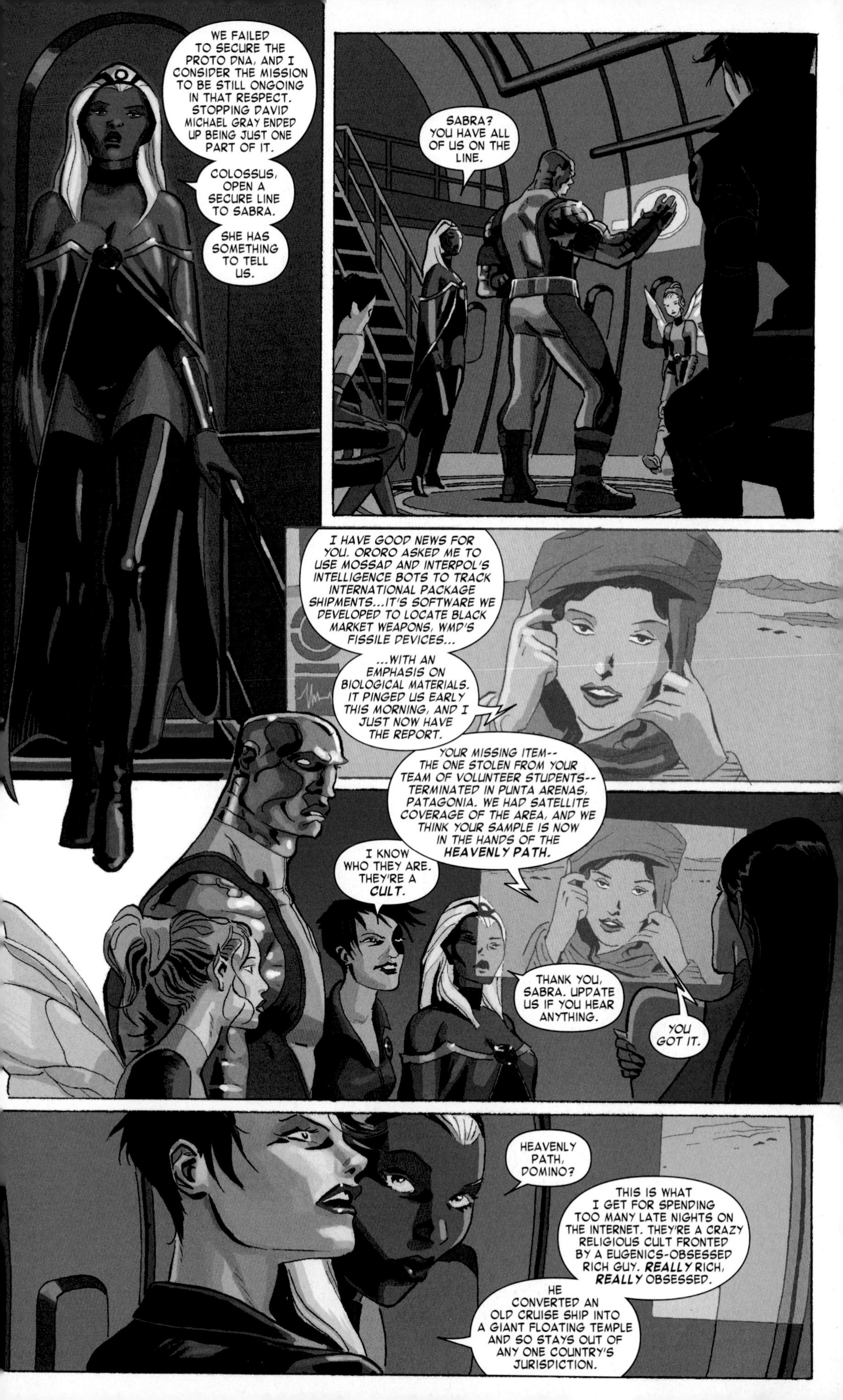
WE FAILED TO SECURE THE PROTO DNA, AND I CONSIDER THE MISSION TO BE STILL ONGOING IN THAT RESPECT. STOPPING DAVID MICHAEL GRAY ENDED UP BEING JUST ONE PART OF IT.
COLOSSUS, OPEN A SECURE LINE TO SABRA.
SHE HAS SOMETHING TO TELL US.
SABRA? YOU HAVE ALL OF US ON THE LINE.
I HAVE GOOD NEWS FOR YOU. ORORO ASKED ME TO USE MOSSAD AND INTERPOL'S INTELLIGENCE BOTS TO TRACK INTERNATIONAL PACKAGE SHIPMENTS...IT'S SOFTWARE WE DEVELOPED TO LOCATE BLACK MARKET WEAPONS, WMD'S FISSILE DEVICES...
...WITH AN EMPHASIS ON BIOLOGICAL MATERIALS. IT PINGED US EARLY THIS MORNING, AND I JUST NOW HAVE THE REPORT.
YOUR MISSING ITEM-- THE ONE STOLEN FROM YOUR TEAM OF VOLUNTEER STUDENTS-- TERMINATED IN PUNTA ARENAS, PATAGONIA. WE HAD SATELLITE COVERAGE OF THE AREA, AND WE THINK YOUR SAMPLE IS NOW IN THE HANDS OF THE HEAVENLY PATH.
I KNOW WHO THEY ARE. THEY'RE A CULT.
THANK YOU, SABRA. UPDATE US IF YOU HEAR ANYTHING.
YOU GOT IT.
HEAVENLY PATH, DOMINO?
THIS IS WHAT I GET FOR SPENDING TOO MANY LATE NIGHTS ON THE INTERNET. THEY'RE A CRAZY RELIGIOUS CULT FRONTED BY A EUGENICS-OBSESSED RICH GUY. REALLY RICH, REALLY OBSESSED.
HE CONVERTED AN OLD CRUISE SHIP INTO A GIANT FLOATING TEMPLE AND SO STAYS OUT OF ANY ONE COUNTRY'S JURISDICTION.

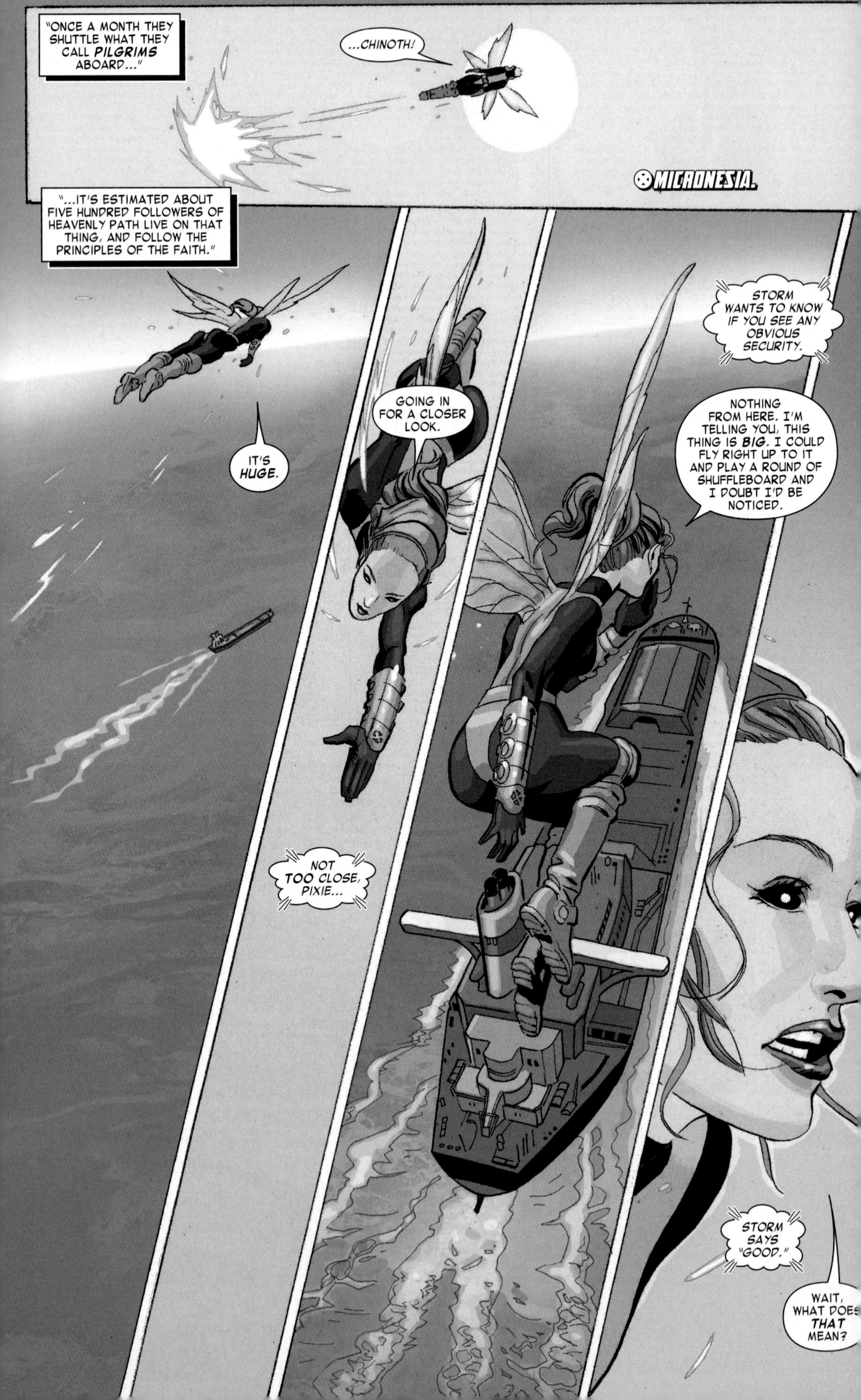
"ONCE A MONTH THEY SHUTTLE WHAT THEY CALL PILGRIMS ABOARD..."
...CHINOTH!
MICRONESIA.
"...IT'S ESTIMATED ABOUT FIVE HUNDRED FOLLOWERS OF HEAVENLY PATH LIVE ON THAT THING, AND FOLLOW THE PRINCIPLES OF THE FAITH."
IT'S HUGE.
GOING IN FOR A CLOSER LOOK.
NOT TOO CLOSE, PIXIE...
STORM WANTS TO KNOW IF YOU SEE ANY OBVIOUS SECURITY.
NOTHING FROM HERE. I'M TELLING YOU, THIS THING IS BIG. I COULD FLY RIGHT UP TO IT AND PLAY A ROUND OF SHUFFLEBOARD AND I DOUBT I'D BE NOTICED.
STORM SAYS "GOOD."
WAIT, WHAT DOE THAT MEAN?

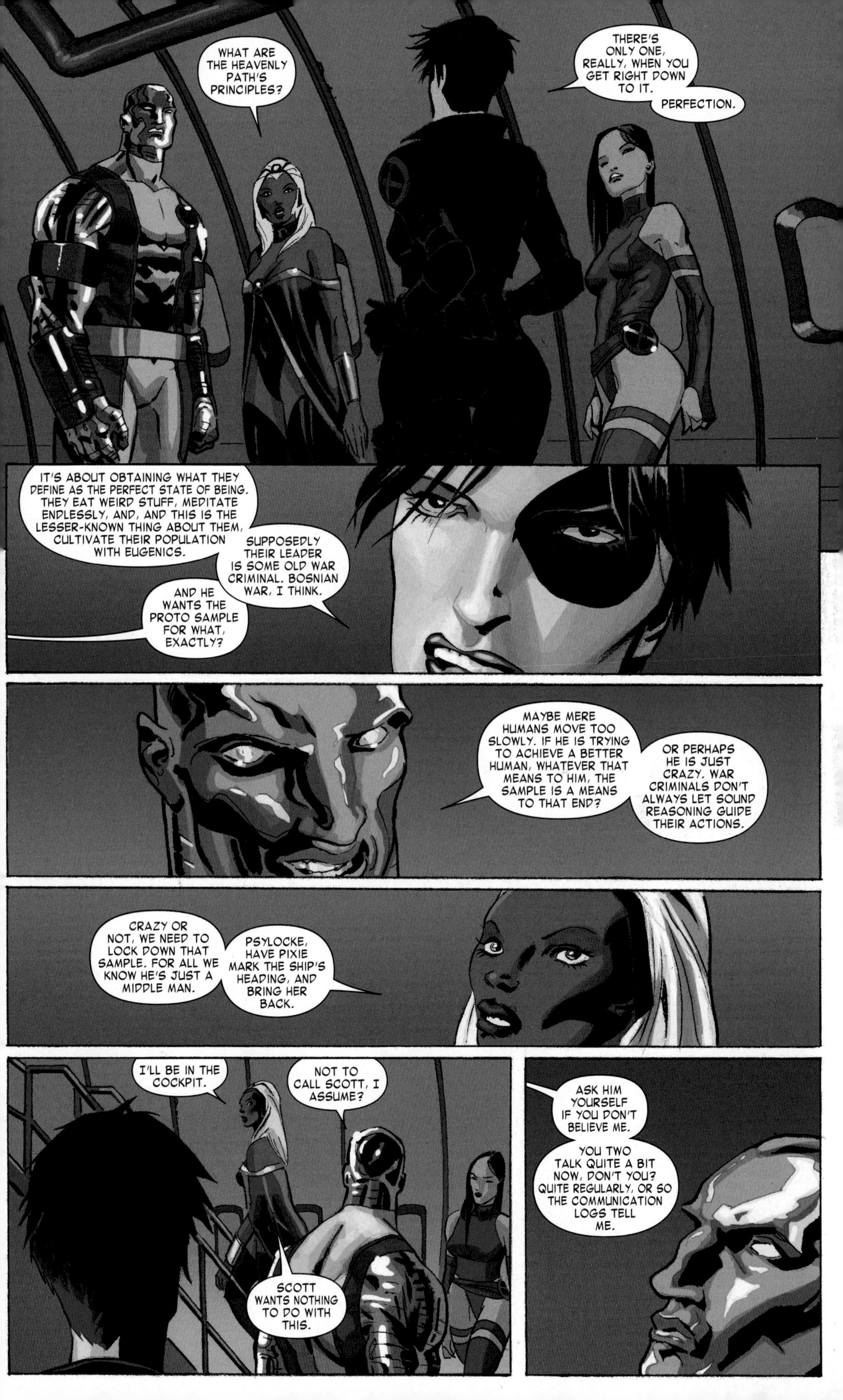
WHAT ARE THE HEAVENLY PATH'S PRINCIPLES?
THERE'S ONLY ONE, REALLY, WHEN YOU GET RIGHT DOWN TO IT.
PERFECTION.
IT'S ABOUT OBTAINING WHAT THEY DEFINE AS THE PERFECT STATE OF BEING. THEY EAT WEIRD STUFF, MEDITATE ENDLESSLY, AND, AND THIS IS THE LESSER-KNOWN THING ABOUT THEM, CULTIVATE THEIR POPULATION WITH EUGENICS.
SUPPOSEDLY THEIR LEADER IS SOME OLD WAR CRIMINAL. BOSNIAN WAR, I THINK.
AND HE WANTS THE PROTO SAMPLE FOR WHAT, EXACTLY?
MAYBE MERE HUMANS MOVE TOO SLOWLY. IF HE IS TRYING TO ACHIEVE A BETTER HUMAN, WHATEVER THAT MEANS TO HIM, THE SAMPLE IS A MEANS TO THAT END?
OR PERHAPS HE IS JUST CRAZY. WAR CRIMINALS DON'T ALWAYS LET SOUND REASONING GUIDE THEIR ACTIONS.
CRAZY OR NOT, WE NEED TO LOCK DOWN THAT SAMPLE. FOR ALL WE KNOW HE'S JUST A MIDDLE MAN.
PSYLOCKE, HAVE PIXIE MARK THE SHIP'S HEADING, AND BRING HER BACK.
I'LL BE IN THE COCKPIT.
NOT TO CALL SCOTT, I ASSUME?
SCOTT WANTS NOTHING TO DO WITH THIS.
ASK HIM YOURSELF IF YOU DON'T BELIEVE ME.
YOU TWO TALK QUITE A BIT NOW, DON'T YOU? QUITE REGULARLY, OR SO THE COMMUNICATION LOGS TELL ME.

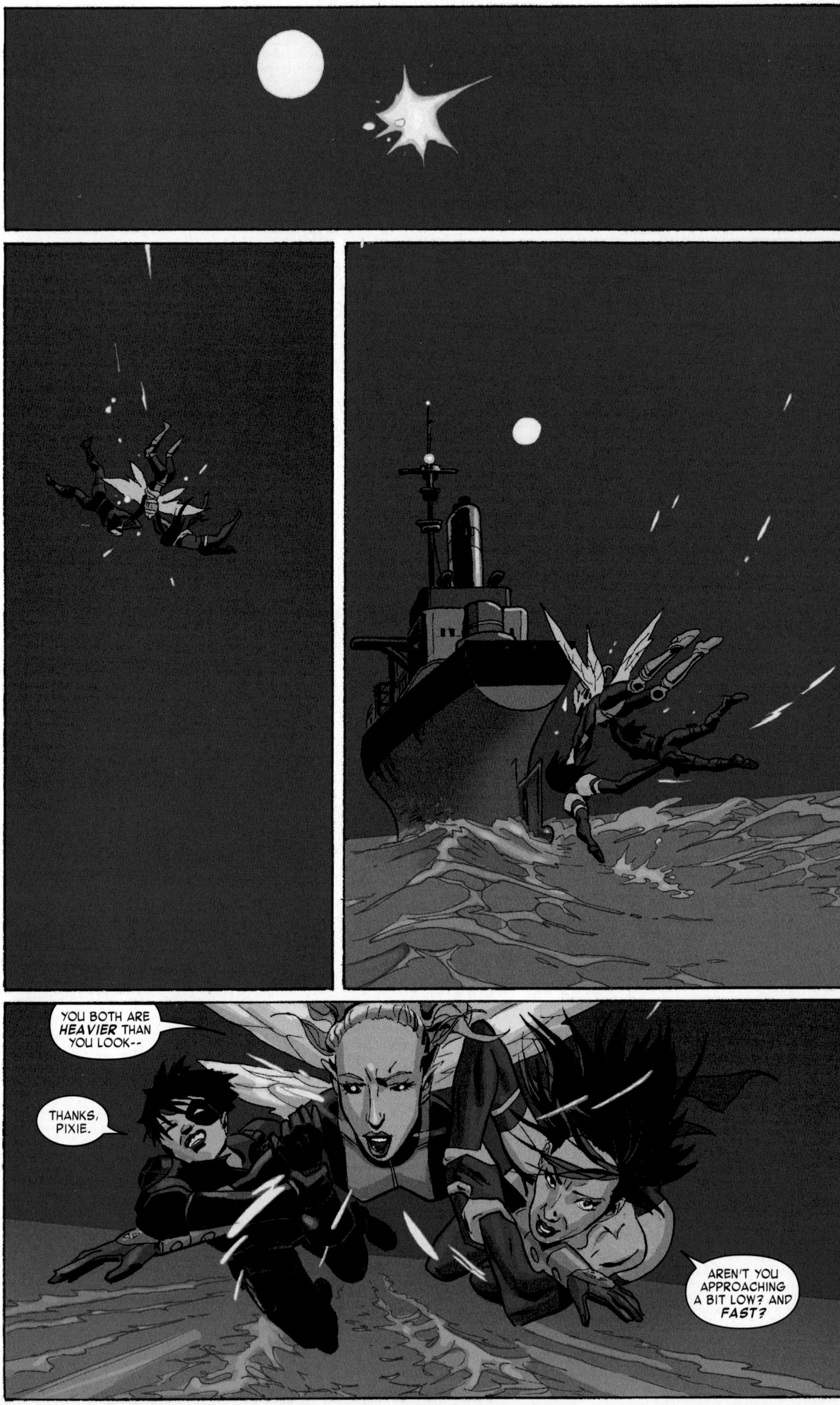
YOU BOTH ARE HEAVIER THAN YOU LOOK--
THANKS, PIXIE.
AREN'T YOU APPROACHING A BIT LOW? AND FAST?

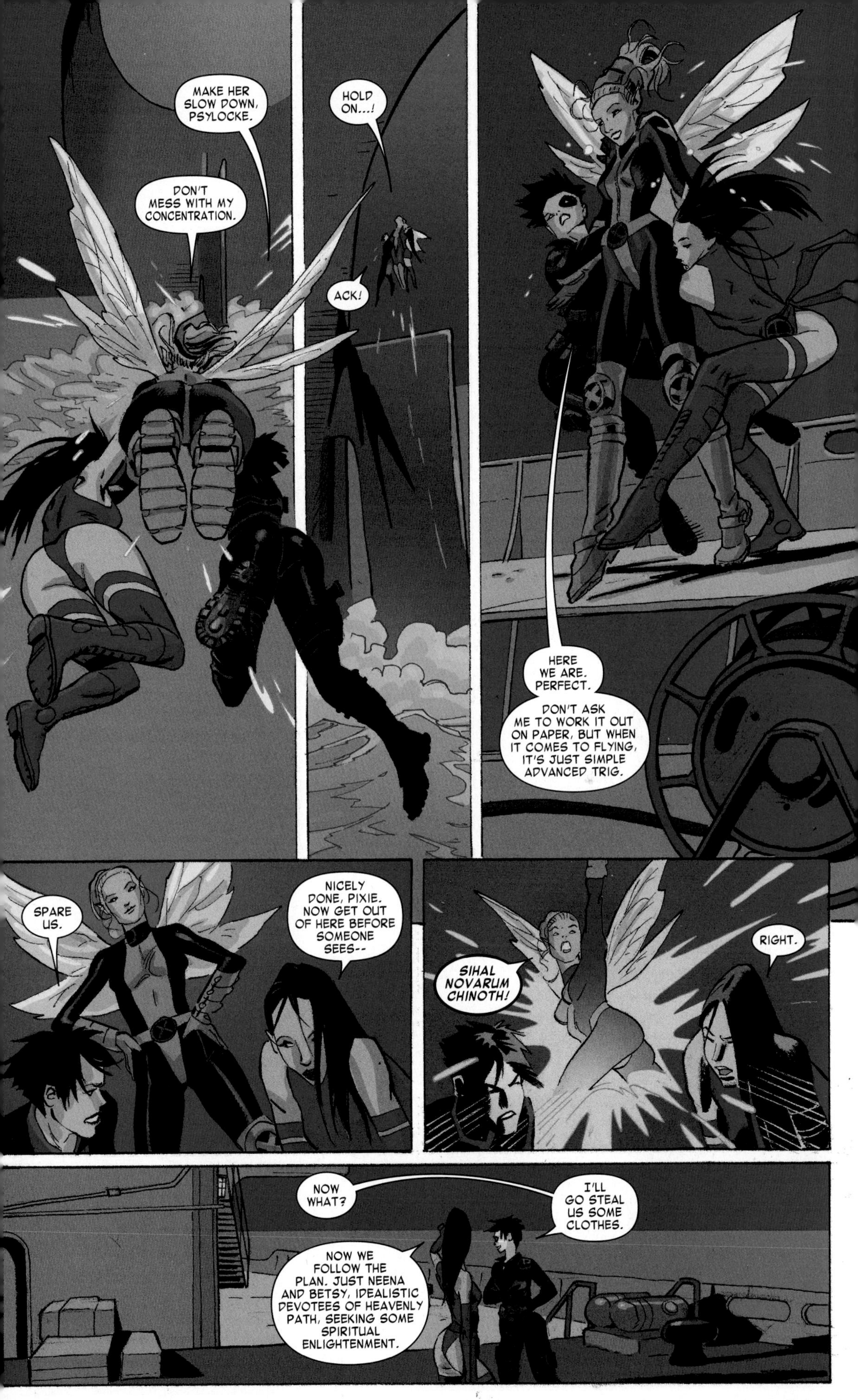
MAKE HER SLOW DOWN, PSYLOCKE.
DON'T MESS WITH MY CONCENTRATION.
HOLD ON...!
ACK!
HERE WE ARE. PERFECT.
DON'T ASK ME TO WORK IT OUT ON PAPER, BUT WHEN IT COMES TO FLYING, IT'S JUST SIMPLE ADVANCED TRIG.
SPARE US.
NICELY DONE, PIXIE. NOW GET OUT OF HERE BEFORE SOMEONE SEES--
SIHAL NOVARUM CHINOTH!
RIGHT.
NOW WHAT?
I'LL GO STEAL US SOME CLOTHES.
NOW WE FOLLOW THE PLAN. JUST NEENA AND BETSY, IDEALISTIC DEVOTEES OF HEAVENLY PATH, SEEKING SOME SPIRITUAL ENLIGHTENMENT.

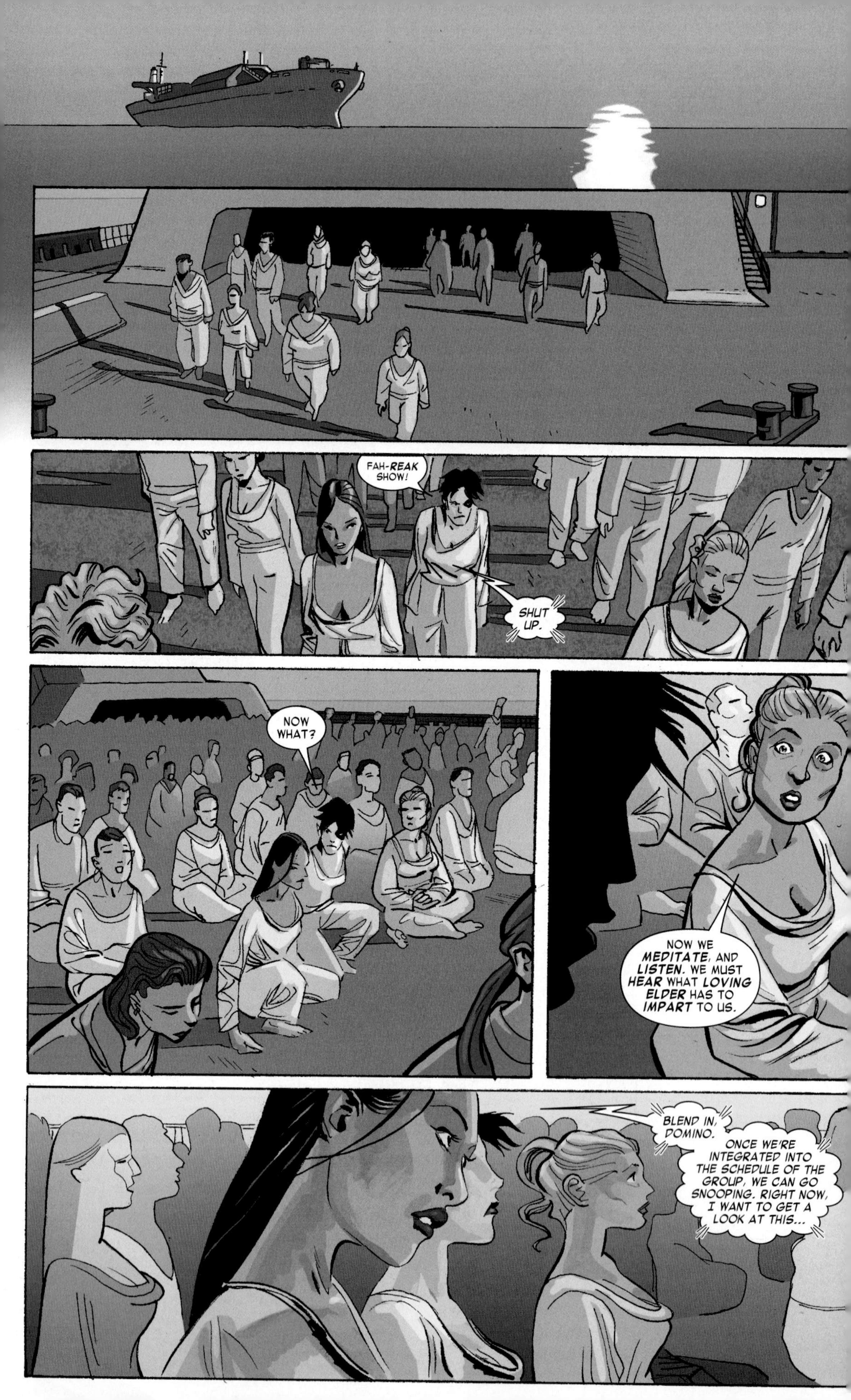
FAH-REAK SHOW!
SHUT UP.
NOW WHAT?
NOW WE MEDITATE, AND LISTEN. WE MUST HEAR WHAT LOVING ELDER HAS TO IMPART TO US.
BLEND IN, DOMINO.
ONCE WE'RE INTEGRATED INTO THE SCHEDULE OF THE GROUP, WE CAN GO SNOOPING. RIGHT NOW, I WANT TO GET A LOOK AT THIS...

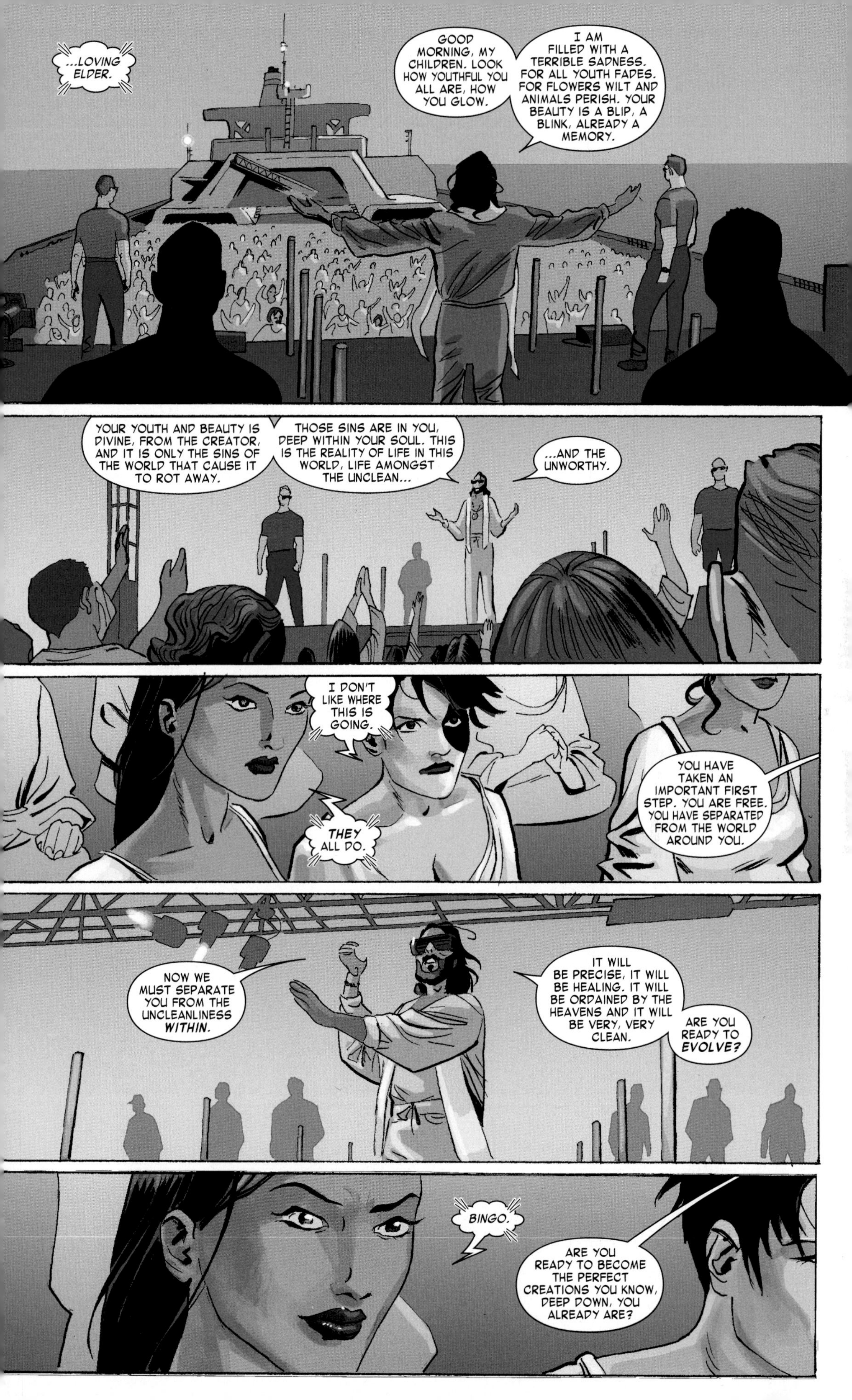
...LOVING ELDER.
GOOD MORNING, MY CHILDREN. LOOK HOW YOUTHFUL YOU ALL ARE, HOW YOU GLOW.
I AM FILLED WITH A TERRIBLE SADNESS. FOR ALL YOUTH FADES. FOR FLOWERS WILT AND ANIMALS PERISH. YOUR BEAUTY IS A BLIP, A BLINK, ALREADY A MEMORY.
YOUR YOUTH AND BEAUTY IS DIVINE, FROM THE CREATOR, AND IT IS ONLY THE SINS OF THE WORLD THAT CAUSE IT TO ROT AWAY.
THOSE SINS ARE IN YOU, DEEP WITHIN YOUR SOUL. THIS IS THE REALITY OF LIFE IN THIS WORLD, LIFE AMONGST THE UNCLEAN...
...AND THE UNWORTHY.
I DON'T LIKE WHERE THIS IS GOING.
THEY ALL DO.
YOU HAVE TAKEN AN IMPORTANT FIRST STEP. YOU ARE FREE. YOU HAVE SEPARATED FROM THE WORLD AROUND YOU.
NOW WE MUST SEPARATE YOU FROM THE UNCLEANLINESS WITHIN.
IT WILL BE PRECISE, IT WILL BE HEALING. IT WILL BE ORDAINED BY THE HEAVENS AND IT WILL BE VERY, VERY CLEAN.
ARE YOU READY TO EVOLVE?
BINGO.
ARE YOU READY TO BECOME THE PERFECT CREATIONS YOU KNOW, DEEP DOWN, YOU ALREADY ARE?

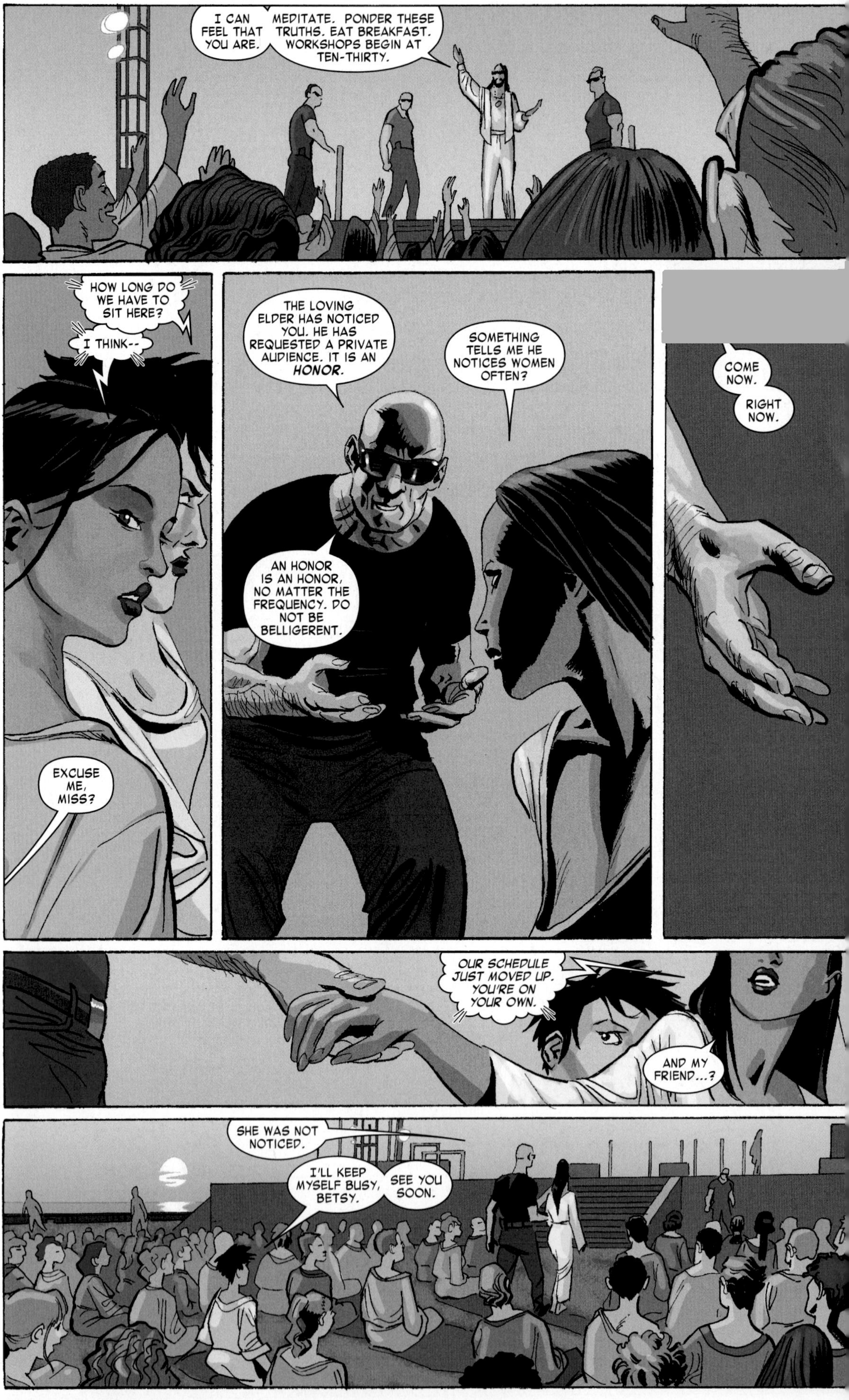
I CAN FEEL THAT YOU ARE.
MEDITATE. PONDER THESE TRUTHS. EAT BREAKFAST. WORKSHOPS BEGIN AT TEN-THIRTY.
HOW LONG DO WE HAVE TO SIT HERE?
I THINK--
EXCUSE ME, MISS?
THE LOVING ELDER HAS NOTICED YOU. HE HAS REQUESTED A PRIVATE AUDIENCE. IT IS AN HONOR.
SOMETHING TELLS ME HE NOTICES WOMEN OFTEN?
AN HONOR IS AN HONOR, NO MATTER THE FREQUENCY. DO NOT BE BELLIGERENT.
COME NOW.
RIGHT NOW.
OUR SCHEDULE JUST MOVED UP. YOU'RE ON YOUR OWN.
AND MY FRIEND...?
SHE WAS NOT NOTICED.
I'LL KEEP MYSELF BUSY, BETSY.
SEE YOU SOON.

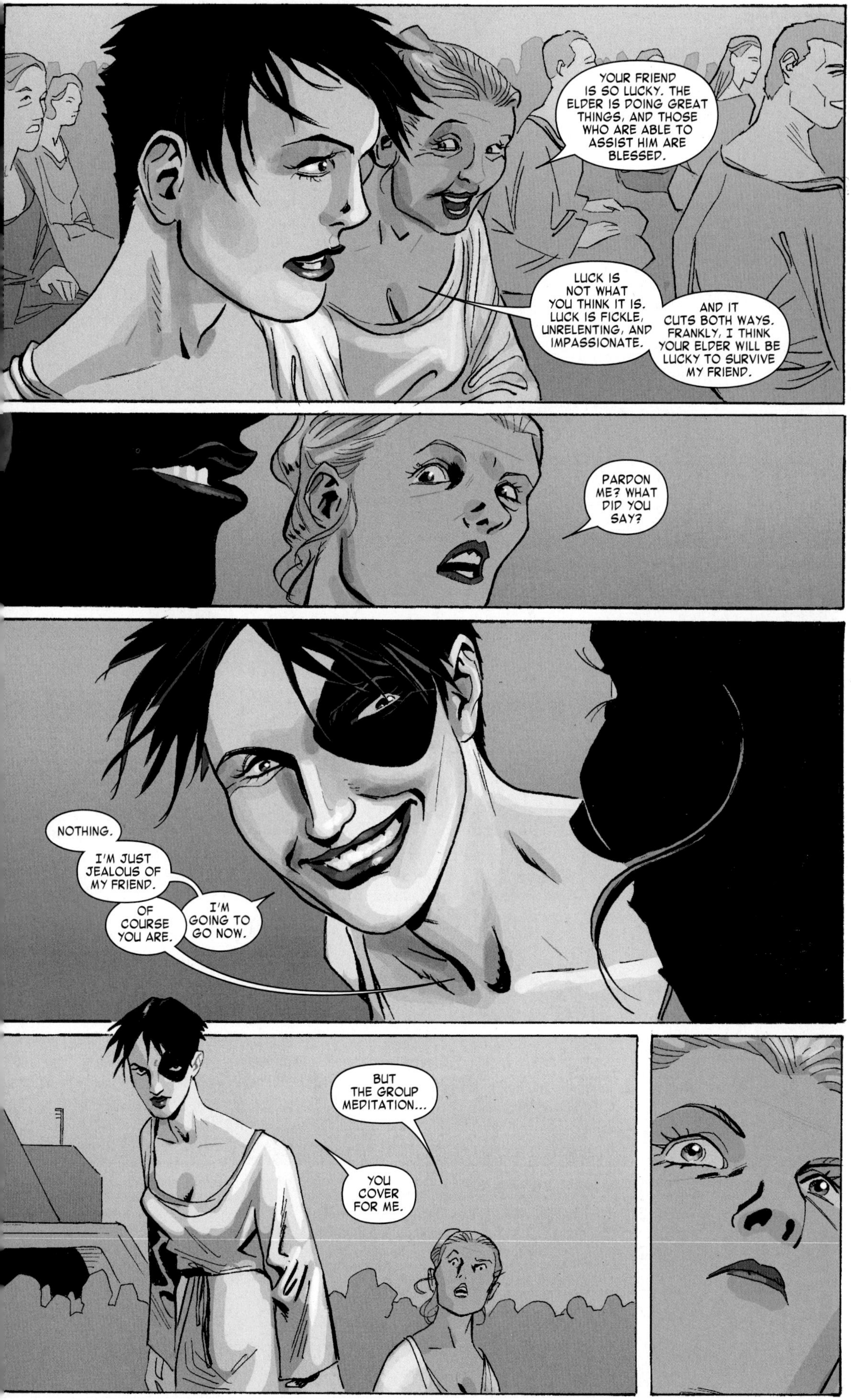

YOUR FRIEND IS SO LUCKY. THE ELDER IS DOING GREAT THINGS, AND THOSE WHO ARE ABLE TO ASSIST HIM ARE BLESSED.
LUCK IS NOT WHAT YOU THINK IT IS. LUCK IS FICKLE, UNRELENTING, AND IMPASSIONATE.
AND IT CUTS BOTH WAYS. FRANKLY, I THINK YOUR ELDER WILL BE LUCKY TO SURVIVE MY FRIEND.
PARDON ME? WHAT DID YOU SAY?
NOTHING.
I'M JUST JEALOUS OF MY FRIEND.
OF COURSE YOU ARE.
I'M GOING TO GO NOW.
BUT THE GROUP MEDITATION...
YOU COVER FOR ME.

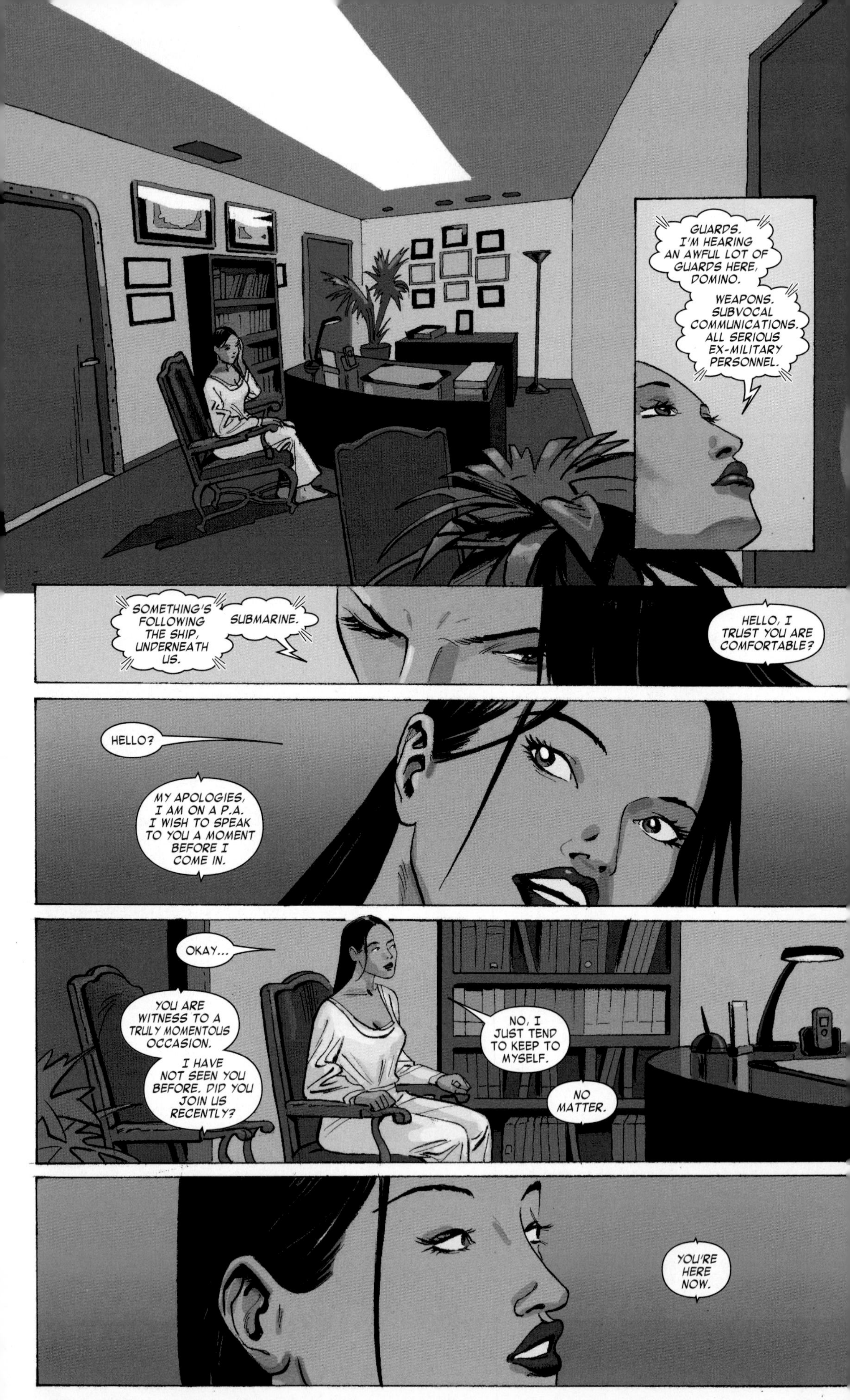
GUARDS. I'M HEARING AN AWFUL LOT OF GUARDS HERE, DOMINO.
WEAPONS. SUBVOCAL COMMUNICATIONS. ALL SERIOUS EX-MILITARY PERSONNEL.
SOMETHING'S FOLLOWING THE SHIP, UNDERNEATH US.
SUBMARINE.
HELLO, I TRUST YOU ARE COMFORTABLE?
HELLO?
MY APOLOGIES, I AM ON A P.A. I WISH TO SPEAK TO YOU A MOMENT BEFORE I COME IN.
OKAY...
YOU ARE WITNESS TO A TRULY MOMENTOUS OCCASION.
I HAVE NOT SEEN YOU BEFORE. DID YOU JOIN US RECENTLY?
NO, I JUST TEND TO KEEP TO MYSELF.
NO MATTER.
YOU'RE HERE NOW.

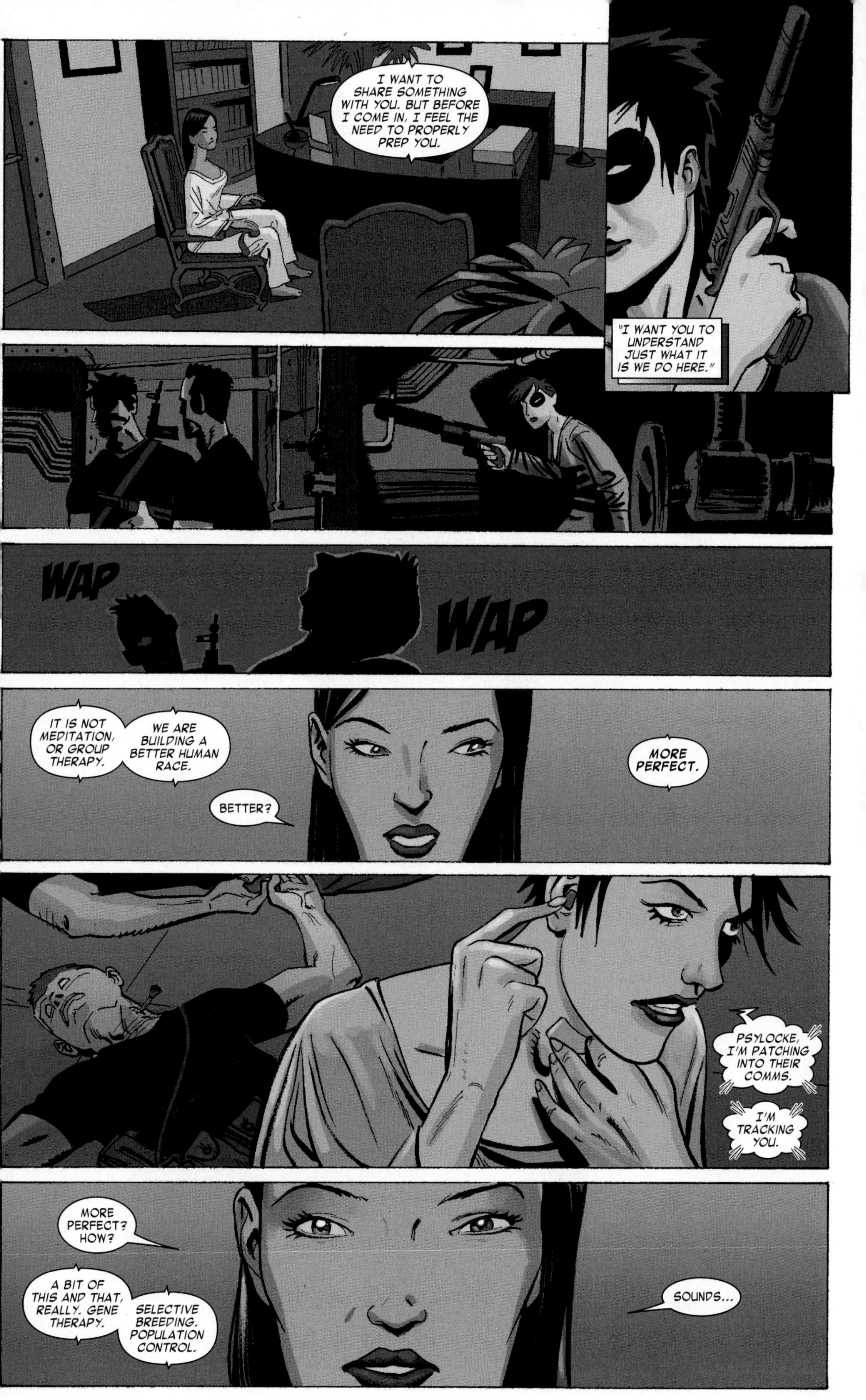

I WANT TO SHARE SOMETHING WITH YOU. BUT BEFORE I COME IN, I FEEL THE NEED TO PROPERLY PREP YOU.
"I WANT YOU TO UNDERSTAND JUST WHAT IT IS WE DO HERE."
WAP
WAP
IT IS NOT MEDITATION, OR GROUP THERAPY.
WE ARE BUILDING A BETTER HUMAN RACE.
BETTER?
MORE PERFECT.
PSYLOCKE, I'M PATCHING INTO THEIR COMMS.
I'M TRACKING YOU.
MORE PERFECT? HOW?
A BIT OF THIS AND THAT, REALLY. GENE THERAPY.
SELECTIVE BREEDING. POPULATION CONTROL.
SOUNDS...

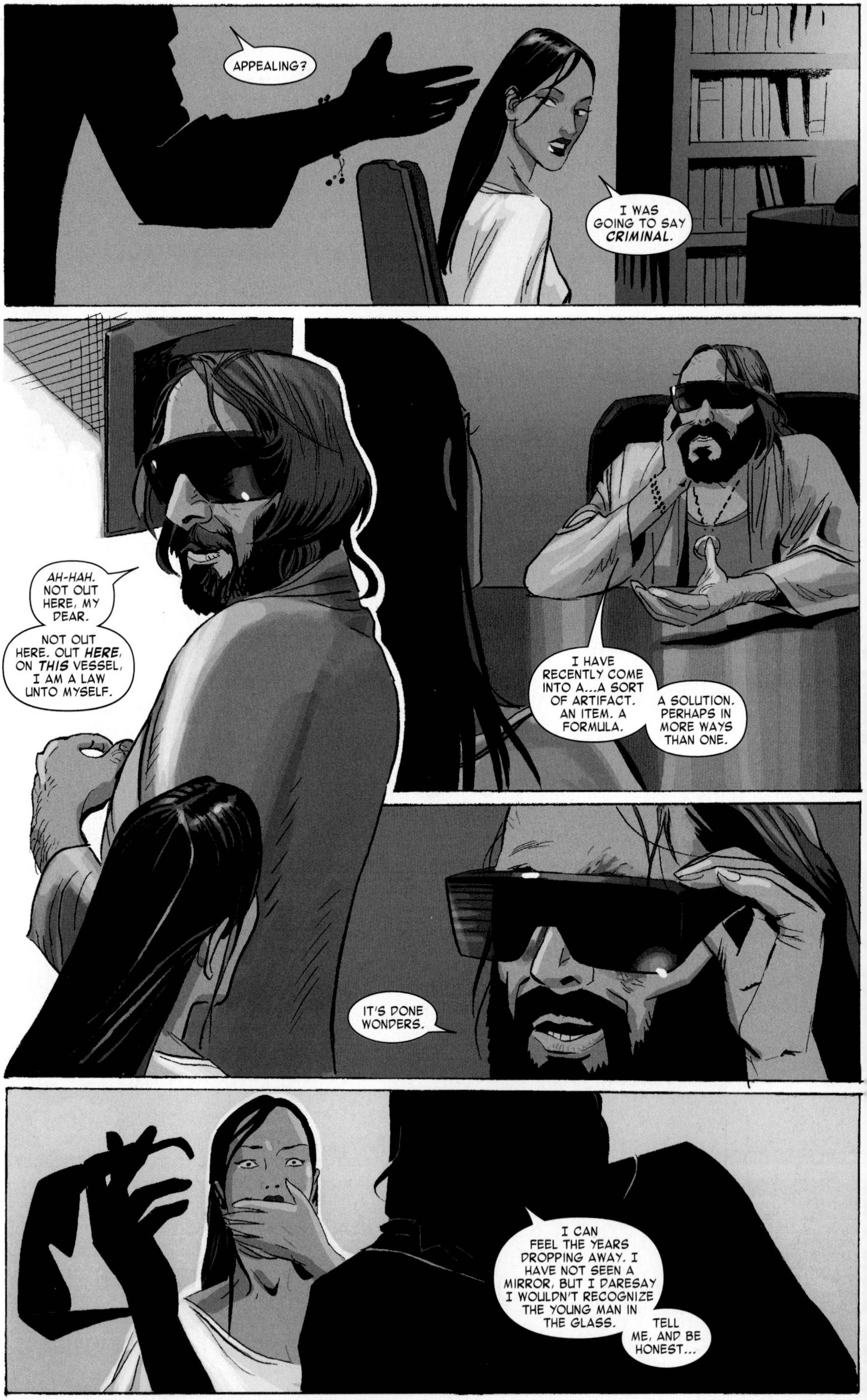
APPEALING?
I WAS GOING TO SAY CRIMINAL.
AH-HAH. NOT OUT HERE, MY DEAR.
NOT OUT HERE. OUT HERE, ON THIS VESSEL, I AM A LAW UNTO MYSELF.
I HAVE RECENTLY COME INTO A...A SORT OF ARTIFACT. AN ITEM. A FORMULA.
A SOLUTION. PERHAPS IN MORE WAYS THAN ONE.
IT'S DONE WONDERS.
I CAN FEEL THE YEARS DROPPING AWAY. I HAVE NOT SEEN A MIRROR, BUT I DARESAY I WOULDN'T RECOGNIZE THE YOUNG MAN IN THE GLASS.
TELL ME, AND BE HONEST...

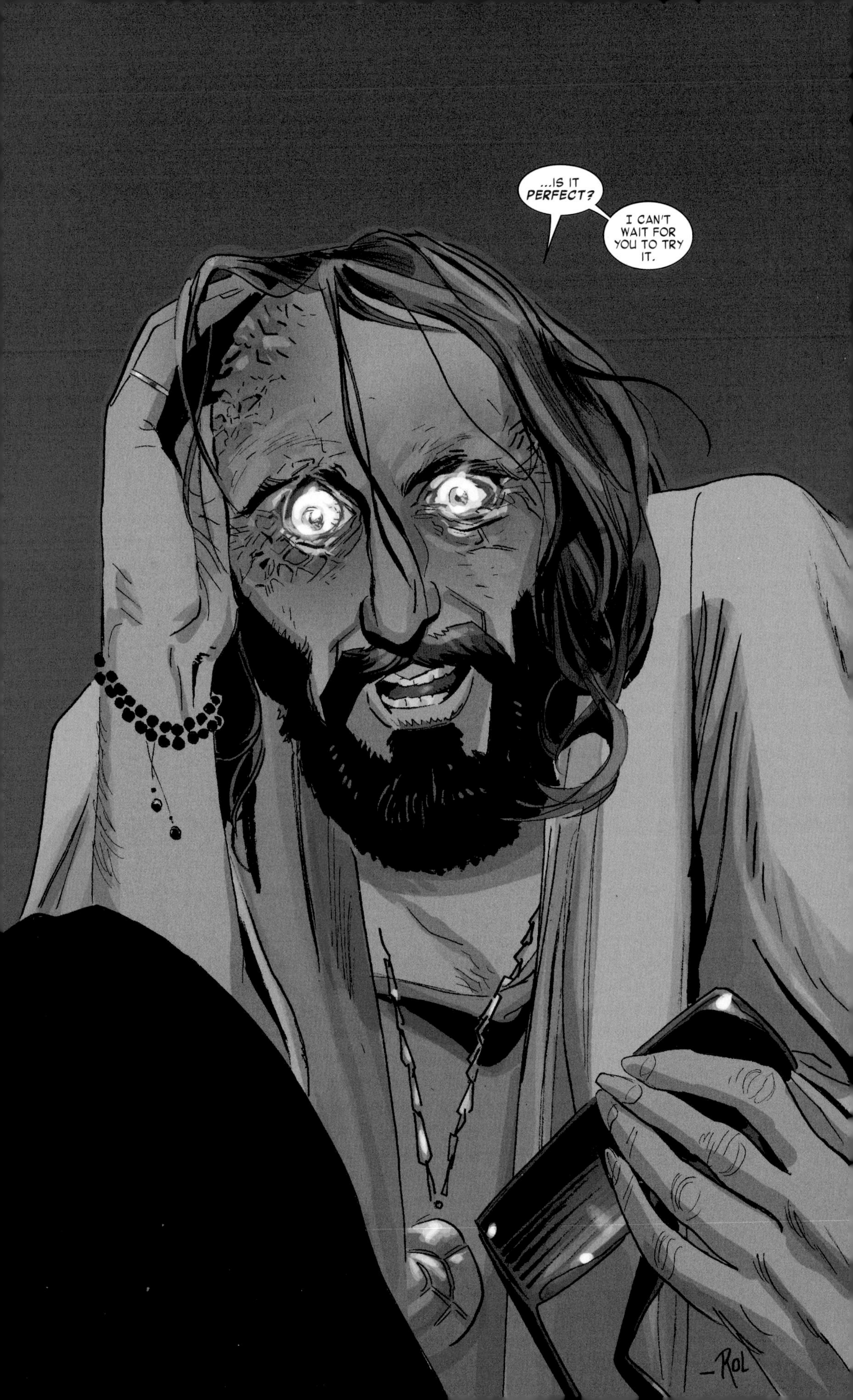
...IS IT PERFECT?
I CAN'T WAIT FOR YOU TO TRY IT.

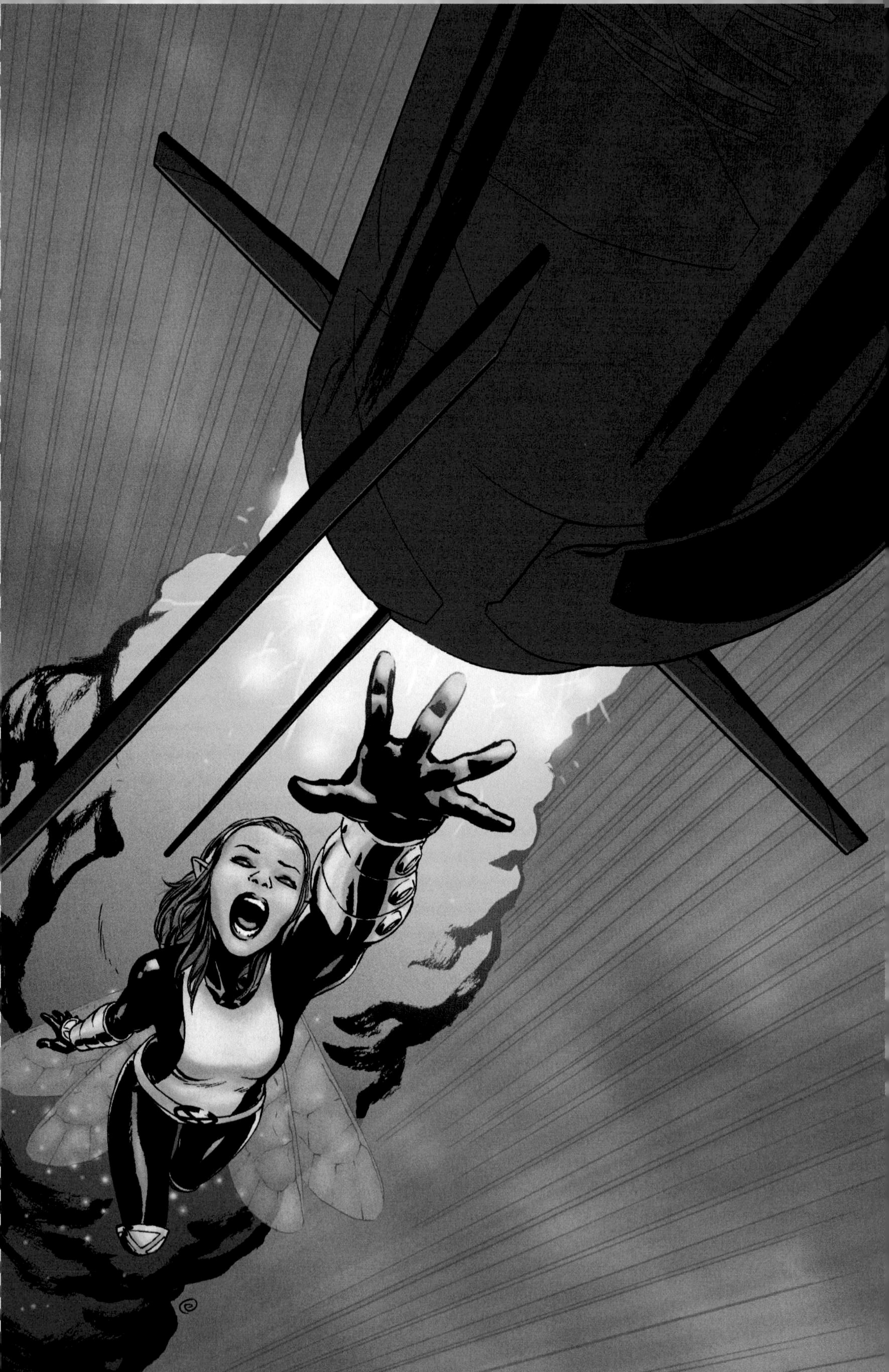

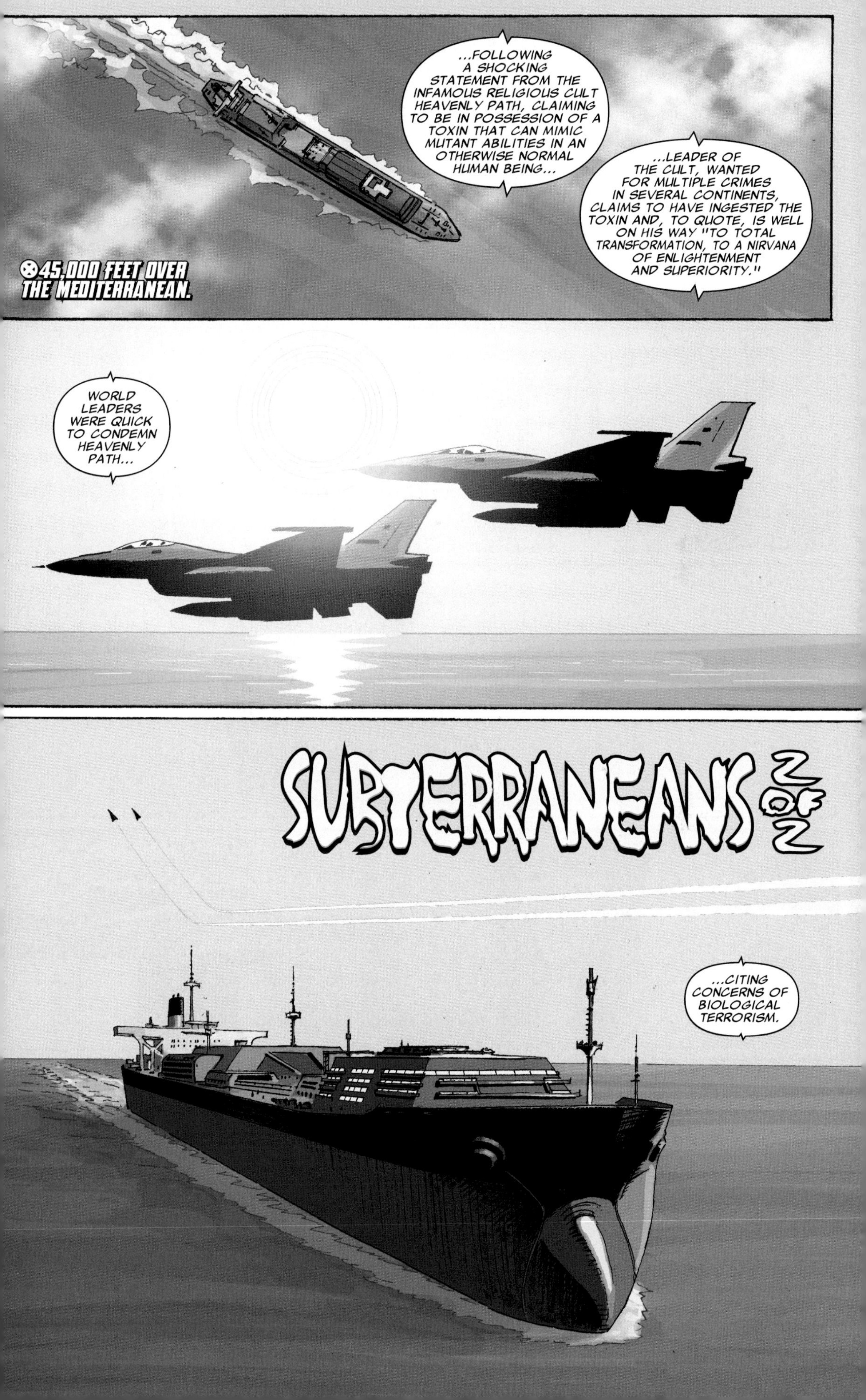
45,000 FEET OVER THE MEDITERRANEAN.
...FOLLOWING A SHOCKING STATEMENT FROM THE INFAMOUS RELIGIOUS CULT HEAVENLY PATH, CLAIMING TO BE IN POSSESSION OF A TOXIN THAT CAN MIMIC MUTANT ABILITIES IN AN OTHERWISE NORMAL HUMAN BEING...
...LEADER OF THE CULT, WANTED FOR MULTIPLE CRIMES IN SEVERAL CONTINENTS, CLAIMS TO HAVE INGESTED THE TOXIN AND, TO QUOTE, IS WELL ON HIS WAY "TO TOTAL TRANSFORMATION, TO A NIRVANA OF ENLIGHTENMENT AND SUPERIORITY."
WORLD LEADERS WERE QUICK TO CONDEMN HEAVENLY PATH...
SUBTERRANEANS
2 OF 2
...CITING CONCERNS OF BIOLOGICAL TERRORISM.

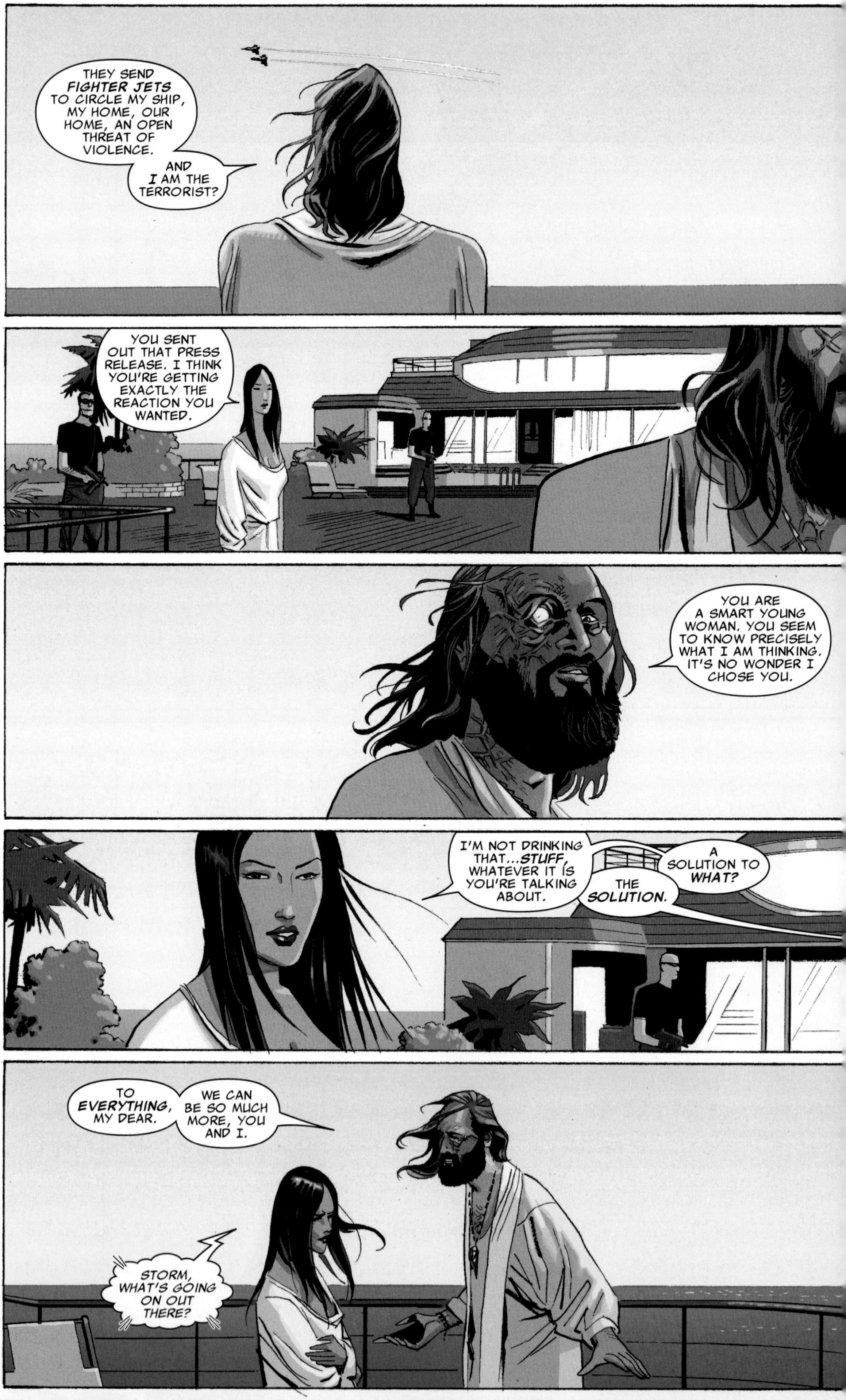
THEY SEND FIGHTER JETS TO CIRCLE MY SHIP, MY HOME, OUR HOME, AN OPEN THREAT OF VIOLENCE.
AND I AM THE TERRORIST?
YOU SENT OUT THAT PRESS RELEASE. I THINK YOU'RE GETTING EXACTLY THE REACTION YOU WANTED.
YOU ARE A SMART YOUNG WOMAN. YOU SEEM TO KNOW PRECISELY WHAT I AM THINKING. IT'S NO WONDER I CHOSE YOU.
I'M NOT DRINKING THAT...STUFF, WHATEVER IT IS YOU'RE TALKING ABOUT.
THE SOLUTION.
A SOLUTION TO WHAT?
TO EVERYTHING, MY DEAR.
WE CAN BE SO MUCH MORE, YOU AND I.
STORM, WHAT'S GOING ON OUT THERE?

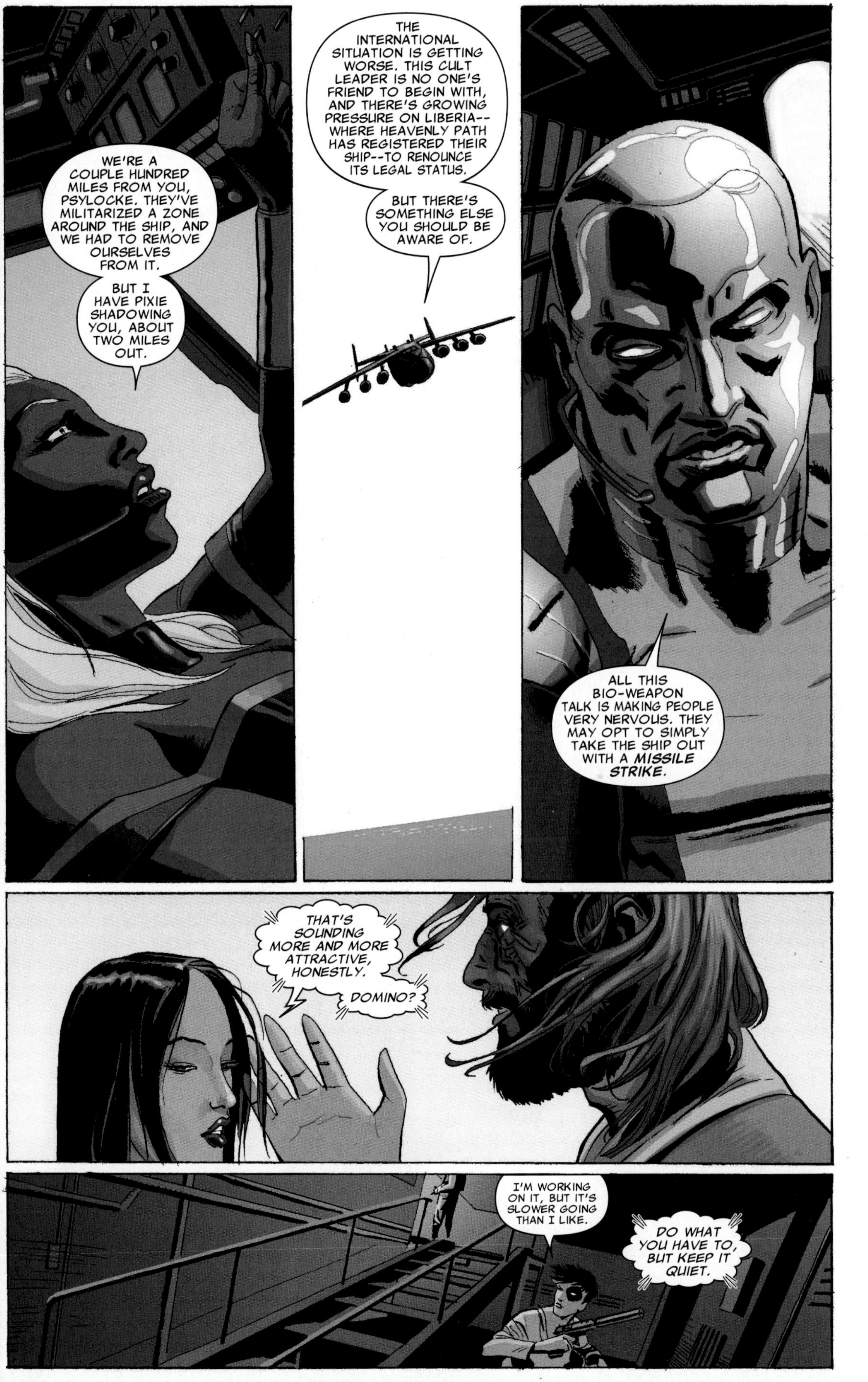
WE'RE A COUPLE HUNDRED MILES FROM YOU, PSYLOCKE. THEY'VE MILITARIZED A ZONE AROUND THE SHIP, AND WE HAD TO REMOVE OURSELVES FROM IT.
BUT I HAVE PIXIE SHADOWING YOU, ABOUT TWO MILES OUT.
THE INTERNATIONAL SITUATION IS GETTING WORSE. THIS CULT LEADER IS NO ONE'S FRIEND TO BEGIN WITH, AND THERE'S GROWING PRESSURE ON LIBERIA--WHERE HEAVENLY PATH HAS REGISTERED THEIR SHIP--TO RENOUNCE ITS LEGAL STATUS.
BUT THERE'S SOMETHING ELSE YOU SHOULD BE AWARE OF.
ALL THIS BIO-WEAPON TALK IS MAKING PEOPLE VERY NERVOUS. THEY MAY OPT TO SIMPLY TAKE THE SHIP OUT WITH A *MISSILE STRIKE.*
THAT'S SOUNDING MORE AND MORE ATTRACTIVE, HONESTLY.
DOMINO?
I'M WORKING ON IT, BUT IT'S SLOWER GOING THAN I LIKE.
DO WHAT YOU HAVE TO, BUT KEEP IT QUIET.

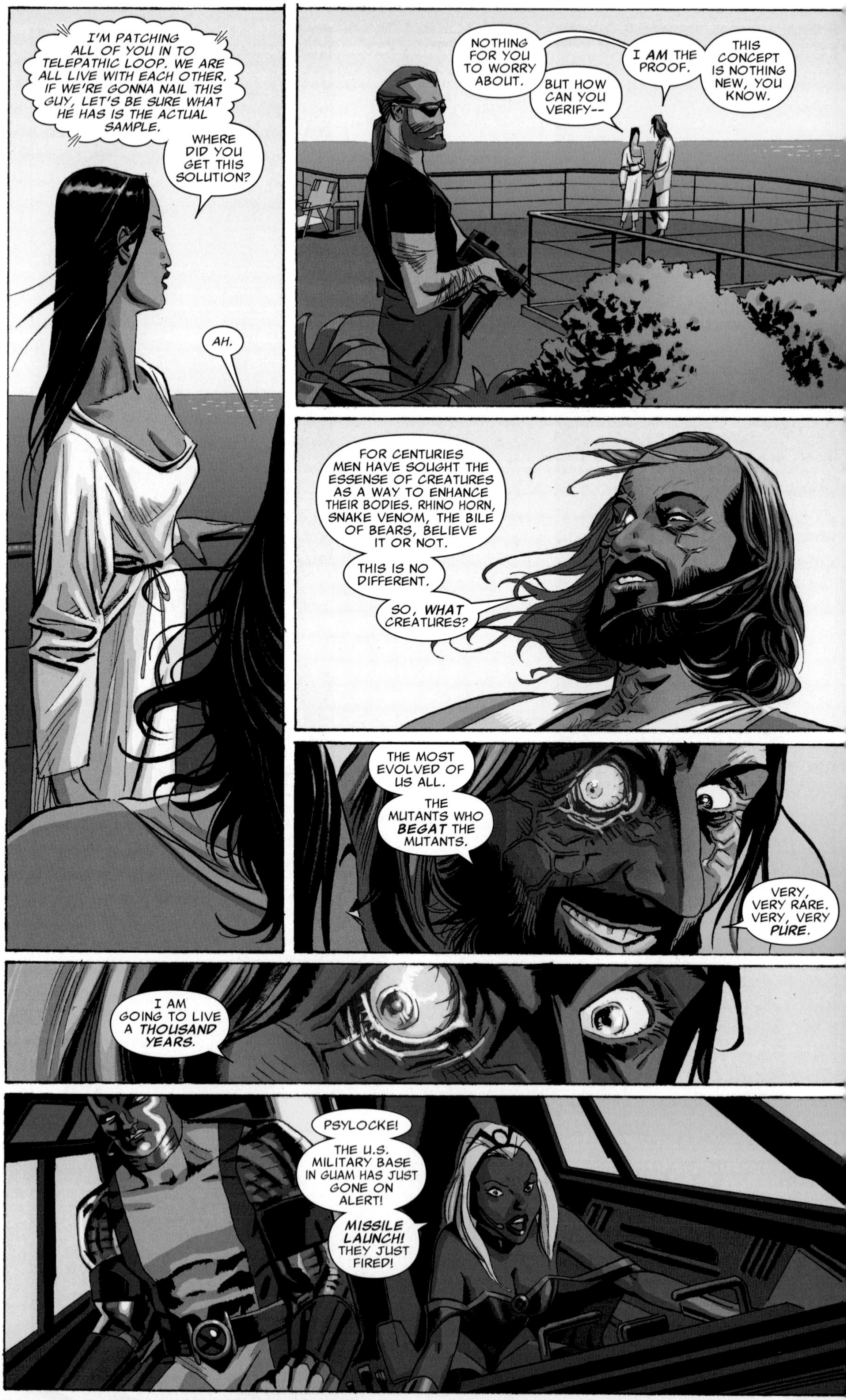
I'M PATCHING ALL OF YOU IN TO TELEPATHIC LOOP. WE ARE ALL LIVE WITH EACH OTHER. IF WE'RE GONNA NAIL THIS GUY, LET'S BE SURE WHAT HE HAS IS THE ACTUAL SAMPLE.
WHERE DID YOU GET THIS SOLUTION?
AH.
NOTHING FOR YOU TO WORRY ABOUT.
BUT HOW CAN YOU VERIFY--
I AM THE PROOF.
THIS CONCEPT IS NOTHING NEW, YOU KNOW.
FOR CENTURIES MEN HAVE SOUGHT THE ESSENSE OF CREATURES AS A WAY TO ENHANCE THEIR BODIES. RHINO HORN, SNAKE VENOM, THE BILE OF BEARS, BELIEVE IT OR NOT.
THIS IS NO DIFFERENT.
SO, WHAT CREATURES?
THE MOST EVOLVED OF US ALL.
THE MUTANTS WHO BEGAT THE MUTANTS.
VERY, VERY RARE. VERY, VERY PURE.
I AM GOING TO LIVE A THOUSAND YEARS.
PSYLOCKE!
THE U.S. MILITARY BASE IN GUAM HAS JUST GONE ON ALERT!
MISSILE LAUNCH! THEY JUST FIRED!

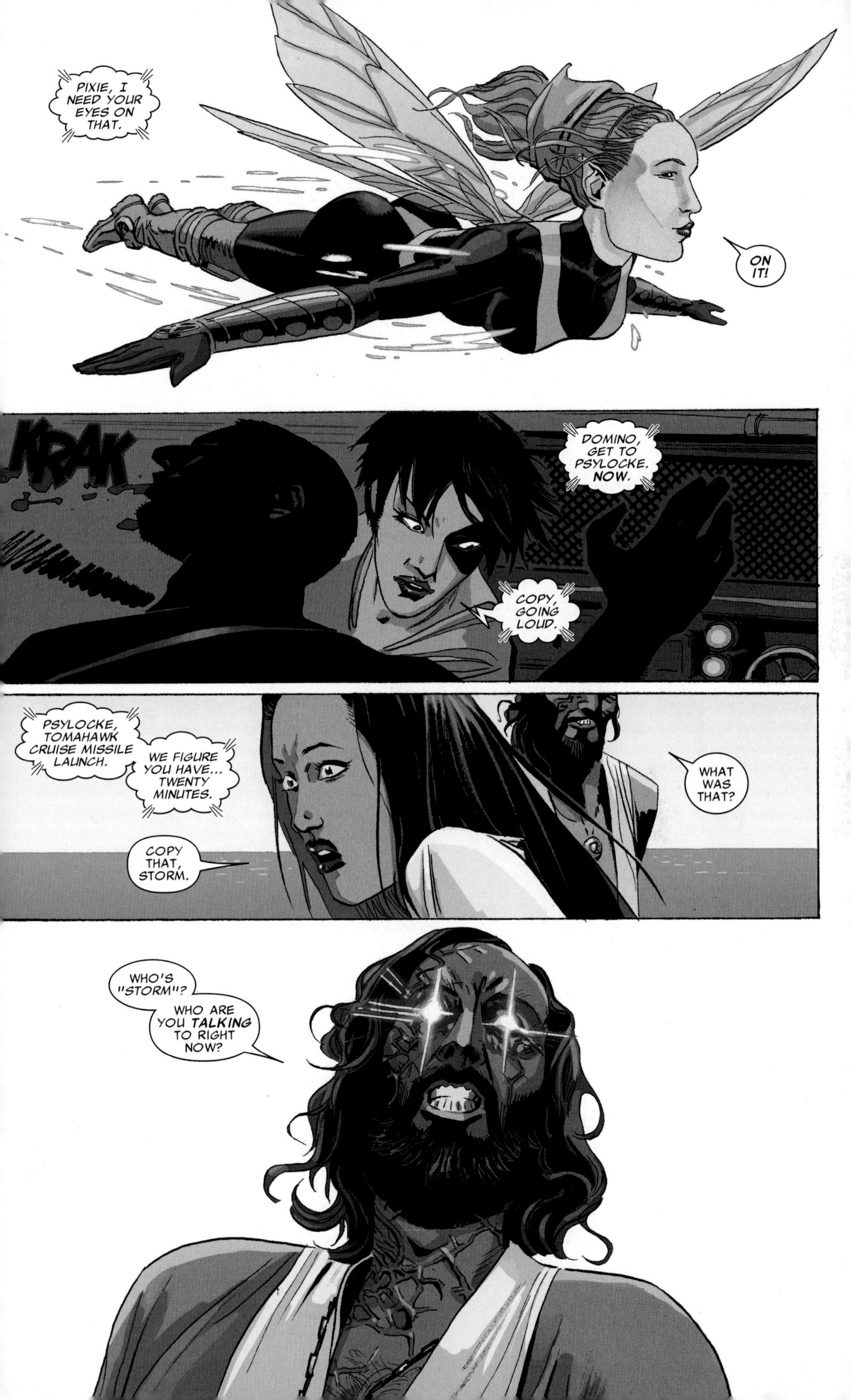
PIXIE, I NEED YOUR EYES ON THAT.
ON IT!
KRAK
DOMINO, GET TO PSYLOCKE. NOW.
COPY, GOING LOUD.
PSYLOCKE, TOMAHAWK CRUISE MISSILE LAUNCH.
WE FIGURE YOU HAVE... TWENTY MINUTES.
WHAT WAS THAT?
COPY THAT, STORM.
WHO'S "STORM"?
WHO ARE YOU TALKING TO RIGHT NOW?

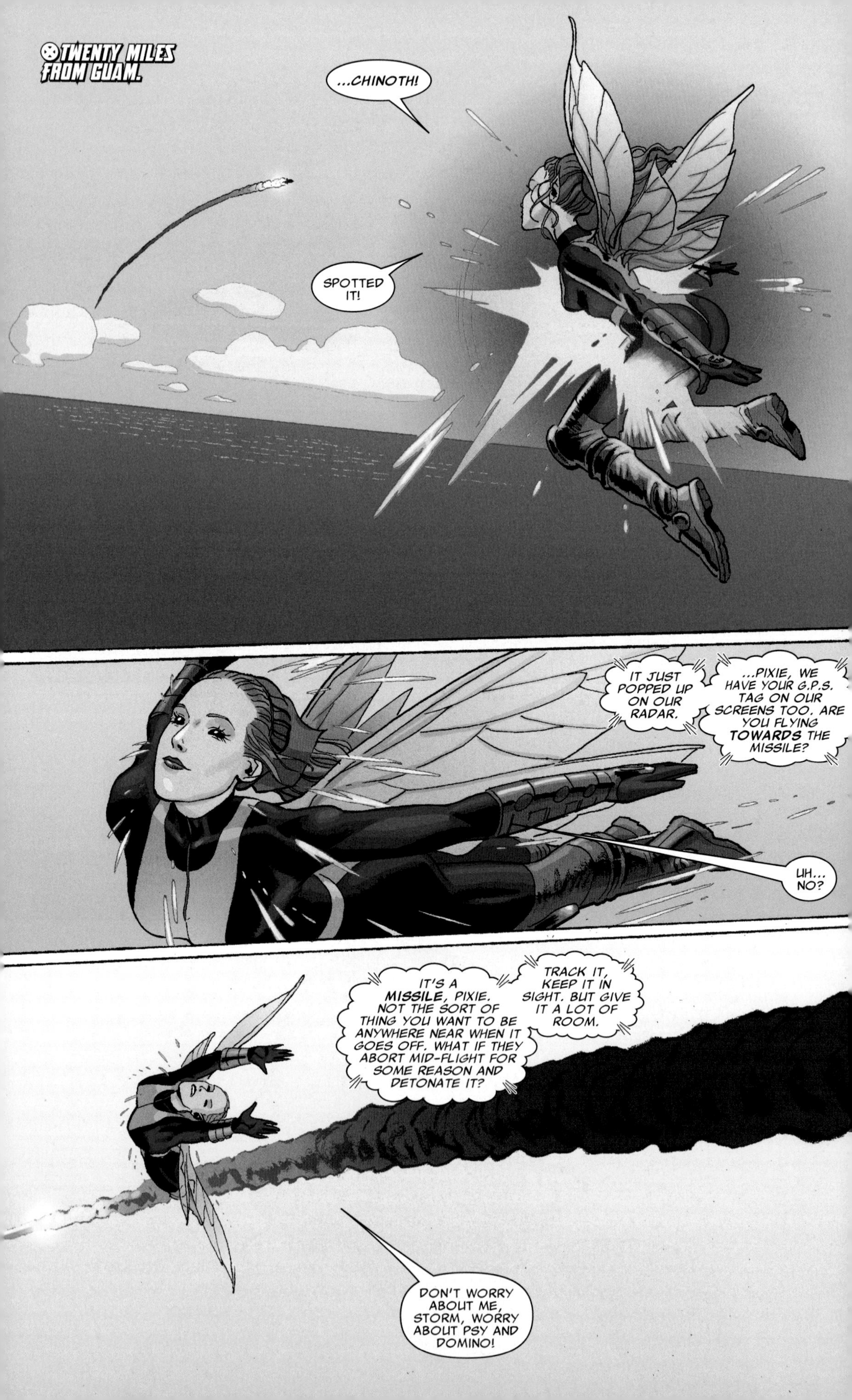
TWENTY MILES FROM GUAM.
...CHINOTH!
SPOTTED IT!
IT JUST POPPED UP ON OUR RADAR.
...PIXIE, WE HAVE YOUR G.P.S. TAG ON OUR SCREENS TOO. ARE YOU FLYING TOWARDS THE MISSILE?
UH... NO?
IT'S A MISSILE, PIXIE. NOT THE SORT OF THING YOU WANT TO BE ANYWHERE NEAR WHEN IT GOES OFF. WHAT IF THEY ABORT MID-FLIGHT FOR SOME REASON AND DETONATE IT?
TRACK IT, KEEP IT IN SIGHT, BUT GIVE IT A LOT OF ROOM.
DON'T WORRY ABOUT ME, STORM, WORRY ABOUT PSY AND DOMINO!

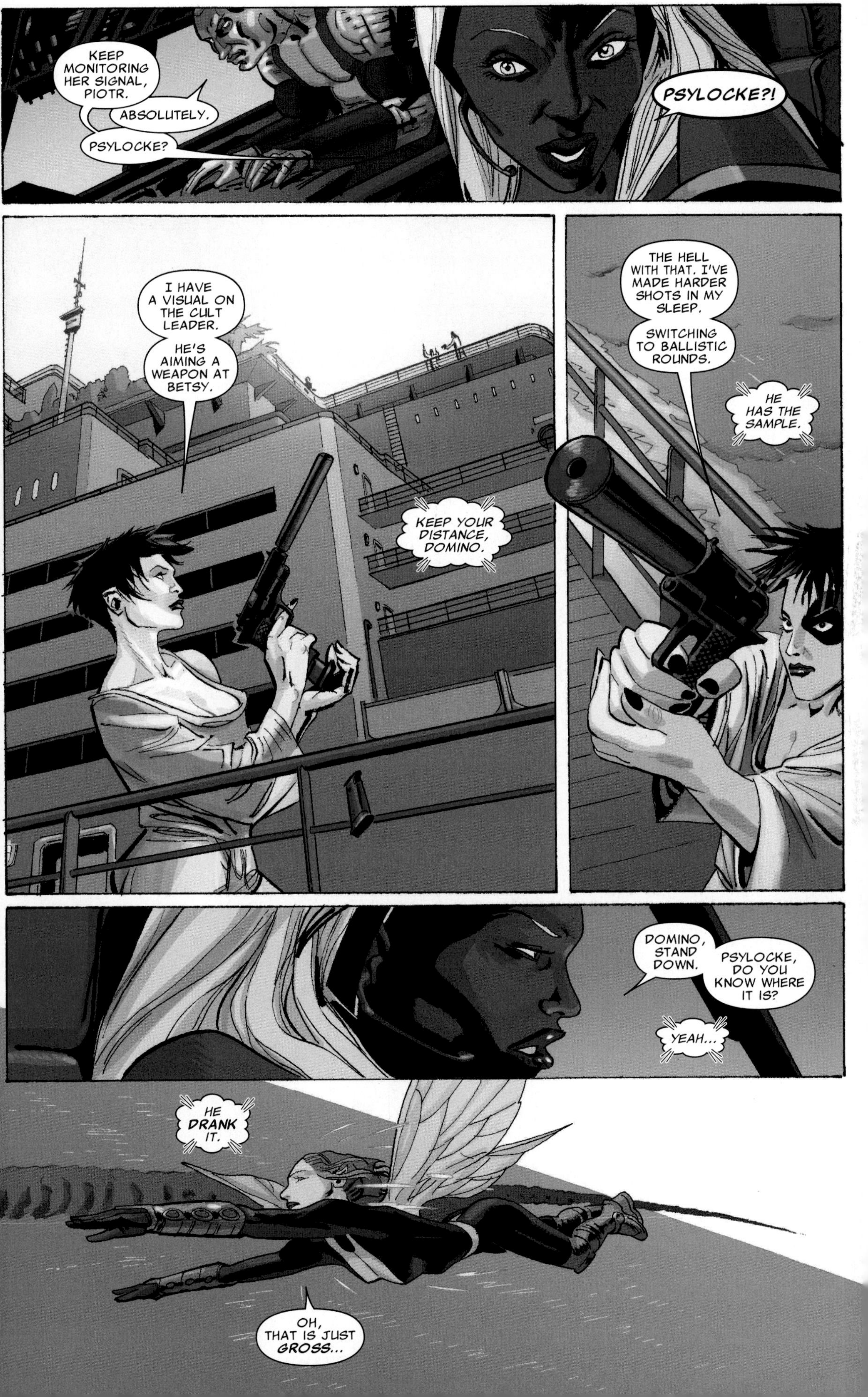
KEEP MONITORING HER SIGNAL, PIOTR.
ABSOLUTELY.
PSYLOCKE?
PSYLOCKE?!
I HAVE A VISUAL ON THE CULT LEADER.
HE'S AIMING A WEAPON AT BETSY.
KEEP YOUR DISTANCE, DOMINO.
THE HELL WITH THAT. I'VE MADE HARDER SHOTS IN MY SLEEP.
SWITCHING TO BALLISTIC ROUNDS.
HE HAS THE SAMPLE.
DOMINO, STAND DOWN.
PSYLOCKE, DO YOU KNOW WHERE IT IS?
YEAH...
HE DRANK IT.
OH, THAT IS JUST GROSS...

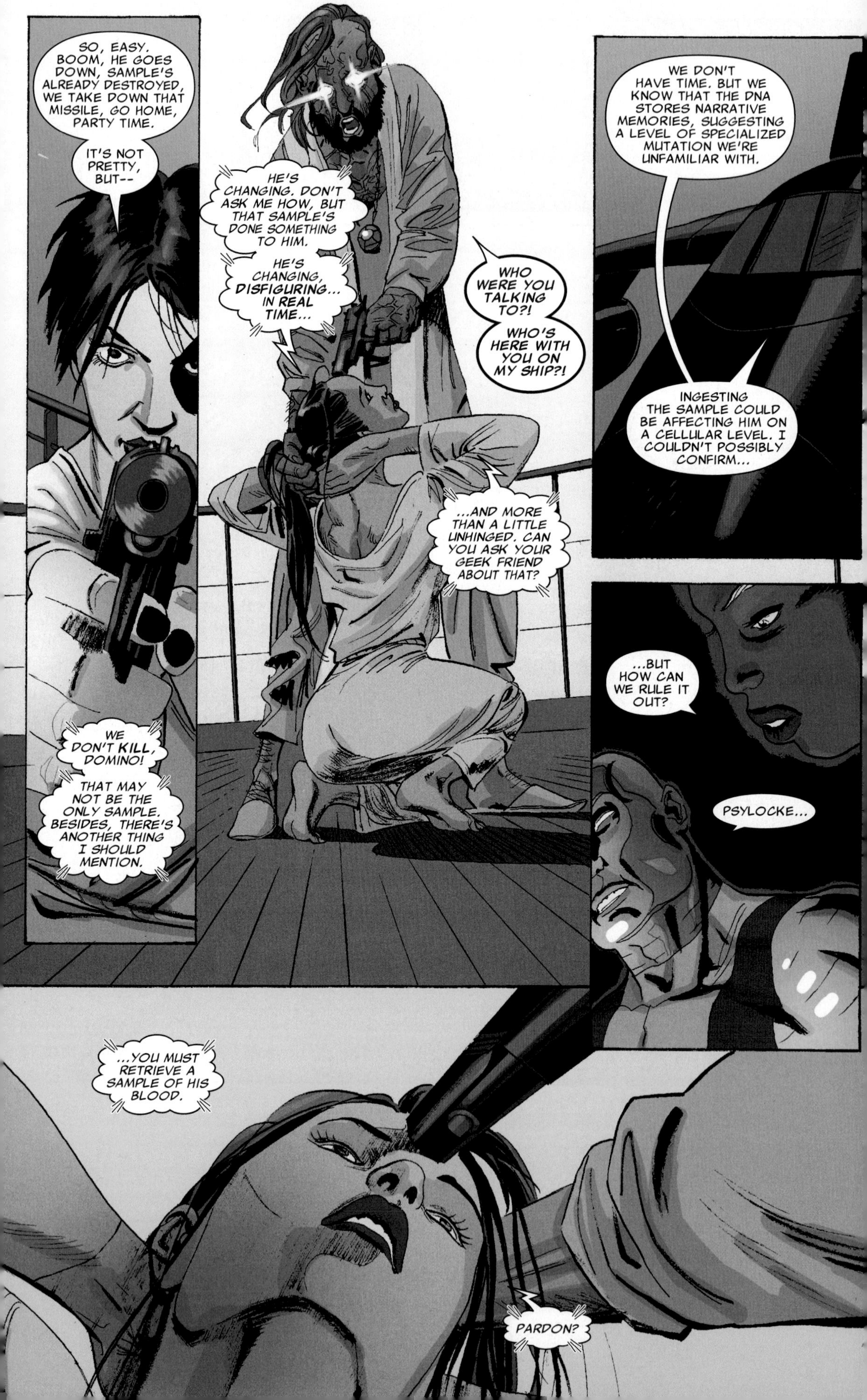
SO, EASY. BOOM, HE GOES DOWN, SAMPLE'S ALREADY DESTROYED, WE TAKE DOWN THAT MISSILE, GO HOME, PARTY TIME.
IT'S NOT PRETTY, BUT--
HE'S CHANGING. DON'T ASK ME HOW, BUT THAT SAMPLE'S DONE SOMETHING TO HIM.
HE'S CHANGING, DISFIGURING... IN REAL TIME...
WHO WERE YOU TALKING TO?!
WHO'S HERE WITH YOU ON MY SHIP?!
...AND MORE THAN A LITTLE UNHINGED. CAN YOU ASK YOUR GEEK FRIEND ABOUT THAT?
WE DON'T KILL, DOMINO!
THAT MAY NOT BE THE ONLY SAMPLE. BESIDES, THERE'S ANOTHER THING I SHOULD MENTION.
WE DON'T HAVE TIME. BUT WE KNOW THAT THE DNA STORES NARRATIVE MEMORIES, SUGGESTING A LEVEL OF SPECIALIZED MUTATION WE'RE UNFAMILIAR WITH.
INGESTING THE SAMPLE COULD BE AFFECTING HIM ON A CELLULAR LEVEL. I COULDN'T POSSIBLY CONFIRM...
...BUT HOW CAN WE RULE IT OUT?
PSYLOCKE...
...YOU MUST RETRIEVE A SAMPLE OF HIS BLOOD.
PARDON?

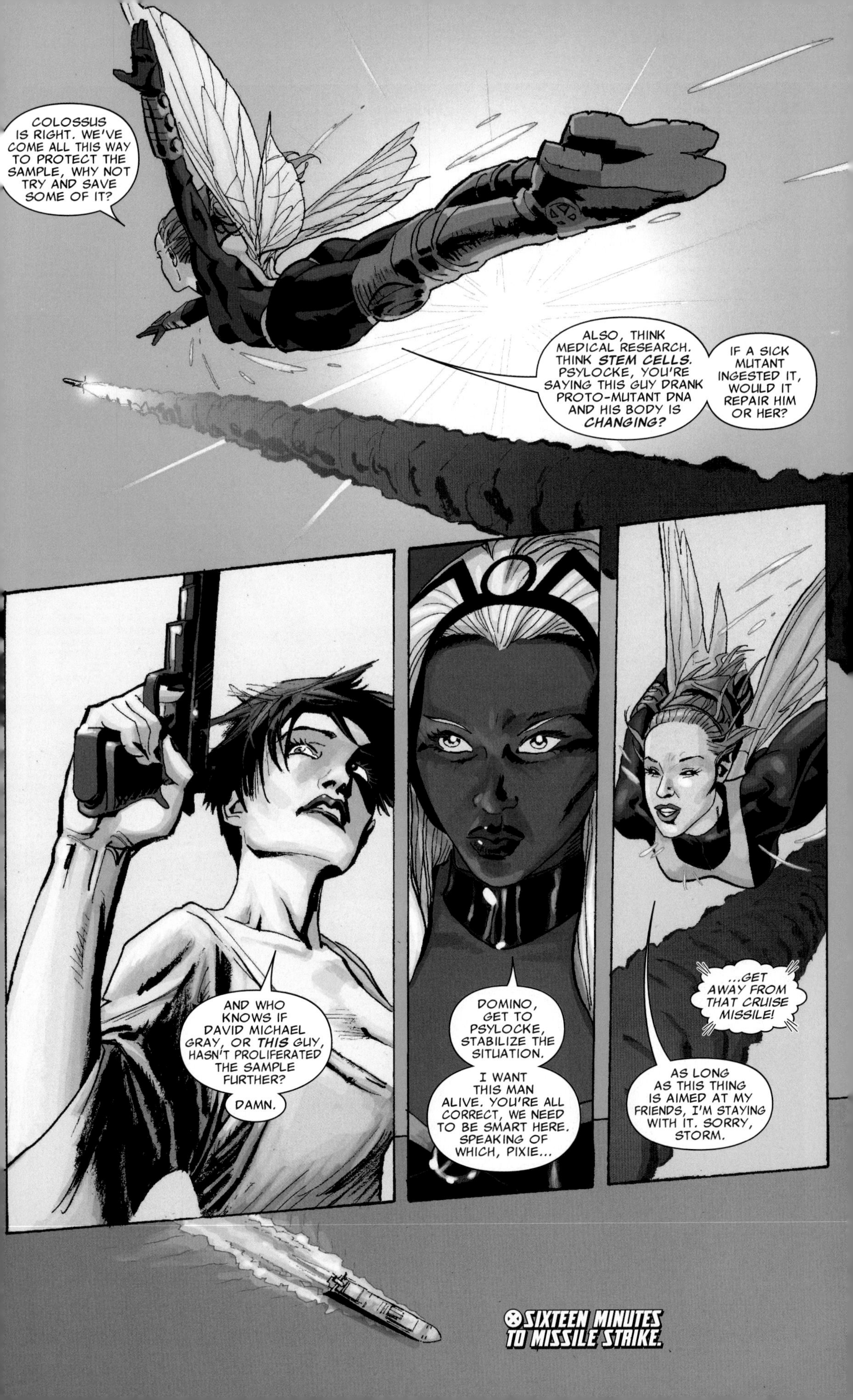
COLOSSUS IS RIGHT. WE'VE COME ALL THIS WAY TO PROTECT THE SAMPLE, WHY NOT TRY AND SAVE SOME OF IT?
ALSO, THINK MEDICAL RESEARCH. THINK STEM CELLS. PSYLOCKE, YOU'RE SAYING THIS GUY DRANK PROTO-MUTANT DNA AND HIS BODY IS CHANGING?
IF A SICK MUTANT INGESTED IT, WOULD IT REPAIR HIM OR HER?
AND WHO KNOWS IF DAVID MICHAEL GRAY, OR THIS GUY, HASN'T PROLIFERATED THE SAMPLE FURTHER?
DAMN.
DOMINO, GET TO PSYLOCKE, STABILIZE THE SITUATION.
I WANT THIS MAN ALIVE. YOU'RE ALL CORRECT, WE NEED TO BE SMART HERE. SPEAKING OF WHICH, PIXIE...
...GET AWAY FROM THAT CRUISE MISSILE!
AS LONG AS THIS THING IS AIMED AT MY FRIENDS, I'M STAYING WITH IT. SORRY, STORM.
SIXTEEN MINUTES TO MISSILE STRIKE.

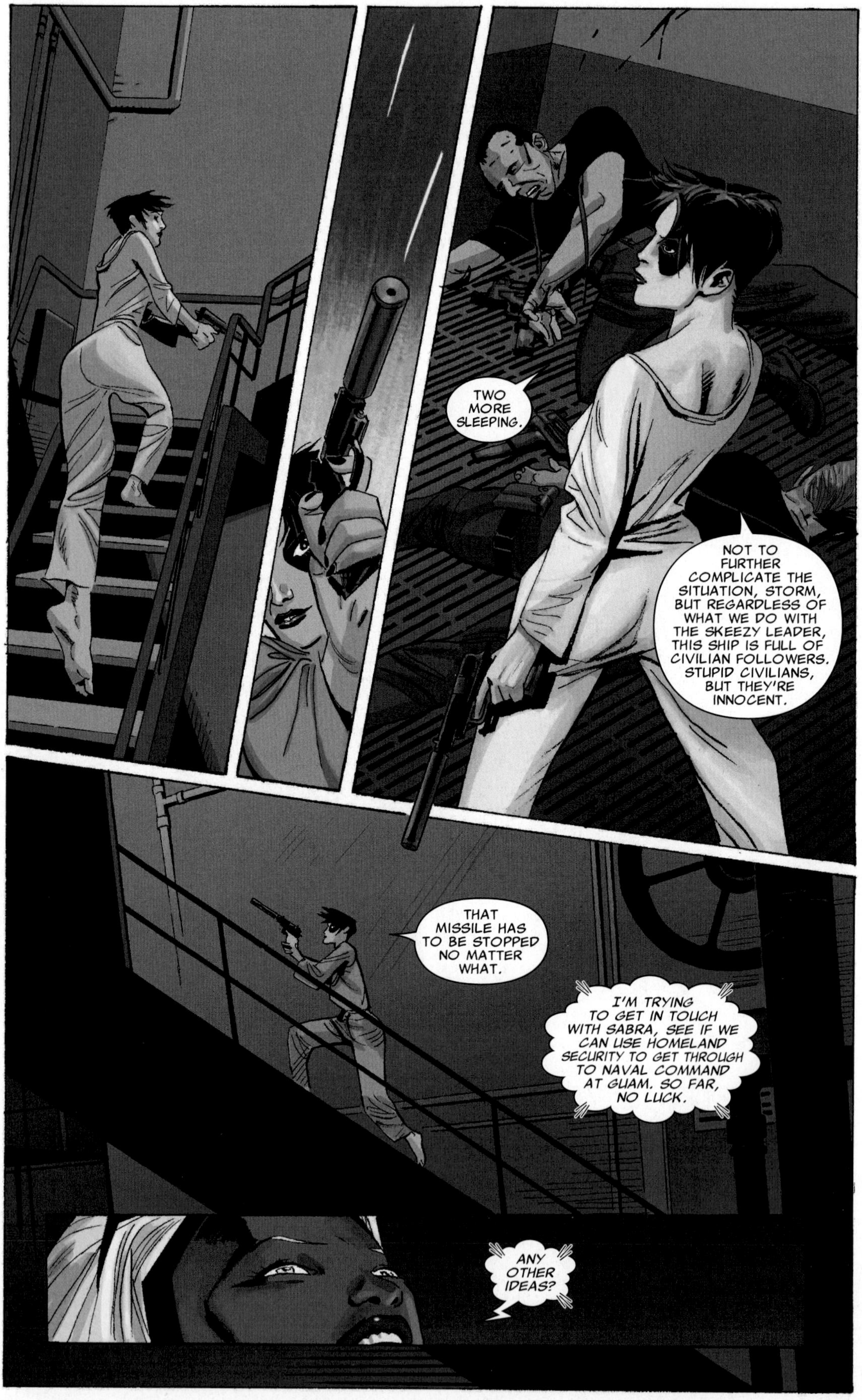
TWO MORE SLEEPING.
NOT TO FURTHER COMPLICATE THE SITUATION, STORM, BUT REGARDLESS OF WHAT WE DO WITH THE SKEEZY LEADER, THIS SHIP IS FULL OF CIVILIAN FOLLOWERS. STUPID CIVILIANS, BUT THEY'RE INNOCENT.
THAT MISSILE HAS TO BE STOPPED NO MATTER WHAT.
I'M TRYING TO GET IN TOUCH WITH SABRA, SEE IF WE CAN USE HOMELAND SECURITY TO GET THROUGH TO NAVAL COMMAND AT GUAM. SO FAR, NO LUCK.
ANY OTHER IDEAS?

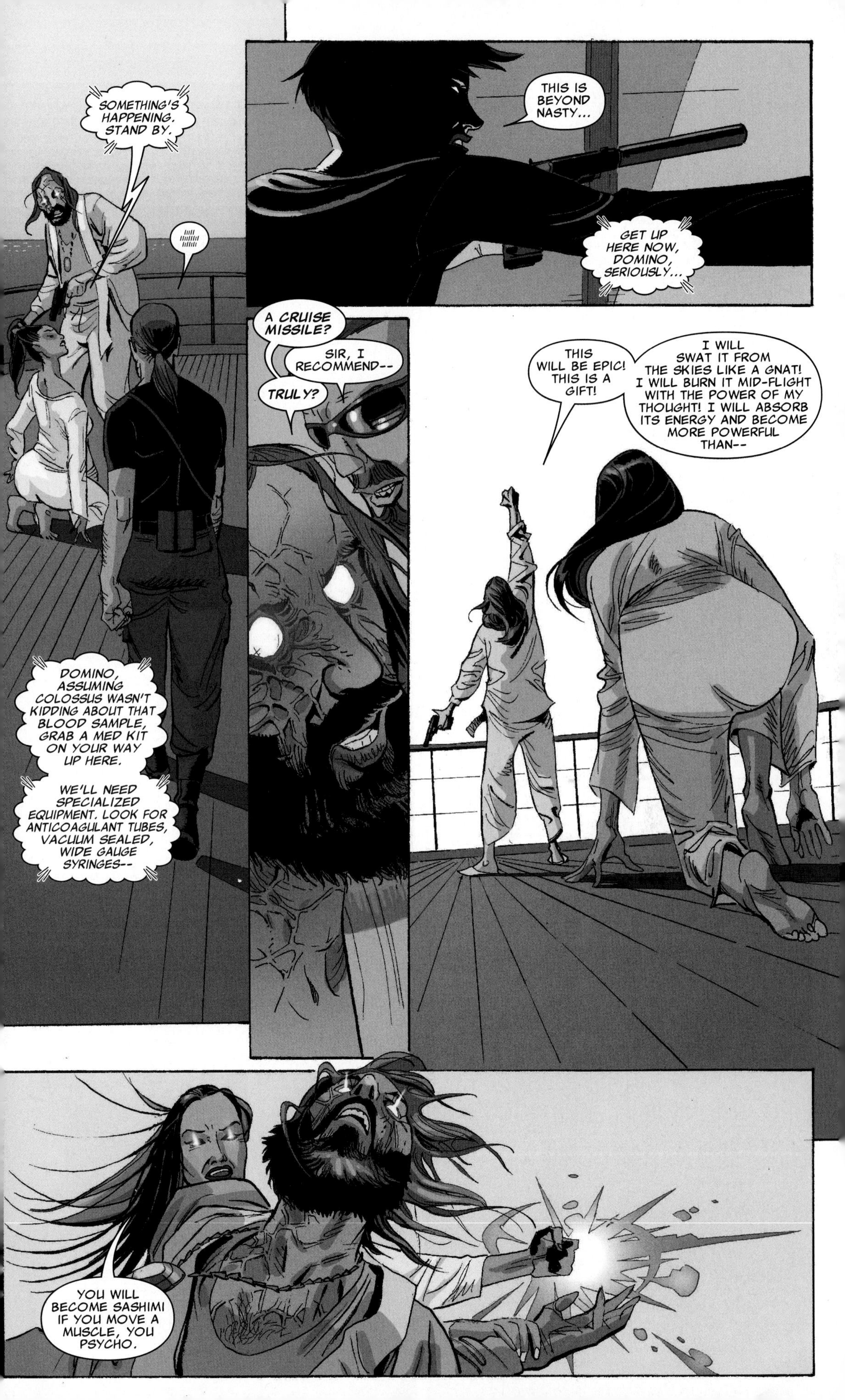
SOMETHING'S HAPPENING. STAND BY.
!!!!!
THIS IS BEYOND NASTY...
GET UP HERE NOW, DOMINO, SERIOUSLY...
DOMINO, ASSUMING COLOSSUS WASN'T KIDDING ABOUT THAT BLOOD SAMPLE, GRAB A MED KIT ON YOUR WAY UP HERE.
WE'LL NEED SPECIALIZED EQUIPMENT. LOOK FOR ANTICOAGULANT TUBES, VACUUM SEALED, WIDE GAUGE SYRINGES--
A CRUISE MISSILE?
SIR, I RECOMMEND--
TRULY?
THIS WILL BE EPIC! THIS IS A GIFT!
I WILL SWAT IT FROM THE SKIES LIKE A GNAT! I WILL BURN IT MID-FLIGHT WITH THE POWER OF MY THOUGHT! I WILL ABSORB ITS ENERGY AND BECOME MORE POWERFUL THAN--
YOU WILL BECOME SASHIMI IF YOU MOVE A MUSCLE, YOU PSYCHO.

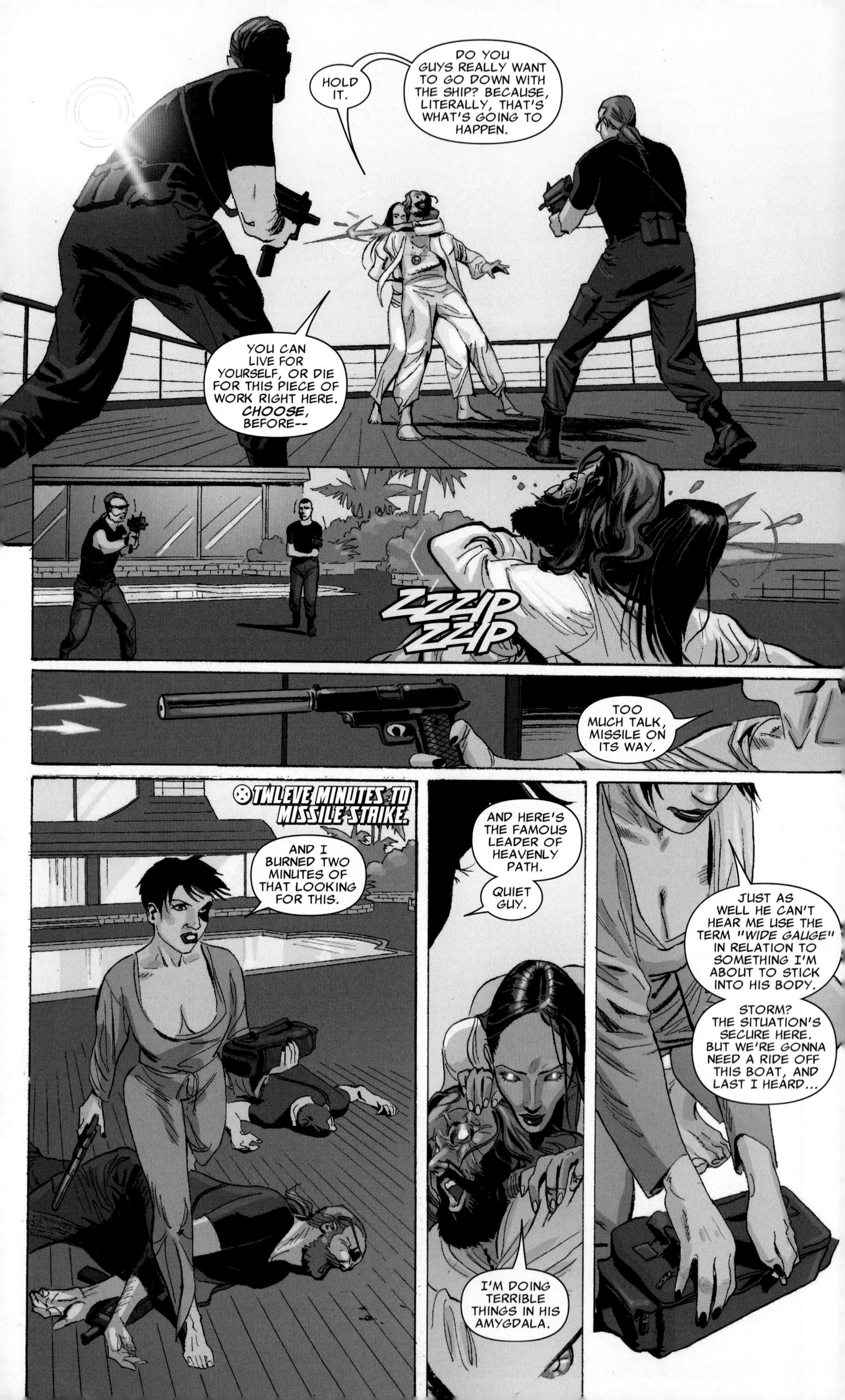
HOLD IT.
DO YOU GUYS REALLY WANT TO GO DOWN WITH THE SHIP? BECAUSE, LITERALLY, THAT'S WHAT'S GOING TO HAPPEN.
YOU CAN LIVE FOR YOURSELF, OR DIE FOR THIS PIECE OF WORK RIGHT HERE. *CHOOSE*, BEFORE--
ZZZIP ZZIP
TOO MUCH TALK, MISSILE ON ITS WAY.
TWLEVE MINUTES TO MISSILE STRIKE.
AND I BURNED TWO MINUTES OF THAT LOOKING FOR THIS.
AND HERE'S THE FAMOUS LEADER OF HEAVENLY PATH.
QUIET GUY.
I'M DOING TERRIBLE THINGS IN HIS AMYGDALA.
JUST AS WELL HE CAN'T HEAR ME USE THE TERM "*WIDE GAUGE*" IN RELATION TO SOMETHING I'M ABOUT TO STICK INTO HIS BODY.
STORM? THE SITUATION'S SECURE HERE. BUT WE'RE GONNA NEED A RIDE OFF THIS BOAT, AND LAST I HEARD...

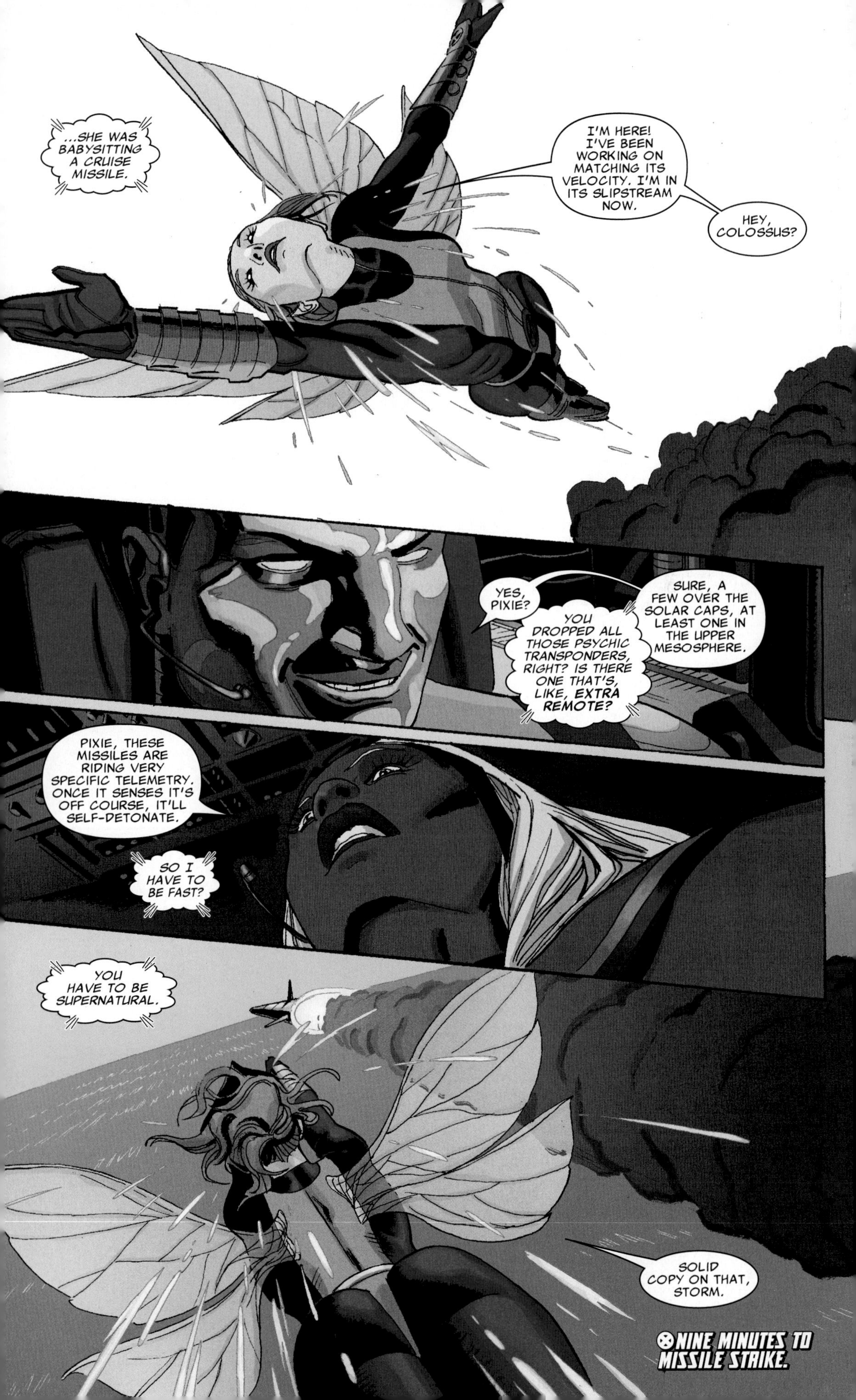
...SHE WAS BABYSITTING A CRUISE MISSILE.
I'M HERE! I'VE BEEN WORKING ON MATCHING ITS VELOCITY. I'M IN ITS SLIPSTREAM NOW.
HEY, COLOSSUS?
YES, PIXIE?
YOU DROPPED ALL THOSE PSYCHIC TRANSPONDERS, RIGHT? IS THERE ONE THAT'S, LIKE, EXTRA REMOTE?
SURE, A FEW OVER THE SOLAR CAPS, AT LEAST ONE IN THE UPPER MESOSPHERE.
PIXIE, THESE MISSILES ARE RIDING VERY SPECIFIC TELEMETRY. ONCE IT SENSES IT'S OFF COURSE, IT'LL SELF-DETONATE.
SO I HAVE TO BE FAST?
YOU HAVE TO BE SUPERNATURAL.
SOLID COPY ON THAT, STORM.
NINE MINUTES TO MISSILE STRIKE.

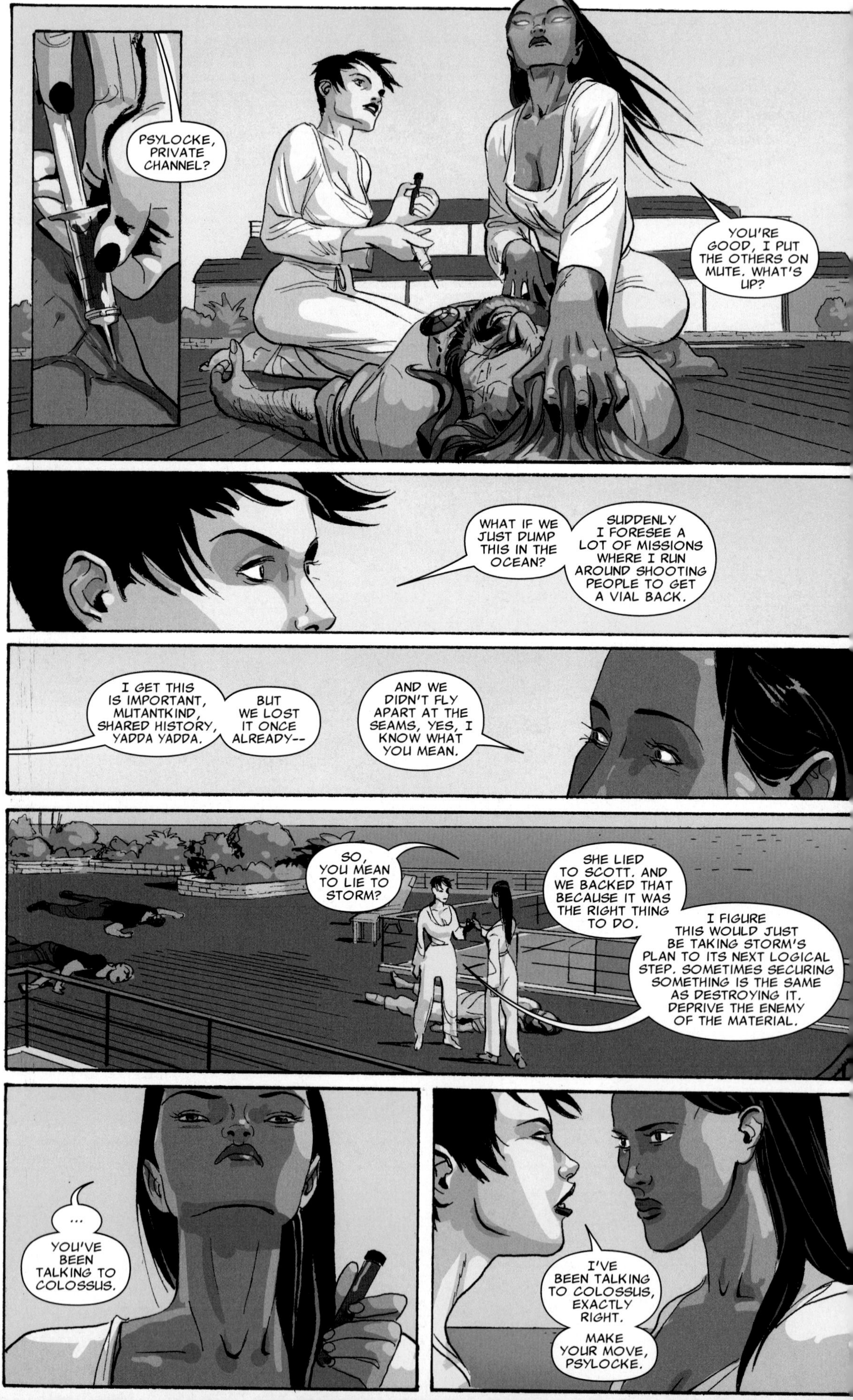
PSYLOCKE, PRIVATE CHANNEL?
YOU'RE GOOD, I PUT THE OTHERS ON MUTE. WHAT'S UP?
WHAT IF WE JUST DUMP THIS IN THE OCEAN?
SUDDENLY I FORESEE A LOT OF MISSIONS WHERE I RUN AROUND SHOOTING PEOPLE TO GET A VIAL BACK.
I GET THIS IS IMPORTANT, MUTANTKIND, SHARED HISTORY, YADDA YADDA.
BUT WE LOST IT ONCE ALREADY--
AND WE DIDN'T FLY APART AT THE SEAMS, YES, I KNOW WHAT YOU MEAN.
SO, YOU MEAN TO LIE TO STORM?
SHE LIED TO SCOTT. AND WE BACKED THAT BECAUSE IT WAS THE RIGHT THING TO DO.
I FIGURE THIS WOULD JUST BE TAKING STORM'S PLAN TO ITS NEXT LOGICAL STEP. SOMETIMES SECURING SOMETHING IS THE SAME AS DESTROYING IT. DEPRIVE THE ENEMY OF THE MATERIAL.
...
YOU'VE BEEN TALKING TO COLOSSUS.
I'VE BEEN TALKING TO COLOSSUS, EXACTLY RIGHT.
MAKE YOUR MOVE, PSYLOCKE.

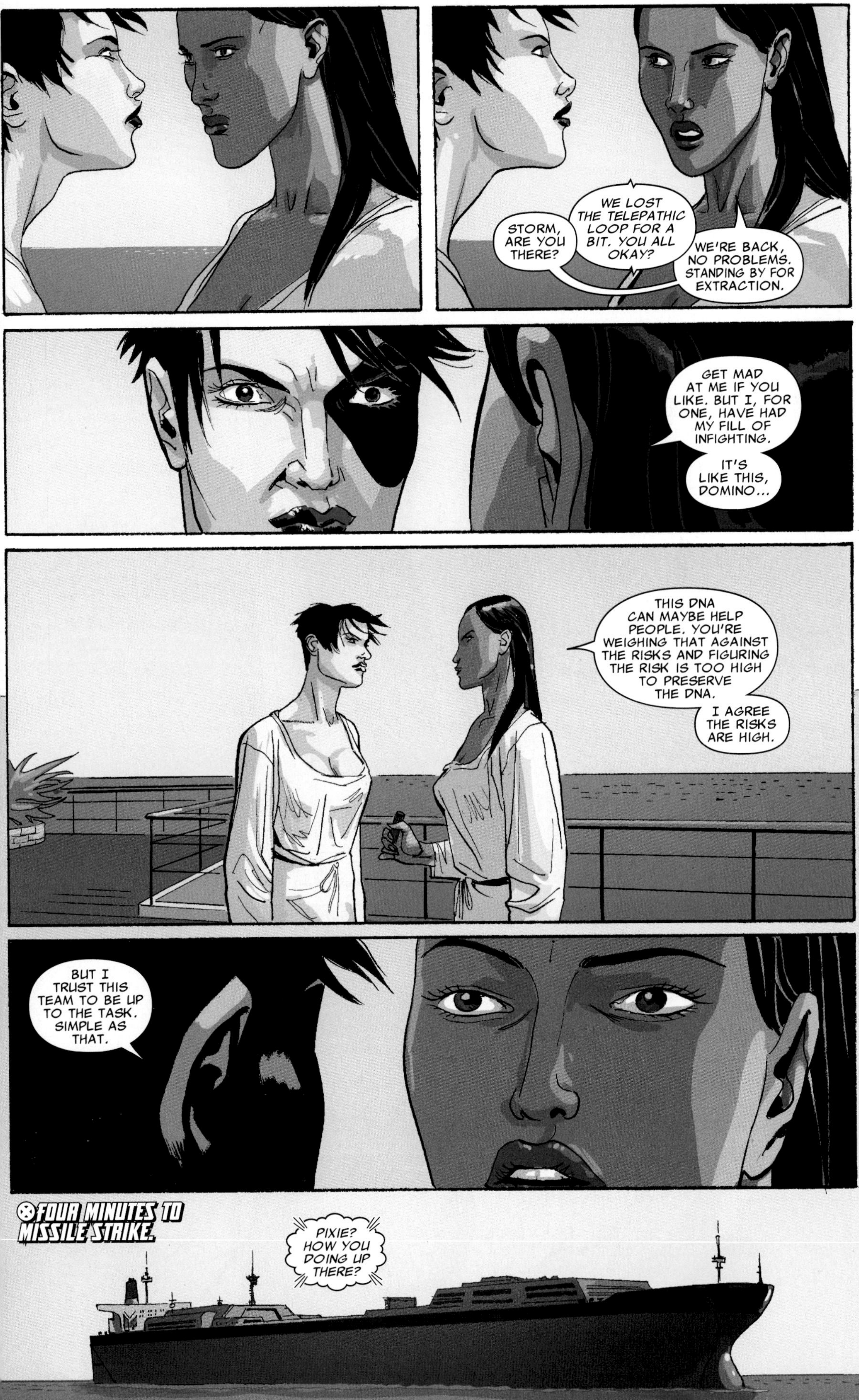
STORM, ARE YOU THERE?
WE LOST THE TELEPATHIC LOOP FOR A BIT. YOU ALL OKAY?
WE'RE BACK, NO PROBLEMS. STANDING BY FOR EXTRACTION.
GET MAD AT ME IF YOU LIKE. BUT I, FOR ONE, HAVE HAD MY FILL OF INFIGHTING.
IT'S LIKE THIS, DOMINO...
THIS DNA CAN MAYBE HELP PEOPLE. YOU'RE WEIGHING THAT AGAINST THE RISKS AND FIGURING THE RISK IS TOO HIGH TO PRESERVE THE DNA.
I AGREE THE RISKS ARE HIGH.
BUT I TRUST THIS TEAM TO BE UP TO THE TASK. SIMPLE AS THAT.
FOUR MINUTES TO MISSILE STRIKE.
PIXIE? HOW YOU DOING UP THERE?

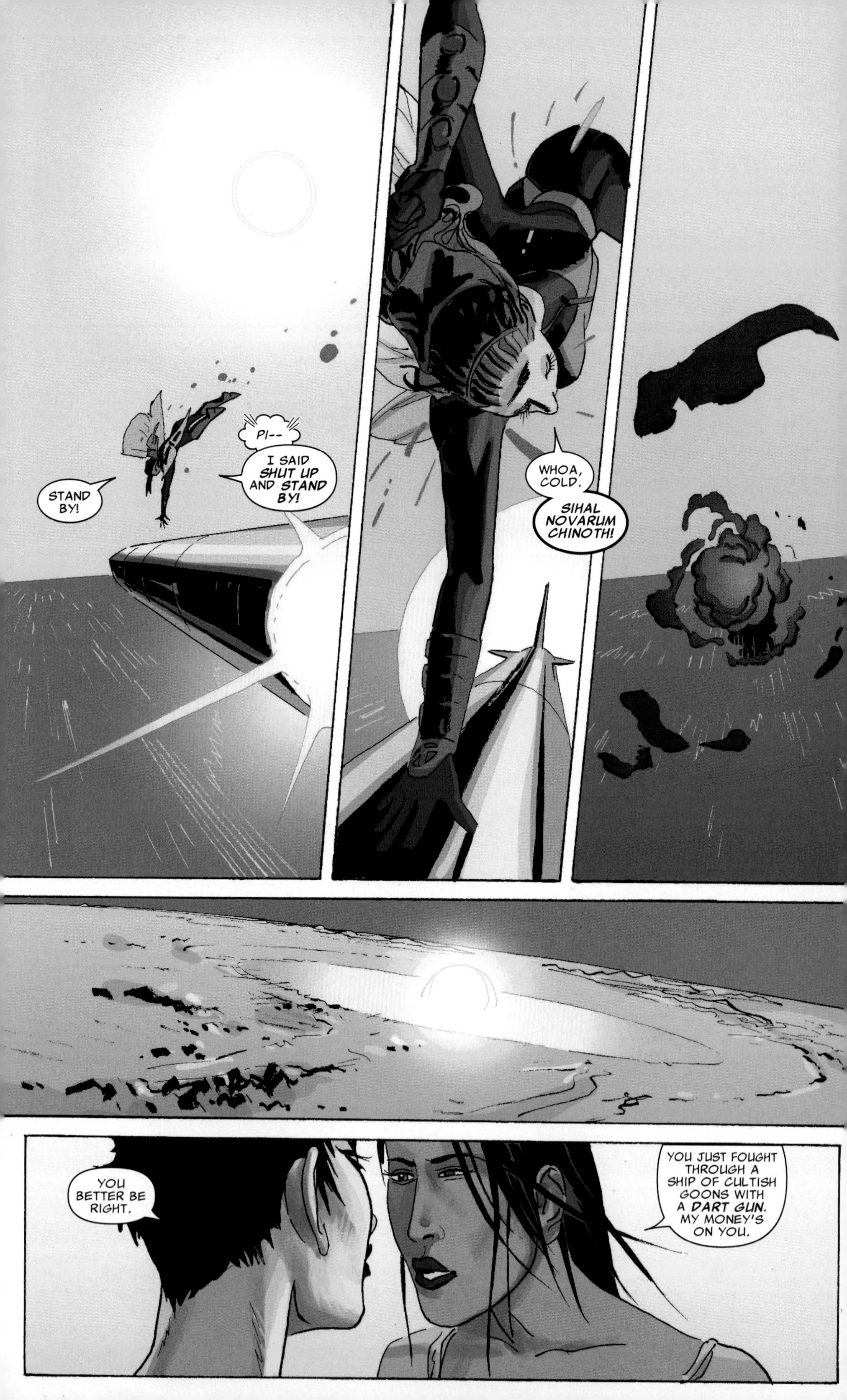
STAND BY!
PI--
I SAID SHUT UP AND STAND BY!
WHOA, COLD.
SIHAL NOVARUM CHINOTH!
YOU BETTER BE RIGHT.
YOU JUST FOUGHT THROUGH A SHIP OF CULTISH GOONS WITH A DART GUN. MY MONEY'S ON YOU.

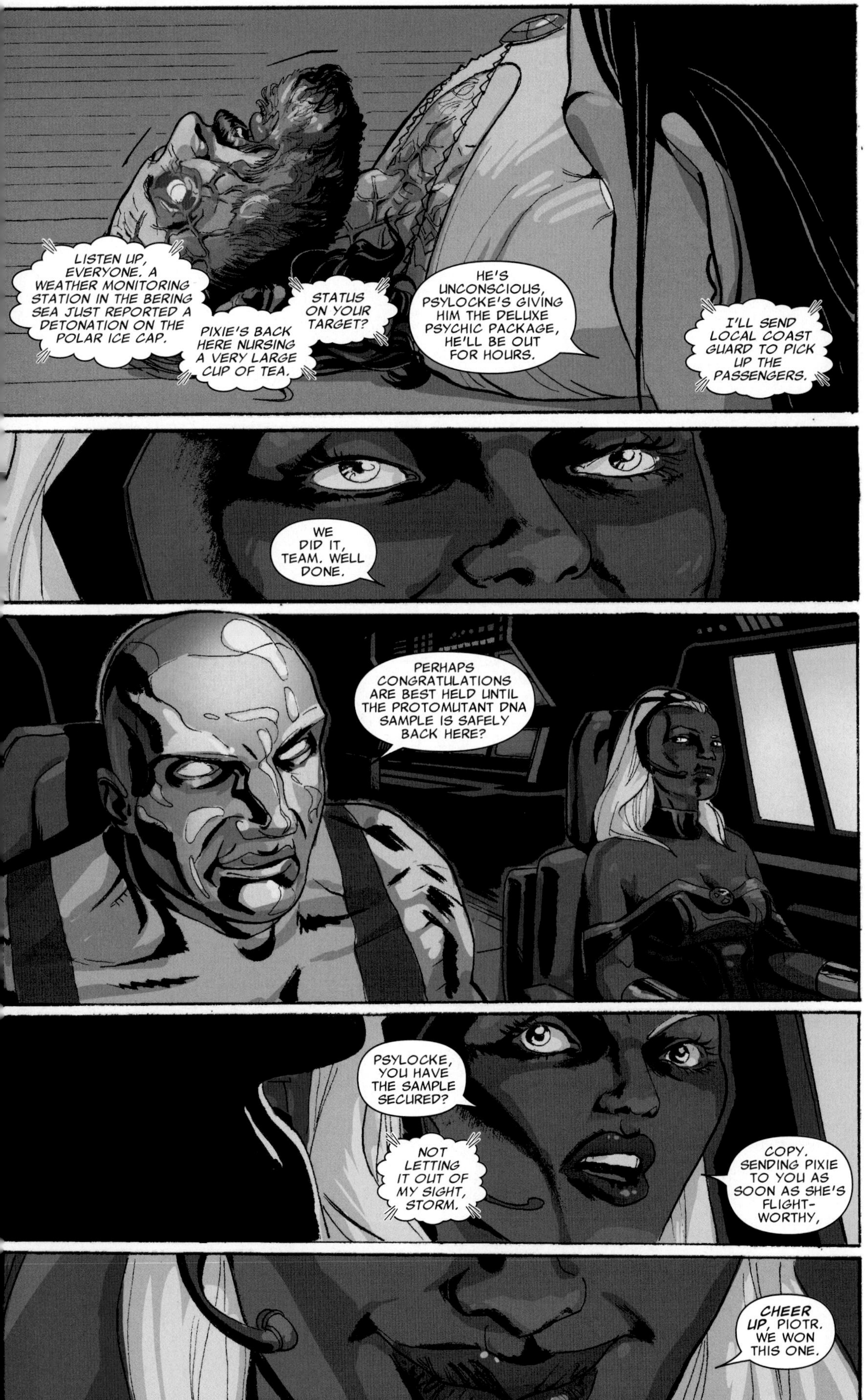
LISTEN UP, EVERYONE. A WEATHER MONITORING STATION IN THE BERING SEA JUST REPORTED A DETONATION ON THE POLAR ICE CAP.
PIXIE'S BACK HERE NURSING A VERY LARGE CUP OF TEA.
STATUS ON YOUR TARGET?
HE'S UNCONSCIOUS, PSYLOCKE'S GIVING HIM THE DELUXE PSYCHIC PACKAGE, HE'LL BE OUT FOR HOURS.
I'LL SEND LOCAL COAST GUARD TO PICK UP THE PASSENGERS.
WE DID IT, TEAM. WELL DONE.
PERHAPS CONGRATULATIONS ARE BEST HELD UNTIL THE PROTOMUTANT DNA SAMPLE IS SAFELY BACK HERE?
PSYLOCKE, YOU HAVE THE SAMPLE SECURED?
NOT LETTING IT OUT OF MY SIGHT, STORM.
COPY. SENDING PIXIE TO YOU AS SOON AS SHE'S FLIGHT-WORTHY,
CHEER UP, PIOTR. WE WON THIS ONE.

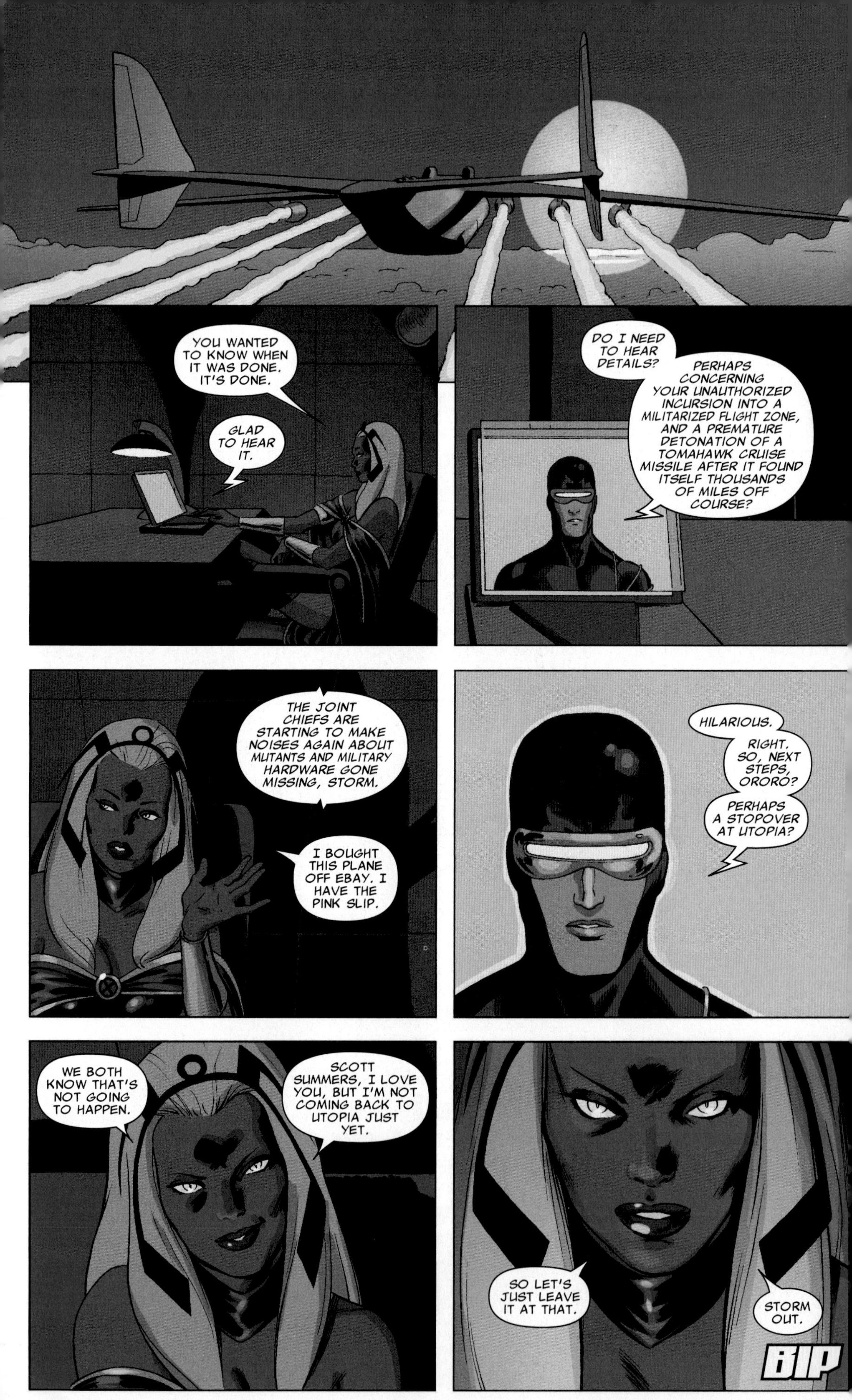
YOU WANTED TO KNOW WHEN IT WAS DONE. IT'S DONE.
GLAD TO HEAR IT.
DO I NEED TO HEAR DETAILS?
PERHAPS CONCERNING YOUR UNAUTHORIZED INCURSION INTO A MILITARIZED FLIGHT ZONE, AND A PREMATURE DETONATION OF A TOMAHAWK CRUISE MISSILE AFTER IT FOUND ITSELF THOUSANDS OF MILES OFF COURSE?
THE JOINT CHIEFS ARE STARTING TO MAKE NOISES AGAIN ABOUT MUTANTS AND MILITARY HARDWARE GONE MISSING, STORM.
I BOUGHT THIS PLANE OFF EBAY. I HAVE THE PINK SLIP.
HILARIOUS.
RIGHT. SO, NEXT STEPS, ORORO?
PERHAPS A STOPOVER AT UTOPIA?
WE BOTH KNOW THAT'S NOT GOING TO HAPPEN.
SCOTT SUMMERS, I LOVE YOU, BUT I'M NOT COMING BACK TO UTOPIA JUST YET.
SO LET'S JUST LEAVE IT AT THAT.
STORM OUT.
BIP

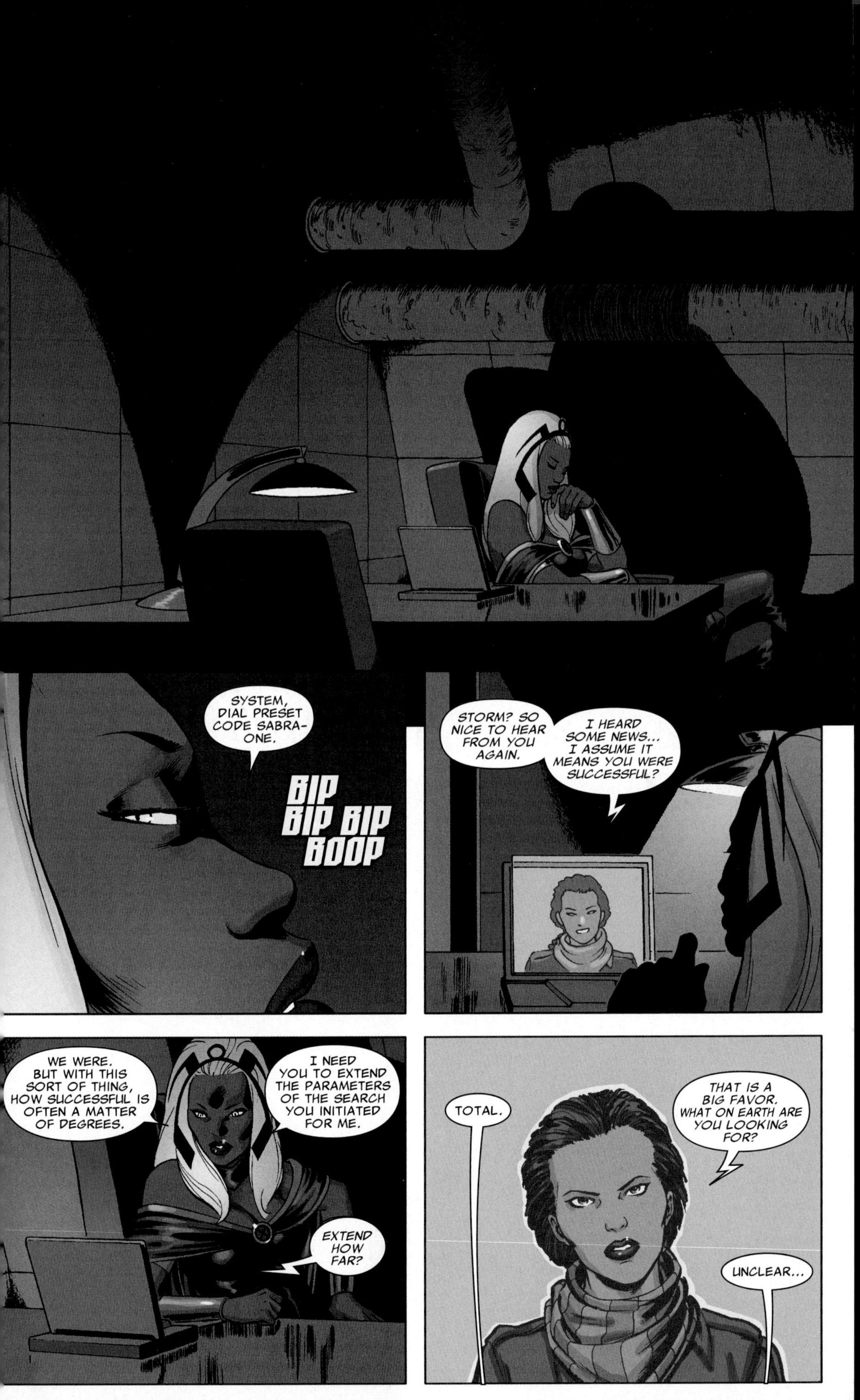
SYSTEM, DIAL PRESET CODE SABRA-ONE.
BIP BIP BIP BOOP
STORM? SO NICE TO HEAR FROM YOU AGAIN.
I HEARD SOME NEWS... I ASSUME IT MEANS YOU WERE SUCCESSFUL?
WE WERE. BUT WITH THIS SORT OF THING, HOW SUCCESSFUL IS OFTEN A MATTER OF DEGREES.
I NEED YOU TO EXTEND THE PARAMETERS OF THE SEARCH YOU INITIATED FOR ME.
EXTEND HOW FAR?
TOTAL.
THAT IS A BIG FAVOR. WHAT ON EARTH ARE YOU LOOKING FOR?
UNCLEAR...

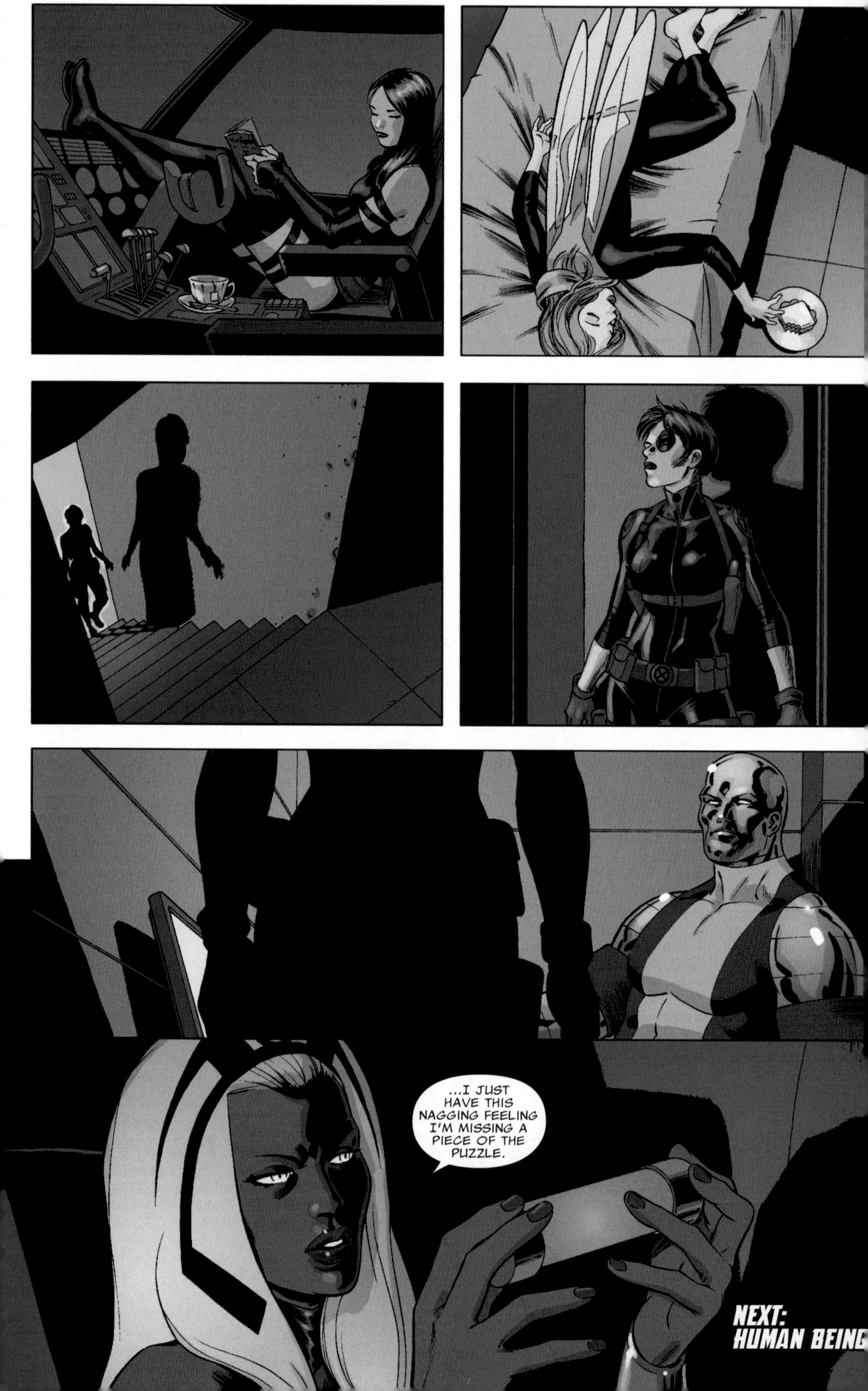
...I JUST HAVE THIS NAGGING FEELING I'M MISSING A PIECE OF THE PUZZLE.
NEXT: HUMAN BEING

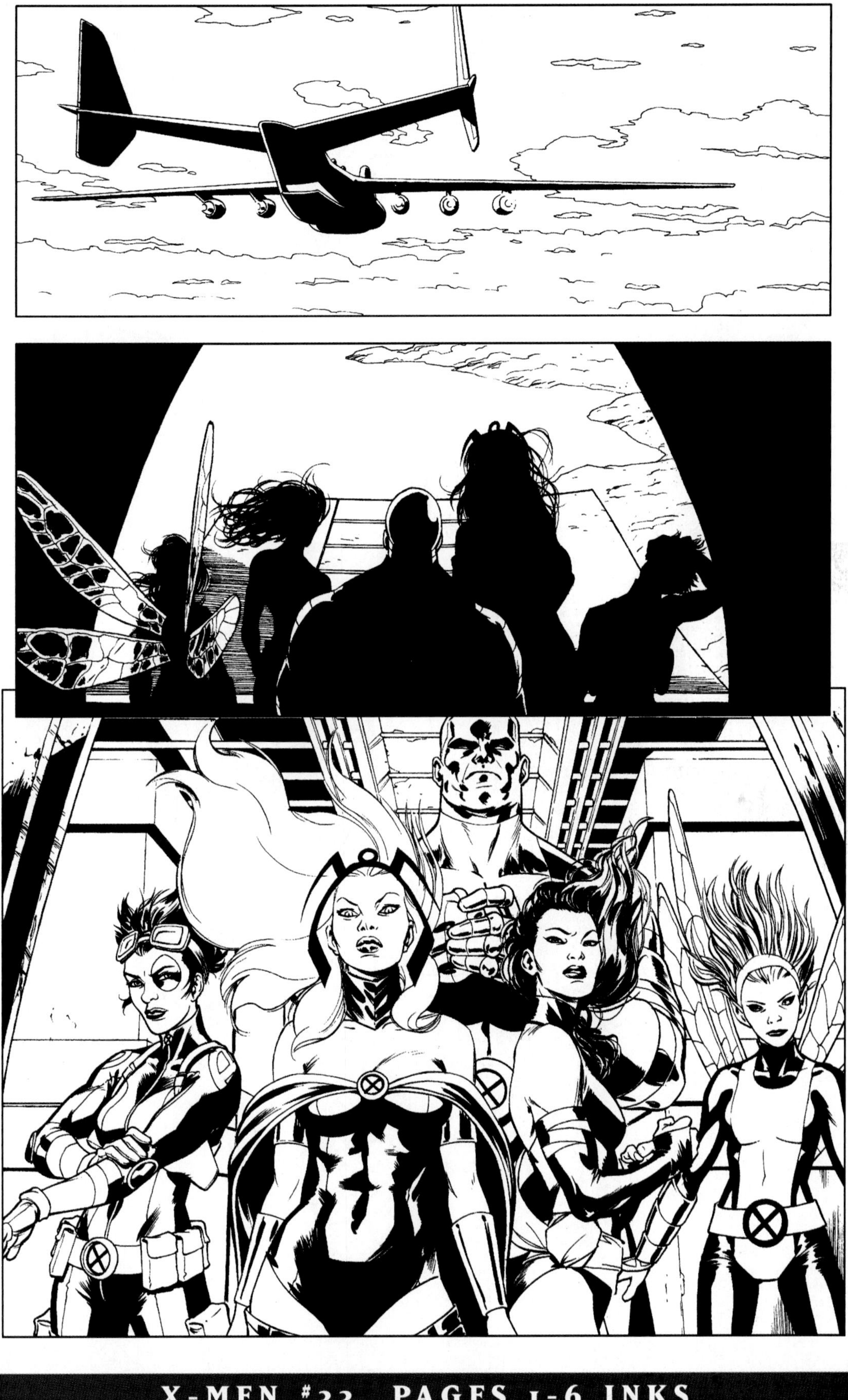

X-MEN #33, PAGES 1-6 INKS
BY DAVID LÓPEZ & ÁLVARO LÓPEZ

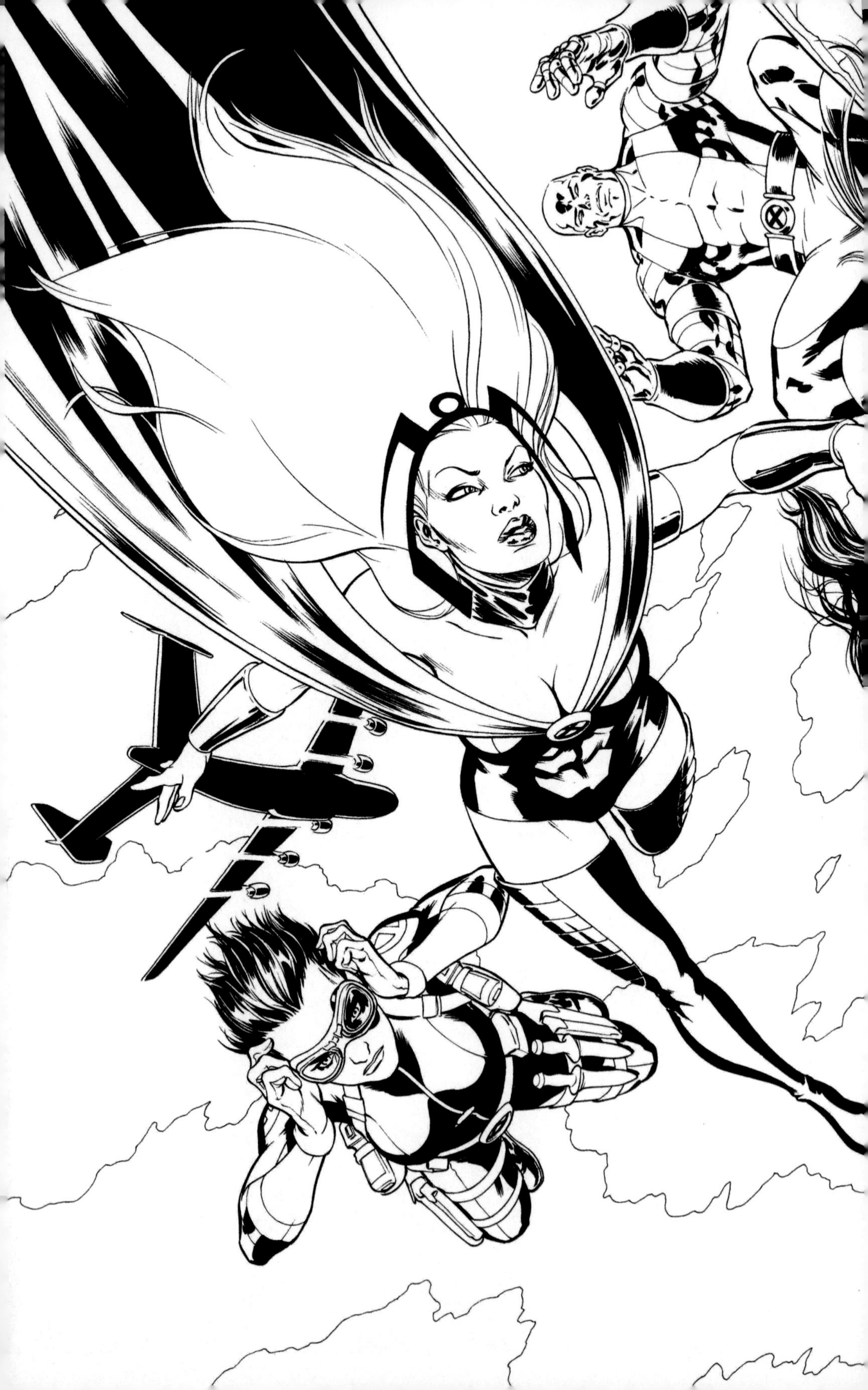

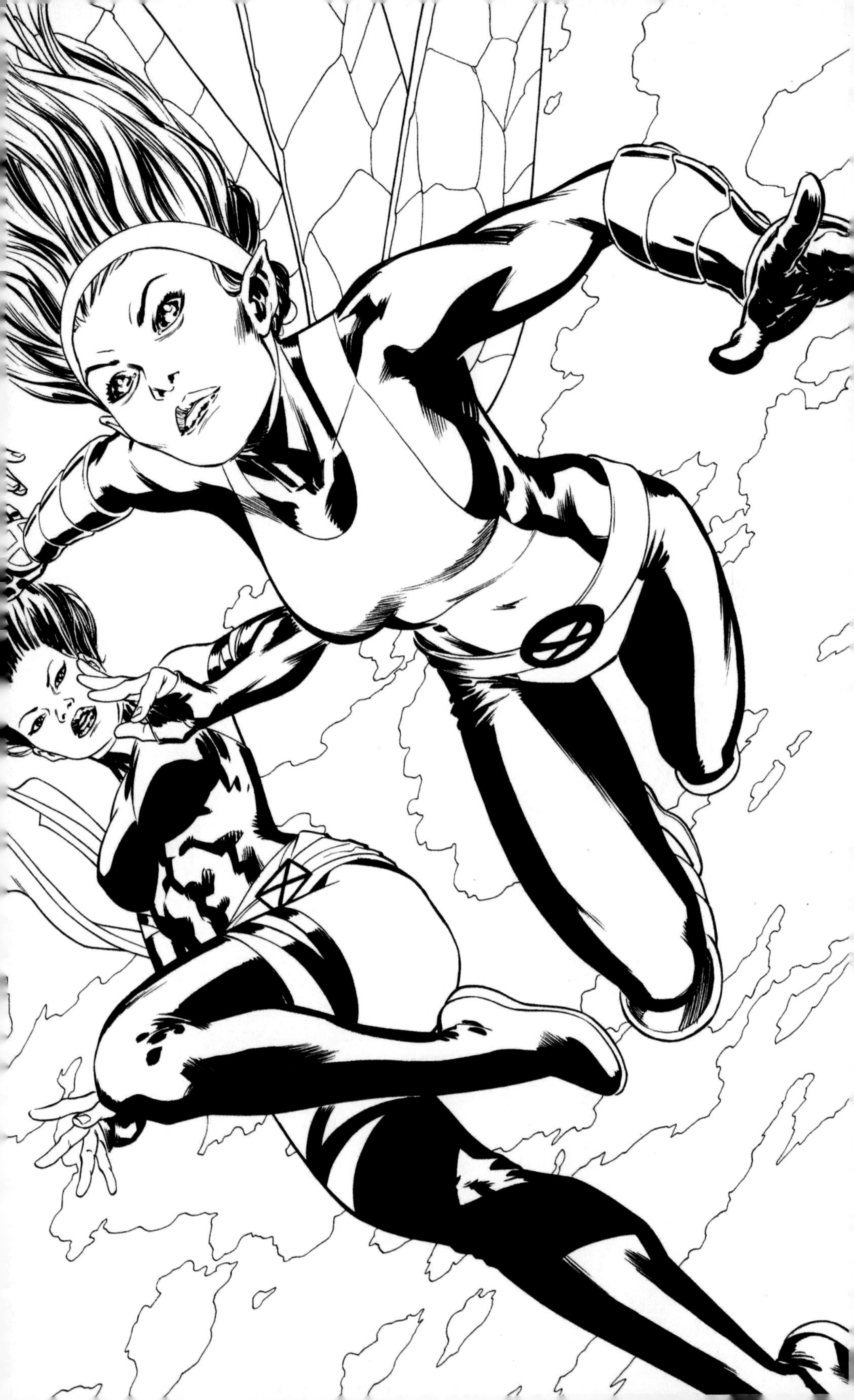

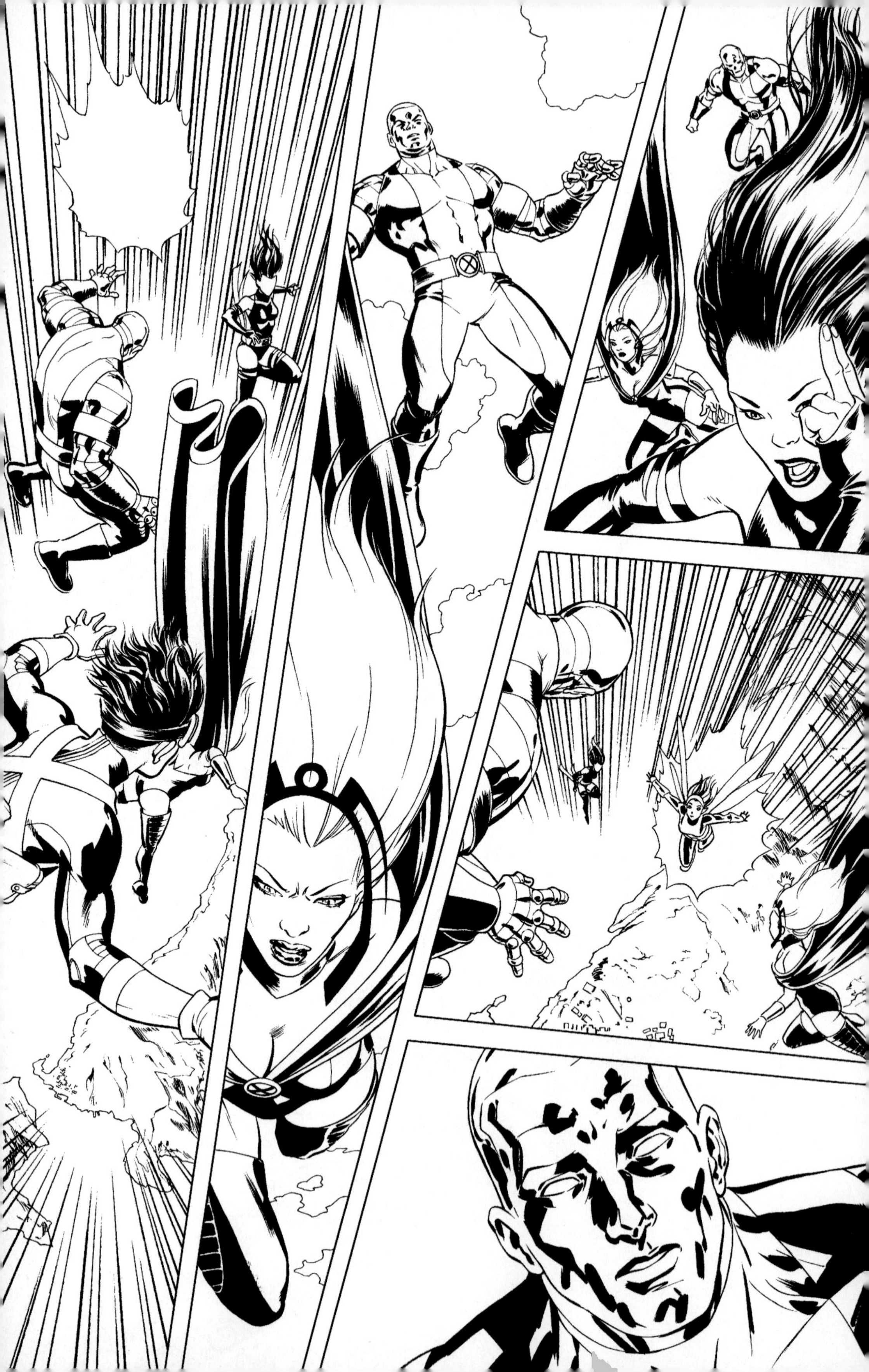

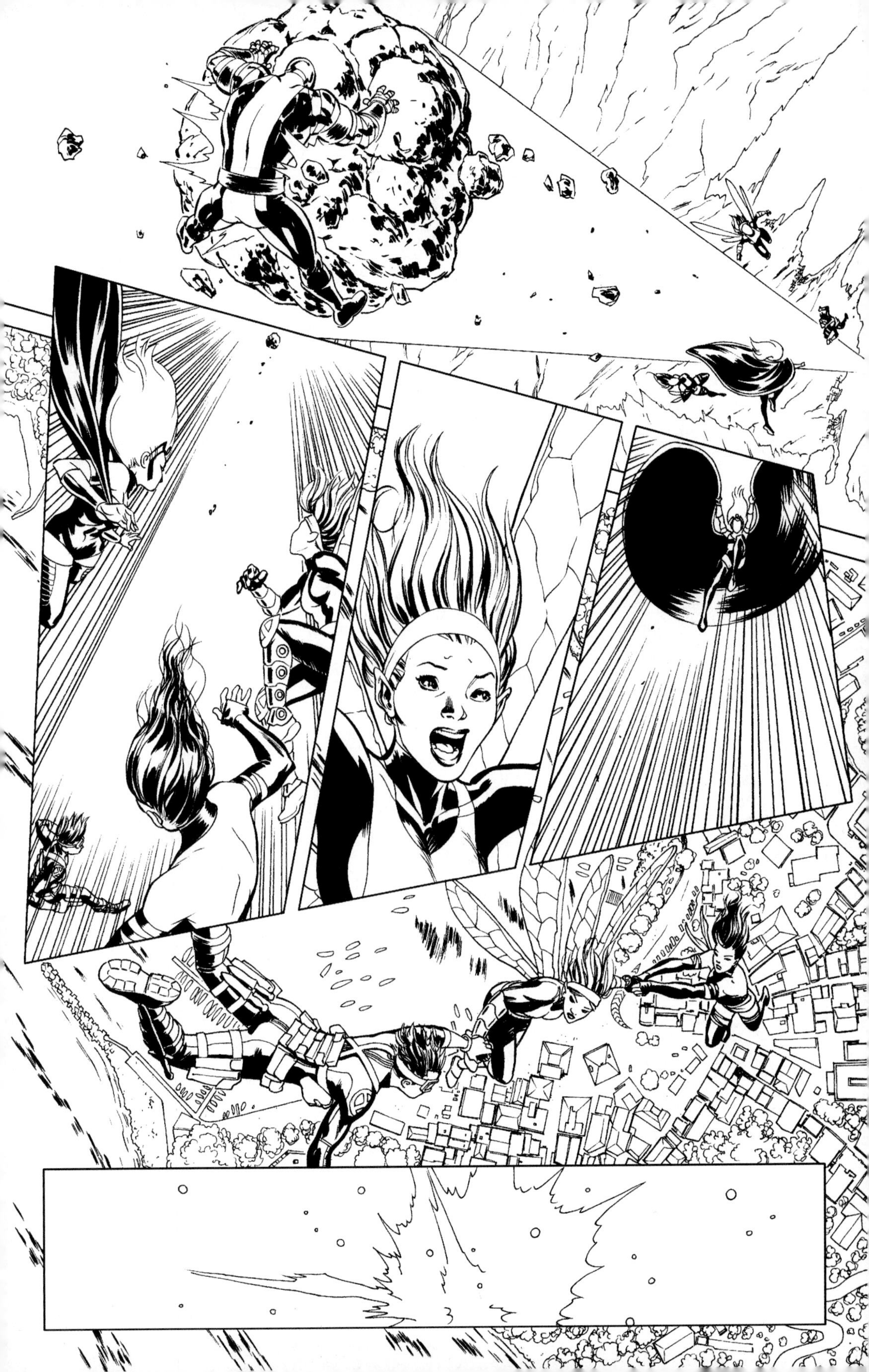

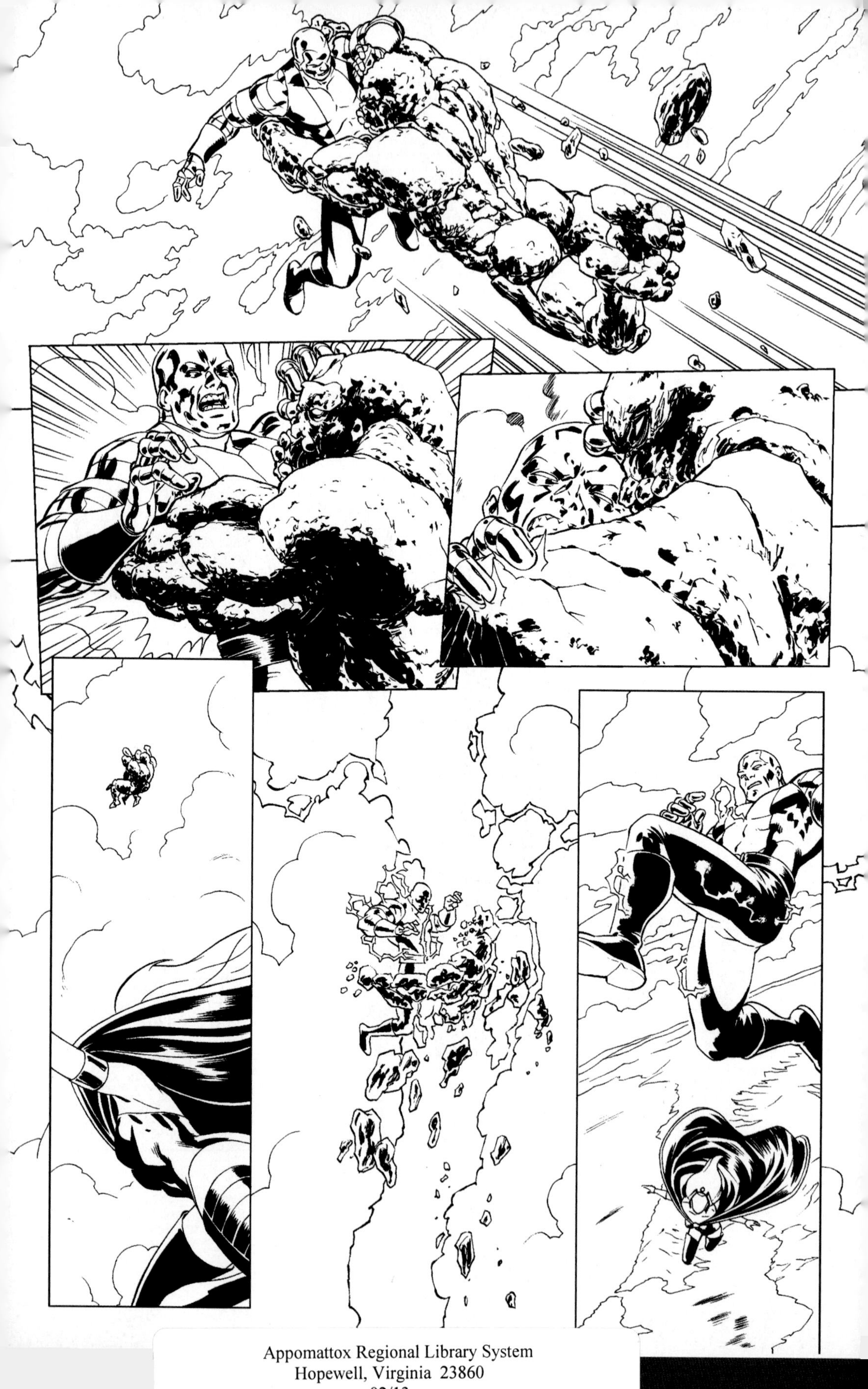